Ready® | 6 Mathematics PRACTICE AND PROBLEM SOLVING

Vice President-Product Development: Adam Berkin
Editorial Director: Cynthia Tripp
Editorial: Stacie Cartwright, Pam Halloran, Kathy Kellman, Lauren Van Wart
Project Manager: Grace Izzi
Cover Designer and Illustrator: Matt Pollock
Illustrator: Sam Valentino
Photography Credit: wk1003mike/Shutterstock (front cover background)

ISBN 978-1-4957-0483-3
©2016—Curriculum Associates, LLC
North Billerica, MA 01862

Table of Contents

Family Letter available with every lesson.

Table of Contents

Family Letter available with every lesson.

Dear Family,

> **Your child is learning about ratios.**

You use a ratio when you compare two different quantities. For example, you might use a ratio when you describe the quantities needed to make a batch of granola. If you use 2 cups of almonds and 7 cups of oats, you could describe the quantities in the following ways.

- The ratio of almonds to oats is 2 to 7.

- The ratio of oats to almonds is 7 to 2.

- The ratio of almonds to the entire batch of granola is 2 to 9.

You can think of a ratio as comparing two quantities. Sometimes ratios compare parts, and sometimes they compare parts and wholes.

- When you compare the quantity of almonds to oats or the quantity of oats to almonds, you compare parts to each other.

- When you compare the quantity of almonds to the entire batch of granola, you compare one part to the whole.

A ratio can be written with words, with a colon, or as a fraction: 2 to 7, 2 : 7, or $\frac{2}{7}$.

Consider the following example:

A recipe for fruit salad calls for 1 apple, 3 oranges, and 4 bananas. How can you use a ratio to compare the quantities of oranges to bananas and to compare the quantity of oranges to the total amount of fruit in the salad?

The next page shows two different ways in which your child might write ratios to compare the quantities of fruit.

NEXT

A recipe for fruit salad calls for 1 apple, 3 oranges, and 4 bananas. How can you use a ratio to compare the quantities of oranges to bananas and to compare the quantity of oranges to the total amount of fruit in the salad?

To compare the quantities of fruit, think about the parts and the whole. Each quantity of apples, oranges, and bananas is a part. All the fruit together makes up the whole.

One way: Use a picture to represent the quantities.

The ratio of oranges to bananas is: 3 to 4, 3 : 4, or $\frac{3}{4}$.

The ratio of oranges to the total amount of fruit is: 3 to 8, 3 : 8, or $\frac{3}{8}$.

Another way: Use a tape diagram to show how the quantities of each kind of fruit compare to each other and to the whole.

Apples
Oranges
Bananas
Total fruit

The ratio of oranges to bananas is 3 to 4, 3 : 4, or $\frac{3}{4}$.

The ratio of oranges to the total amount of fruit is 3 to 8, 3 : 8, or $\frac{3}{8}$.

Answer: Both methods show that the ratio of oranges to bananas is 3 to 4, 3 : 4, or $\frac{3}{4}$, meaning that there are 3 oranges for every 4 bananas. Both methods also show that the ratio of oranges to the total amount of fruit is 3 to 8, 3 : 8, or $\frac{3}{8}$, meaning that there are 3 oranges for every 8 pieces of fruit in the salad.

Ratios

Name: _____

Prerequisite: Relating Patterns

Study the example showing how to describe the relationship between two patterns. Then solve problems 1–6.

Example

The school store sells headbands for $2 each and T-shirts for $8 each. Write ordered pairs to compare the cost of headbands to T-shirts for 0, 1, 2, 3, 4, and 5 of each item.

Use a table to show the two numerical patterns.

Cost of Headbands ($)	Cost of T-shirts ($)	Ordered Pairs
0	0	(0, 0)
2	8	(2, 8)
4	16	(4, 16)
6	24	(6, 24)
8	32	(8, 32)
10	40	(10, 40)

The cost of headbands follows the rule "add 2."

    0, 2, 4, 6, 8, 10

The cost of T-shirts follows the rule "add 8."

    0, 8, 16, 24, 32, 40

Then write the corresponding terms as ordered pairs.

1 Use the rule "add 8" to find the cost of 6 T-shirts. Explain how you found your answer.

_____

_____

_____

_____

2 For each ordered pair in the table, how does the second number compare to the first number?

_____

3 If the cost of headbands is $20, what is the corresponding cost for T-shirts? _____

Vocabulary

corresponding terms numbers that are in the same place in two or more related patterns.

ordered pair a pair of numbers that locate a point on a coordinate plane.

Solve.

4 One pattern starts at 0 and follows the rule "add 2." Another pattern starts at 0 and follows the rule "add 5." Write the first 6 numbers in each pattern. How do the terms in the first pattern compare to the corresponding terms in the second pattern?

Show your work.

Solution: _____

_____

5 Complete the table below. Then describe the relationship between corresponding terms.

x	y	Ordered pairs (x, y)
0	0	
6	3	
12	6	

6 A shop sells matching hats and scarves. The scarves cost 1.5 times as much as the hats. Write two patterns that could represent the costs of 1, 2, 3, 4, and 5 hats and scarves. List the first 5 terms of each pattern. Then explain how to find the cost of 6 hats and scarves, using the patterns you wrote.

Show your work.

Solution: _____

Name: _____

Compare Quantities Using Ratios

Study the example problem showing how to compare quantities using ratios. Then solve problems 1–8.

Example

A florist makes a bouquet using 4 roses, 5 carnations, and 3 daffodils. What is the ratio of roses to the total number of flowers in the bouquet?

Roses   Carnations   Daffodils

There are 4 roses in the bouquet.

The total number of flowers is $4 + 5 + 3 = 12$.

There are 12 flowers in the bouquet.

You can express the ratio "4 roses to 12 total flowers" as $\frac{4}{12}$, 4 : 12, or 4 to 12.

---

1 Write the ratio of carnations to daffodils in three different ways.

_____

2 What is the ratio of the total number of flowers to carnations? Write the ratio in three different ways.

_____

3 Describe a ratio in words about the flowers that compares one part of the bouquet to another part. Write the ratio in at least two different ways.

_____

_____

Solve.

Ben has a collection of 15 coins in quarters and dimes. There are 7 quarters in the collection.

4 Write the ratio of quarters to dimes in at least two different ways.

_____

5 Write the ratio of dimes to total number of coins in at least two different ways.

_____

6 Describe a ratio in words about the coins that compares the whole coin collection to one part of it. Then write the ratio in at least two different ways.

_____

_____

_____

7 Is the ratio of quarters to dimes the same as the ratio of dimes to quarters? Explain.

_____

_____

_____

_____

8 Pradip and Pam each have a plate of apple slices and orange slices. The ratio of apple slices to the total number of slices on Pradip's plate is 4 to 11. The ratio of the total number of slices to orange slices on Pam's plate is 13 : 6. Neither person has more than 20 total slices. Who has more orange slices? Explain.

_____

_____

_____

_____

6 **Lesson 1** Ratios

Name: _____

Ratios

Solve the problems.

1 Alicia has pencils and markers as shown in the tape diagram. Write the ratio of markers to pencils in three different ways.

Be sure the terms in each ratio are in the correct order.

Pencils

Markers

_____

2 Kenny has 2 red marbles, 3 blue marbles, and 4 black marbles. Which ratio compares a part to the whole?

The whole in this problem is the total of the red, blue, and black marbles.

A 2 to 7   **C** 5 to 4

B 3 : 9   **D** 9 : 5

3 Mrs. Adams buys 4 bananas and 6 apples. Tell whether each statement is *True* or *False*.

Does the ratio compare part to part or part to whole?

a. The ratio of bananas to apples is 6 : 4.   ☐ True ☐ False

b. The ratio of apples to total fruit is 10 to 6.   ☐ True ☐ False

c. The ratio of bananas to total fruit is 4 to 10.   ☐ True ☐ False

d. The ratio of total fruit to apples is $\frac{6}{10}$.   ☐ True ☐ False

Solve.

4 For his exercise last weekend, Benito walked 5 miles and jogged 2 miles. What is the ratio of the miles walked to the total number of miles of exercise?

   A 5 to 2   **C** 5 : 7

   B 2 : 7   **D** 7 to 5

   Elsa chose **A** as the correct answer. How did she get that answer?

   Are you finding a ratio that compares part to part or part to whole?

   _____

   _____

   _____

   _____

5 The ratio of boys to girls in Mr. Smith's class is 3 : 2. Which statement is correct? Circle all that apply.

   A For every 3 boys, there are 2 girls.

   B For every 2 boys, there are 3 girls.

   C There are exactly 5 students in Mr. Smith's class.

   D The ratio of the number of boys in the class to the total number of students is 3 : 5.

   E The ratio of the number of students in the class to the number of girls is 5 to 2.

   Does the statement describing the ratio match the numerical ratio given in the problem?

6 Kelly buys a hat and gloves. The price of the hat is 4 times as much as the gloves. The hat costs $8. What is the ratio of the cost of the gloves to the total cost for both items?

   Show your work.

   How can you find the cost of the gloves?

   Solution: _____

Dear Family,

> ## Your child is learning about unit rates.

Rates and unit rates are often used in everyday life. Some examples that you are probably familiar with are miles per hour, price per pound, and earnings per hour. You might use rates and unit rates when you are grocery shopping, traveling, or figuring out payments to a babysitter.

Rates and unit rates are related to ratios. A ratio compares two quantities, such as 6 cups of flour to 3 cups of sugar in a recipe. A rate compares the first quantity to just *one* of the second quantity. In the recipe example, the rate of flour to sugar is 2 cups of flour to 1 cup of sugar. The unit rate comparing flour to sugar is 2 because that is the part of the rate that is compared to 1.

Consider the following example:

A train travels 360 miles in 6 hours. The train makes no stops and travels at the same speed for the entire time. How could you use the ratio of miles to hours to find the related rate and unit rate to describe how fast the train traveled?

On the next page you will see two ways your child may find a rate and a unit rate.

Vocabulary

ratio a way to compare two different quantities.

rate an equivalent ratio that compares the first quantity in a ratio to only one of the second quantity.

unit rate the part of the rate that is being compared to 1.

Understand Unit Rate: Sample Solution

A train went 360 miles in 6 hours. The train makes no stops and travels at the same speed for the entire time. Use the ratio of miles to hours to find a related rate and unit rate that describe how fast the train traveled.

One way:

- Write the ratio of miles to hours as a fraction. $\frac{360}{6}$

- Write an equivalent fraction with a denominator of 1 to find the rate. $\frac{60}{1}$

- The unit rate is the part of the rate that is compared to 1.   60

Another way:

Use a double number line to find the rate and unit rate.

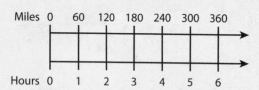

- Show *miles* on the top number line and *hours* on the bottom number line.

- Label the number of miles traveled, 360, and the number of hours spent traveling, 6.

- Since there are 6 hours of travel time, break up the distance of 360 miles into 6 equal parts, too.

- Find the number of miles traveled in 1 hour.

Answer: Both methods show that the ratio of $\frac{360}{60}$ has a related rate of $\frac{60}{1}$ and a unit rate of 60. This means that the train traveled at a rate of 60 miles per hour and that the unit rate, or the number of miles traveled in 1 hour, is 60.

Name: _____

Study the example problem showing how to write a division problem as a fraction. Then solve problems 1–7.

Example

There are 3 bags of popcorn to divide equally among 2 students. How much popcorn will each student get?

There are 3 bags of popcorn for 2 students to share, which is $3 \div 2$.

Divide each of the 3 bags into 2 equal parts. Each student will get $\frac{1}{2}$ of each bag.

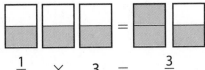

$$\frac{1}{2} \quad \times \quad 3 \quad = \quad \frac{3}{2}$$

$3 \div 2 = \frac{3}{2}$

Each student will get $\frac{3}{2}$ bags of popcorn.

---

1 How many whole bags plus how many one-half bags of popcorn would each student get?

_____ whole bag(s) _____ one-half bag(s)

2 How can you combine your answers in problem 1 to write how many bags of popcorn each student will get as a mixed number?

_____

3 Nine yards of ribbon are cut into 8 equal pieces. What is the length of each piece of ribbon? Write a division expression to represent the problem and solve.

_____

Solve.

4 How could you model 5 students sharing 4 bags of popcorn equally? How much will each student get?

_____

_____

5 In a store, 60 cans of soup are arranged to be displayed in 10 equal rows. Why does the fraction $\frac{10}{60}$ not represent this situation? Explain.

_____

_____

_____

6 Emilio bakes 2 pies. He shares them equally among 3 friends. How much pie does each person get? Express your answer as a fraction.

Show your work.

Solution: _____

7 Isabel is making lemonade for a party with 12 guests. She wants to make equal servings that are least 2 cups each. She makes 7 quarts of lemonade. Does she have enough lemonade for each guest? (1 quart = 4 cups)

Show your work.

Solution: _____

_____

Name: _____

Find Unit Rates

Study the example showing how a double number line is used to find rate and unit rates. Then solve problems 1–6.

Example

The double number line below shows the relationship between the numbers of hours and weeks Linda works. Linda worked 320 hours in 8 weeks.

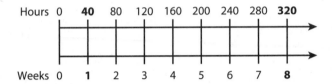

The ratio of hours to weeks is 320 to 8.

The rate is 40 hours to 1 week. The unit rate is 40.

1 Choose a corresponding pair of numbers from the top and bottom number lines. Write a multiplication equation to show how the number of weeks and hours are related.

_____

2 Use words to describe the relationship between corresponding numbers of hours and weeks.

_____

_____

_____

Vocabulary

ratio compares two quantities.

rate compares the first quantity in a ratio to only one of the second quantity.

unit rate the numerical part of the rate, without the units.

3 Explain how you can use the answer to problem 2 to verify the unit rate is 40.

_____

_____

_____

_____

Solve.

Use the following situation to solve problems 4–5.

The double number line shows the relationship between dollars earned and cars washed at a school fundraiser. Students earned 48 dollars washing 8 cars. The ratio of dollars earned to cars washed is 48 : 8.

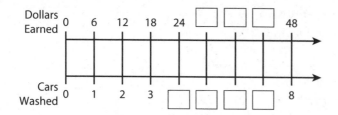

4 What pattern do you see in the dollars earned? Use the pattern to complete the top number line.

_____

What pattern do you see in the number of cars washed? Use the pattern to complete the bottom number line.

_____

Explain how the patterns show the rate of dollars earned to cars washed.

_____

5 The unit rate comparing dollars earned to cars washed is 6. If the fundraiser earned $318, how many cars were washed? Explain.

_____

_____

6 There are 50 campers at day camp and 10 counselors. Write the ratio of campers to counselors as a fraction. Explain how to use equivalent fractions to write a related rate and unit rate. What does the unit rate tell you?

_____

_____

14 **Lesson 2** *Understand* Unit Rate

Name: _____

Reason and Write

Study the example. Underline two parts that you think make it a particularly good answer and a helpful example.

Example

Mom's muffin recipe uses 10 ounces of berries for 2 dozen muffins. Grandma's muffin recipe uses 12 ounces of berries for 3 dozen muffins. Which recipe has more berries per dozen muffins? How many ounces of berries would you need to make 60 muffins of this recipe? (1 dozen = 12 muffins)

Show your work. Use ratios, unit rates, models, and words to explain your thinking.

In Mom's recipe, the ratio of berries (ounces) to muffins (dozens) is 10 : 2. There are 5 ounces of berries per 1 dozen muffins. So the unit rate is 5.

In Grandma's recipe, the ratio of berries (ounces) to muffins (dozens) is 12 : 3. There are 4 ounces of berries per 1 dozen muffins. So the unit rate is 4.

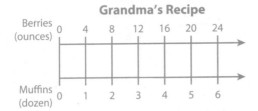

The unit rate of 5 is greater than the unit rate of 4, so Mom's recipe has more berries per dozen.

60 muffins = 5 dozen muffins, so I would need 5 × 5 or 25 ounces of berries for 5 dozen muffins of Mom's recipe.

Where does the example . . .

- answer both parts of the problem?
- use words to explain?
- use numbers to explain?
- use models to explain?
- give details?

Solve the problem. Use what you learned from the model.

You buy 3 tickets for $48 total for the jazz concert on Friday night. Your friend buys 2 tickets for $36 total for the jazz concert on Saturday night. Your brother collected $96 from his friends to buy 6 tickets. Which night can they go to the concert? Did they buy the less expensive tickets? Explain.

Show your work. Use ratios, unit rates, models, and words to explain your thinking.

Where does the example . . .

- answer both parts of the problem?

- use words to explain?

- use numbers to explain?

- use models to explain?

- give details?

Dear Family,

Your child is learning about equivalent ratios.

Your child has already learned that a ratio compares any two quantities and that a ratio has a related rate. Now your child is learning that equivalent ratios are ratios that have the same rate.

You may be familiar with using ratios in recipes, in calculating miles per gallon, or in cost per item. A fruit salad recipe that uses 3 apples for every 2 pints of berries has a 3 to 2 ratio of apples to pints of berries. To double the recipe, multiply each quantity by 2. So use 6 apples and 4 pints of berries. To make three times as much fruit salad, multiply both quantities by 3. You need 9 apples and 6 pints of berries. Both of the ratios, 6 to 4 and 9 to 3, are equivalent to the ratio 3 to 2.

Consider the following example:

A cook uses 12 cartons of berries to make 4 jars of jam. How many cartons of berries are needed to make 6 jars of jam?

The next page shows two ways your child may use equivalent ratios to find the number of cartons of berries needed.

Vocabulary

equivalent ratios two or more ratios that are equal to one another.

ratio a way to compare two different quantities.

rate an equivalent ratio that compares the first quantity in a ratio to only one of the second quantity.

unit rate the part of the rate that is being compared to 1.

NEXT →

Equivalent Ratios: Sample Solution

How many cartons of berries are needed to make 6 jars of jam when it takes 12 cartons of berries to make 4 jars of jam?

To find how many cartons of berries are needed to make 6 jars of jam, write a ratio that is equivalent to the ratio 12 to 4.

One way: Draw a diagram to represent a ratio of 12 cartons of berries to 4 jars of jam.

- The ratio of berries to jam is 12 cartons to 4 jars.

- The related rate is 3 cartons to 1 jar.

- Multiply both quantities in the rate to find an equivalent ratio for 6 jars.

  $3 \times 6 = 18$ and $1 \times 6 = 6$

An equivalent ratio is 18 to 6.

Another way:
Use a table to show equivalent ratios.

- Divide both quantities in the ratio 12 to 4 by 4 to find the related rate 3 to 1.

  $12 \div 4 = 3$ and $4 \div 4 = 1$

- Multiply to find equivalent ratios.

	$3 \times 1 = 3$	$3 \times 2 = 6$	$3 \times 3 = 9$	$3 \times 4 = 12$	$3 \times 5 = 15$	$3 \times 6 = 18$
Cartons of Berries	3	6	9	**12**	15	18
Jars of Jam	1	2	3	**4**	5	6
	$1 \times 1 = 1$	$1 \times 2 = 2$	$1 \times 3 = 3$	$1 \times 4 = 4$	$1 \times 5 = 5$	$1 \times 6 = 6$

An equivalent ratio is 18 to 6.

Answer: Both methods show that the ratio 12 to 4 is equivalent to the ratio 18 to 6. This means that 18 cartons of berries are needed to make 6 jars of jam.

Equivalent Ratios

Name: _____

Prerequisite: Compare Quantities Using Ratios

Study the example problem showing how to use ratios to compare two quantities. Then solve problems 1–6.

Example

Noelle buys 5 peaches, 3 bananas, and 4 oranges at a local fruit stand to make fruit punch. What is the ratio of the number of bananas to the number of peaches she bought?

A tape diagram can help you compare the quantities.

Peaches

Bananas

Oranges

Total Fruit

There are 3 bananas and 5 peaches.

The ratio of bananas to peaches can be written as 3 to 5, $3 : 5$, or $\frac{3}{5}$.

---

1 What is the ratio of peaches to oranges?

_____

2 What is the ratio of the number of bananas to the total number of pieces of fruit?

_____

3 Write a ratio in words to compare a whole to a part. Then write the ratio using numbers.

_____

_____

Vocabulary

ratio a comparison of two quantities.

Solve.

4 In Ellen's sixth-grade class, there are 14 boys and 11 girls. Write each ratio using numbers in two ways.

Number of girls to number of boys

_____

Number of boys to total number of students

_____

Total number of students to number of girls

_____

Number of boys to number of girls

_____

5 For every 4 miles that Pedro runs, he walks 3 miles. Tell whether each statement is *True* or *False*.

a. The ratio of miles walked to miles run is 4 : 3. ☐ True ☐ False

b. The ratio of miles walked to total miles is 3 : 7. ☐ True ☐ False

c. The ratio of miles run to total miles is 7 to 3. ☐ True ☐ False

d. The ratio of total miles to miles run is $\frac{7}{4}$. ☐ True ☐ False

e. The ratio of miles run to miles walked is 4 to 3. ☐ True ☐ False

6 For sixth-grade field day, 6 students in Alice's class are playing volleyball, 5 students are playing soccer, and 9 students are playing basketball. Alice said that the ratio of students playing volleyball to basketball was 6 : 9. Alex said that the ratio of students playing basketball to volleyball was $\frac{9}{6}$. Who is correct? Explain.

_____

_____

_____

_____

Name: _____

Show Equivalent Ratios

Study the example problem showing how to find equivalent ratios. Then solve problems 1–7.

Example

Elena uses 12 red beads to make 4 bracelets. How many red beads will Elena need to make 12 bracelets? How many red beads will Elena need to make 20 bracelets?

You can make a table showing the number of bracelets that can be made with different numbers of red beads. The pairs of numbers in each column show the ratio of red beads to bracelets. Notice the ratios are all equivalent.

Number of Red Beads	3	6	12	24	36	48	60	72
Number of Bracelets	1	2	4	8	12	16	20	24

The table shows Elena will need 36 red beads to make 12 bracelets. Elena will need 60 red beads to make 20 bracelets.

1 How many red beads will Elena need to make 16 bracelets?

_____

2 How many bracelets can Elena make with 24 red beads?

_____

3 Find the rate of red beads per bracelet. Explain how you found your answer.

_____

_____

4 James said that he would need 25 red beads to make 75 bracelets. Is he correct? How did he get that answer?

_____

_____

_____

Solve.

Use the following information to solve problems 5–7.

> The list below shows how many servings of different breakfast items that a restaurant expects to sell every 15 minutes:
>
> | | |
> |---|---|
> | Cups of coffee | 25 |
> | Glasses of orange juice | 10 |
> | Omelets | 6 |

5 How many glasses of orange juice does the restaurant expect to sell in 1 hour?

Show your work.

Solution: _____

6 At this rate, how long will it take to sell 200 cups of coffee?

Show your work.

Solution: _____

7 The restaurant serves breakfast from 6:00 AM until 10:30 AM. They sell 6 omelets every 15 minutes. Should the restaurant expect to sell more than or fewer than 100 omelets? Explain your answer.

_____

_____

_____

_____

_____

Name: _____

Graph Equivalent Ratios

Study the example problem showing how to graph equivalent ratios. Then solve problems 1–10.

Example

The graph compares how far Jorge walks to how many steps he takes. How many feet does he walk in 6 steps? How many steps does Jorge take to walk 30 feet?

Each point on the graph can be represented by an ordered pair. The point represented by (6, 18) shows that Jorge takes 6 steps to walk 18 feet.

The ordered pair for 30 feet is (10, 30), which means that Jorge walks 30 feet in 10 steps.

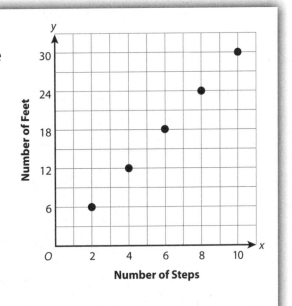

1 What ordered pair represents the number of steps Jorge takes to walk 24 feet?

_____

2 Choose another point on the graph. Write the ordered pair and tell what it represents.

_____

3 What ordered pair represents the number of feet Jorge walks in 3 steps?

_____

4 Joan looks at the graph and says the number of steps is always 3 times the number of feet. Is she correct? Explain your answer.

_____

_____

Solve.

Use the following situation for problems 5–8.

> To make a scarf, Jenny uses blue yarn and white yarn.
> The number of yards of blue yarn she uses is 4 times the
> number of yards of white yarn in each scarf.

5 Write four ratios to show the number of yards of white
   yarn to blue yarn for each scarf.

6 Are the ratios in problem 5 equivalent? Explain how you know.

   _____

   _____

7 Jenny wants to make a scarf that uses 24 yards of blue
   yarn. How many yards of white yarn will she need?

   _____

8 If Jenny wants to keep the ratio of blue yarn to white yarn
   the same, can she make a scarf using 42 yards of blue yarn?
   If so, how much white yarn will she need? If not, why not?

   _____

   _____

   _____

9 Adrianna can read 7 pages in 10 minutes. At this rate,
   how many pages can she read in 25 minutes?

   _____

10 Max calculated that he could read at a rate of 2 pages per
   minute. Is he reading at a faster rate than Adrianna? Explain.

   _____

   _____

   _____

   _____

Name: _____

Equivalent Ratios

Solve the problems.

1 Kate, Mario, Sato, and Den each use a different recipe to make trail mix. Which recipe uses a different ratio of cups of raisins to cereal than the rest?

A Kate uses 3 cups of raisins for every 8 cups of cereal.

B Mario uses 4 cups of raisins for every 12 cups of cereal.

C Sato uses 6 cups of raisins for every 16 cups of cereal.

D Den uses 9 cups of raisins for every 24 cups of cereal.

To find one ratio that's different, I need to find some that are equal to each other.

2 The graph shows the number of teaspoons of lemon juice in cups of lemonade.

Which number is first in an ordered pair?

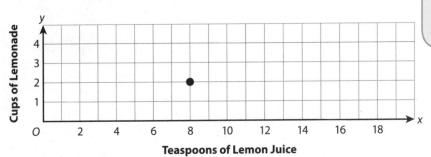

Cups of Lemonade

Teaspoons of Lemon Juice

Which ordered pair represents a ratio equivalent to the ratio of teaspoons of lemon juice to cups of lemonade shown by the point on the graph?

A (4, 16)   **C** (9, 3)

B (6, 1)   **D** (16, 4)

Oscar chose **A** as the correct answer. How did he get that answer?

_____

_____

Solve.

3 Rey buys 4 cards for $10. He plots the point (4, 10) on a graph. All cards are the same price. He wants to see how much it would cost to buy more cards. Tell whether each statement is *True* or *False*.

> Be sure that you understand what Rey's ordered pair means.

a. The point (6, 15) will be on the graph. ☐ True ☐ False

b. Rey buys 1 card for $3.50. ☐ True ☐ False

c. Rey buys 100 cards for less than $40. ☐ True ☐ False

d. The point (14, 35) will be on the graph. ☐ True ☐ False

4 Each table shows four ratios of boys to girls at different sporting events. Which tables show four equivalent ratios of boys to girls? Select all that apply.

> What makes two ratios equivalent?

A

3	5	9	12
5	7	15	20

C

45	25	10	5
18	10	4	2

B

3	4	7	11
12	16	28	44

D

200	150	100	50
50	40	30	20

5 Rosa earns $10 for every 3 hours that she works. Ralph earns $7 for every 2 hours that he works. Who earns more per hour? How much *more* does this person earn after 12 hours of work?

Show your work.

> Be careful not to compare $10 to $7—these represent earnings for different numbers of hours.

Solution: _____

_____

Dear Family,

Your child is learning about solving problems with a unit rate.

Here are some examples of situations involving a unit rate that may be familiar to you.

- You purchase 3 pounds of red peppers for $5.37 at the grocery store. What is the price per pound?

- You drove 120 miles in 2 hours on a car trip. If you drive at the same speed, how long will it take to make a 250-mile trip?

In each situation, you can use a unit rate to figure out the answer. A unit rate gives the price for 1 pound or the distance traveled in 1 hour. In the first situation, which involves a unit rate for price, the unit rate is called a unit price. You often see supermarket shelves labeled with unit prices for various items.

Consider the following example:

Dylan bought 3 pounds of green beans for $7.50. His aunt wants to buy 5 pounds of green beans for a dish that she is making for a party. How much do 5 pounds of green beans cost?

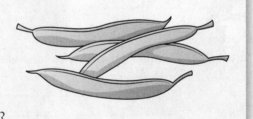

On the next page you will see two ways your child may solve the problem by using a unit rate.

Vocabulary

unit rate the part of the rate that is being compared to 1.

unit price the price for 1 unit.

NEXT

What is the cost of 5 pounds of green beans if 3 pounds of green beans cost $7.50?

To find the cost of 5 pounds, determine the unit price by using the ratio of $7.50 to 3 pounds. Then use the unit price to find the cost of 5 pounds.

One way:
Use a table to determine equivalent ratios and to find the unit rate.

Cost ($)	2.50	5.00	**7.50**	10.00	**12.50**
Pounds	1	2	**3**	4	**5**

- The ratio is $7.50 to 3 pounds.

- Divide both quantities in the ratio $7.50 to 3 by 3. The result is the equivalent ratio $2.50 to 1.

- $2.50 is the unit rate because the cost of 1 unit is $2.50. $2.50 is also the unit price, the cost of 1 pound.

- To find the cost of 5 pounds, multiply the unit price of $2.50 by 5.
    5 × $2.50 = $12.50

Another way:
Add to find the values in a table of equivalent ratios.

Cost ($)	2.50	5.00	7.50	**10.00**	**12.50**
Pounds	1	2	3	**4**	**5**

- Find the unit price as described above. The unit price is $2.50.

- 4 pounds = 3 pounds + 1 pound
    Add the corresponding costs: $7.50 + $2.50 = $10.00

- 5 pounds = 4 pounds + 1 pound
    Add the corresponding costs: $10.00 + $2.50 = $12.50

Answer: Both methods show that the unit price is $2.50, and both methods use the unit price to find that 5 pounds of green beans cost $12.50.

Solve Problems with Unit Rate

Name: _____

Prerequisite: Equivalent Ratios

Study the example problem showing how to find equivalent ratios. Then solve problems 1–6.

Example

Ramon needs 12 oranges to make 3 glasses of juice. How many oranges does he need to make 5 glasses? How many oranges does he need to make 8 glasses?

You can make a table to show ratios of the number of oranges to the number of glasses of juice.

Number of Oranges	4	8	12	16	20	24	28	32
Number of Glasses	1	2	3	4	5	6	7	8

Ramon needs 20 oranges to make 5 glasses of juice.

Ramon needs 32 oranges to make 8 glasses of juice.

1 What ratio is given in the problem for the number of oranges to the number of glasses of juice?

_____

2 What is the unit rate? Explain what it means in this situation.

_____

_____

3 Explain how you can write equivalent ratios.

_____

_____

_____

_____

_____

_____

Vocabulary

equivalent ratios two or more ratios that are equal to one another.

24 : 2, 36 : 3, 48 : 4

Solve.

4 Nathan does push-ups for the same amount of time every day. He does 9 minutes of push-ups in 3 days. How many minutes of push-ups does Nathan do in 7 days? Make a table to show the relationship between the number of minutes and the number of days.

Show your work.

Solution: _____

5 Students are knitting scarves for a fund-raiser. Elaine can knit 4 scarves in 20 days. Mario can knit 2 more scarves than Elaine can in 40 days. What is the difference in the time it takes each of them to knit a scarf? Explain your answers.

Show your work.

Solution: _____

6 There are 24 total customers seated at 4 tables in a restaurant. Each table has the same number of customers. Tell whether each statement is *True* or *False*.

a. Multiply 24 by 4 to find the number of customers per table. ☐ True ☐ False

b. The unit rate for the number of customers per table is 6. ☐ True ☐ False

c. The ratio of customers to tables is 24 : 4. ☐ True ☐ False

d. If all the tables are the same size, a maximum of 30 customers can sit at 6 tables. ☐ True ☐ False

Name: _____

Unit Price

Study the example problem showing how to solve a problem about unit price. Then solve problems 1–7.

Example

All the comic books in a store are the same price. Vera buys 3 comic books for $7.50. How much do 5 comic books cost? How much do 8 comic books cost?

Divide 7.50 by 3 to find the unit price.

$7.50 \div 3 = 2.50$

The price per book is $2.50. You can use the unit price to make a table of equivalent ratios.

Cost ($)	2.50	5.00	7.50	10.00	12.50	15.00	17.50	20.00
Comic Books	1	2	3	4	5	6	7	8

The cost of 5 comic books is $12.50.

The cost of 8 comic books is $20.00.

1 How can you use multiplication to find the cost of 5 comic books?

_____

2 How can you use addition to find the cost of 8 comic books?

_____

3 Explain how to find the number of comic books you could buy with $25.00.

_____

_____

_____

_____

Lesson 4 Solve Problems with Unit Rate   **31**

Solve.

Use the following situation to solve problems 4–7.

All of the used hardcover books at a yard sale are the same price. Hugo paid $4.50 for 6 books.

4 Explain how to find the unit price of the books.

_____

5 Hugo's friends bought used books at the yard sale. Sonia paid $2.25, John paid $6.00, and Keisha paid $3.75. How many books did each friend buy?

Show your work.

Solution: _____

6 Kim bought 10 used books at the yard sale. How much did she pay? Did you use addition or multiplication to solve this problem? Why?

_____

7 The price for the used paperback books at the yard sale was $0.25 less than for the hardcover books. How many more paperback books than hardcover books could someone buy with $3.00?

Show your work.

Solution: _____

Name: _____

Constant Speed

Study the example problem showing how to solve a problem about constant speed. Then solve problems 1–7.

Example

Kenja traveled 120 miles in 3 hours on a train. At this speed, how long will it take her to travel 200 miles?

The unit rate for miles per hour is 120 ÷ 3, or 40. Use the unit rate to make a double number line.

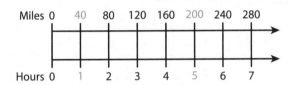

Divide 200 by 40.
200 ÷ 40 = 5

It will take Kenja 5 hours to travel 200 miles.

---

1 How many miles could Kenja travel in 1 hour. Is this the same number of hours it takes Kenja to travel 1 mile? Explain your answer.

_____

_____

_____

2 Explain how to use the unit rate for miles per hour to find how many miles Kenja can travel in 8 hours.

_____

3 Explain how to use the double number line to find how many hours it will take Kenja to travel 220 miles.

_____

_____

_____

Solve.

Use the following situation to solve problems 4–6.

Zachary exercises by jogging at a constant speed. During one week, he jogged 36 miles in 6 hours.

4 Complete the double number line to show the relationship between the number of miles and the hours that Zachary jogs.

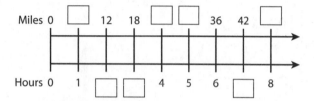

Miles 0 ☐ 12 18 ☐ ☐ 36 42 ☐

Hours 0 1 ☐ ☐ 4 5 6 ☐ 8

5 Explain how you found the number of hours it takes Zachary to jog 18 miles.

_____

_____

6 How many miles does Zachary jog in 4.5 hours? Explain how to use the double number line to find the answer.

_____

_____

7 Alyssa and Caleb both drove 210 miles to the beach in separate cars. They left at the same time. They both drove at a constant speed. Alyssa drove 105 miles in 3.5 hours. Caleb drove 168 miles in 4 hours. Who arrived earlier? How much earlier?

Show your work.

Solution: _____

Converting Measurement Units

Study the example problem showing how to solve a problem involving conversion of measurement units. Then solve problems 1–6.

Example

Hannah needs 78 inches of ribbon to make a picture frame. She knows that there are 60 inches in 5 feet. How many feet of ribbon are in 78 inches?

You can find the unit rate and make a double number line. There are 60 inches in 5 feet, so there are $60 \div 5 =$ 12 inches in 1 foot. The unit rate is 12.

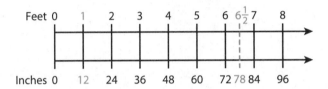

Because the number of inches, 78, is halfway between 72 and 84, the number of feet must be halfway between 6 and 7 feet. There are $6\frac{1}{2}$ feet of ribbon in 78 inches.

---

1 Explain how to use the unit rate without the number lines to find how many feet of ribbon are in 48 inches.

_____

2 How many inches of ribbon are in 3 feet? Explain how to find the answer without using the number lines.

_____

3 What is the difference between using the unit rate to find how many feet are in a given number of inches and using the unit rate to find how many inches are in a given number of feet?

_____

_____

_____

Solve.
Use the following situation to solve problems 4–5.

Antonio measures items in his pocket. He knows there are 50 millimeters in 5 centimeters. His key chain is 3.5 centimeters long. His library card is 80 millimeters long.

4 How many centimeters long is his library card? Explain how to use the unit rate to find the answer.

_____

_____

_____

5 How many millimeters long is his key chain? Draw a double number line to find the answer.

Show your work.

Solution: _____

6 Claire is measuring ingredients for recipes. She knows that there are 12 cups in 6 pints. She also knows that 4 quarts equals 16 cups. Which has more cups, 5 pints or 3 quarts? How many more cups?

Show your work.

Solution: _____

Name: _____

Solve Problems with Unit Rate

Solve the problems.

1 The double number line shows the relationship between the number of minutes and the number of pages that a printer prints. How many pages does the printer print in $4\frac{1}{2}$ minutes?

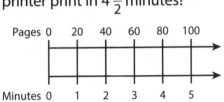

Pages 0   20   40   60   80   100

Minutes 0   1   2   3   4   5

Where is $4\frac{1}{2}$ minutes located on the number line?

A 80 pages   **B** 85 pages   **C** 90 pages   **D** 100 pages

2 A carpenter uses 65 shelves to make 13 bookcases. She uses the same number of shelves for each bookcase. Are 32 shelves enough to build 6 more bookcases?

Show your work.

What is the unit rate?

Solution: _____

3 The price of 6 pretzels is $5.10. Simon and Sofia bought 8 pretzels and shared the cost equally. How much did each person pay?

A $0.85   **C** $6.80

B $3.40   **D** $20.40

One calculation is not enough to solve this problem.

Jacob chose **C** as the correct answer. How did he get that answer?

_____

_____

Solve.

4 Michael drove 350 miles in 7 hours at a constant speed. Tell whether each statement is *True* or *False*.

How can you find a unit rate?

a. The unit rate for miles to hours is 50. ☐ True ☐ False

b. Michael drove 250 miles in 4 hours. ☐ True ☐ False

c. To find the number of miles Michael drove in 3 hours, multiply 3 by 50. ☐ True ☐ False

d. To find the number of hours it took Michael to drive 300 miles, divide 300 by 50. ☐ True ☐ False

5 Jorge says there are 198 inches in 5.5 yards. Is he correct? Explain your answer.

Show your work.

Do you know the unit rate for inches per foot? Do you know the unit rate for feet per yard?

Solution: _____

6 At Teen Tops, a package of 5 T-shirts costs $38. At Bargain City, a package of 4 T-shirts costs $34. Which statement is the most accurate?

Finding unit prices will help you choose the correct answer.

A   Bargain City is the better buy because it sells T-shirts at $8.50 per T-shirt.

B   Teen Tops is the better buy because the package has more T-shirts.

C   Bargain City is the better buy because $34 is less than $38.

D   Teen Tops is the better buy because it sells T-shirts at $7.60 per T-shirt.

Lesson 4 Solve Problems with Unit Rate

Dear Family,

Your child is learning about solving problems with percent.

Your child has already learned about ratios that compare two quantities and about rates that compare a quantity to just one of another quantity. A percent is a special kind of rate that compares a quantity to 100. The symbol % is a percent symbol.

You have most likely seen percent used in a variety of real-life situations. Some examples you might have seen are:

- a store advertises a "25% off" sale

- a student receives a grade of 84% on a test

- a salesperson earns a commission of 7%

- a newscast reports voter turnout for an election was 53%.

An advantage of using a percent in these situations is that you can more easily compare a part to a whole of 100. In the example of a student's grade, it's easier to understand that 84% of the test questions are correct than it is to make sense of the fact that 21 out of 25 questions are correct.

Consider the following example:

Ms. Gartner purchased a new smartphone and plans to pay the total cost of $360 in installments. Her first payment is 25% of the total cost. How much is her first payment?

The next page shows two different ways your child might find a percent of a number.

Vocabulary

percent a rate "for every 100" or "per 100."

> How much is Ms. Gartner's first payment for the smartphone if the payment is 25% of the total cost of $360?

One way:
Use a model.

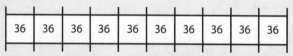

36	36	36	36	36	36	36	36	36	36

0% 10% 20% 30% 40% 50% 60% 70% 80% 90% 100%

- Divide 360 into 10 equal groups of 36.
  Each group of 36 represents 10%.

- 25% is halfway between 20% and 30%.
  20% of 360 is 2 groups of 36, or 72.
  Add another half of a group of 36, or 18, to 72: 72 + 18 = 90.
  So, 25% of 360 is 90.

Another way:
Write an expression. Remember, the word "of" means to multiply.

Use words: 25% of 360

Use numbers: $\frac{25}{100}$ • 360

Multiply: $\frac{25}{100} \cdot \frac{360}{1} = \frac{9,000}{100}$

$= \frac{90}{1}$, or 90

Notice that in this method 25% was written as a fraction. You can write any percent as a fraction with a denominator of 100.

Answer: Both methods show that 25% of 360 is 90. This means that Ms. Gartner's first payment is $90, which represents 25% of the cost of the smartphone, or $360.

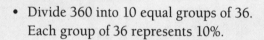

Solve Problems with Percent

Name: _____

Prerequisite: Unit Rate

**Study the example showing how to find the unit rate.
Then solve problems 1–7.**

Example

A bus driver made 100 stops on his route in 5 days. The double number line shows the relationship between the number of stops and the number of days.

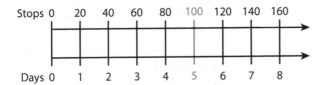

In the diagram, 100 and 5 represent the ratio of 100 stops to 5 days.

You can write a multiplication equation to show how 5 days and 100 stops are related.

$5 \times 20 = 100$

1 Look at the corresponding pairs of numbers on the number lines. Write a multiplication equation to show how 3 days and 60 stops are related. Repeat for two other corresponding pairs of numbers.

_____

2 What is the relationship between the number of stops and each corresponding number of days?

_____

_____

3 What is the rate of stops per day? What is the unit rate?

rate: _____   unit rate: _____

Vocabulary

rate a ratio that compares the first quantity to only one of the second quantity.

unit rate the number in a rate that is being compared to 1.

Solve.

Use the following situation to solve problems 4–5.

Caroline earns $54 babysitting for 6 hours.

4 Fill in the blanks on the double number line to show the relationship between the amount of money Caroline earns and the number of hours she works.

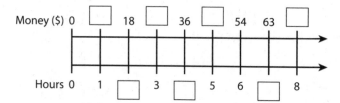

Money ($) 0 ☐ 18 ☐ 36 ☐ 54 63 ☐

Hours 0 1 ☐ 3 ☐ 5 6 ☐ 8

5 What is Caroline's rate, in dollars per hour? What is her unit rate?

_____

6 Ling uses 21 bananas to make 7 fruit smoothies. What is the rate that Ling uses for bananas per each smoothie? What is the unit rate? Explain how to use equivalent fractions to find the answer.

_____

_____

7 Kelly drove 440 miles in 8 hours. Alberto drove 468 miles in 9 hours. Both drove at a constant speed. Who drove farther in 1 hour? How many miles farther?

Show your work.

Solution: _____

Name: _____

Percent of a Number

Study the example problem showing how to find the percent of a number. Then solve problems 1–6.

Example

In an after-school sports program, 70% of 400 students play soccer. How many students play soccer?

You can use a model to find 70% of 400.

40	40	40	40	40	40	40	40	40	40

0% 10% 20% 30% 40% 50% 60% 70% 80% 90% 100%

The model shows 400 divided into groups of 40. Each group of 40 represents 10% of 400, so 7 groups of 40 represent 70% of 400. This means that 70% of 400 is 7 • 40, or 280.

There are 280 students who play soccer.

1 What is 70% written as a fraction? _____

2 Use the fraction to write and evaluate a multiplication expression that represents 70% of 400. Compare the answer to the one you got using the model.

Show your work.

Solution: _____

3 What is 75% of 400? Write and evaluate an expression to find the answer. Then explain how to use the model to justify the answer.

_____

_____

Lesson 5 Solve Problems with Percent   **43**

Solve.

Use the following situation to solve problems 4–5.

The results of a survey show that 40% of 300 students chose conserving natural resources as the top priority for their generation.

4 How many students chose conserving natural resources? Make a model to find the answer.

Show your work.

Solution: _____

5 Suppose only 24% of 300 students chose conserving natural resources. How many students chose conserving natural resources? Explain how you found your answer. How can the model help you justify the answer?

_____

_____

_____

6 There are 50 puzzles in Maggie's puzzle book. Maggie finished 30% of the puzzles. How many puzzles does she have left to do?

Show your work.

Solution: _____

Name: _____

Finding the Whole

Study the example problem showing how to find the whole when a part and the percent are given. Then solve problems 1–6.

Example

Carmen saved $27, which was 30% of the money she earned. How much did Carmen earn?

You can use a double number line to find the whole when a part and the percent are given.

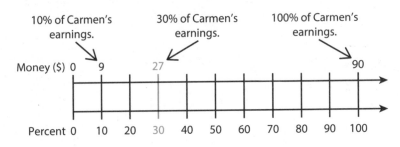

Carmen earned $90.

1 How can you find 10% of Carmen's earnings using the ratio 27 to 30? What is 10% of Carmen's earnings?

_____

_____

_____

2 How many times as great as 10% is 100%?

_____

3 How can you find 100% of Carmen's earnings using the ratio of her earnings to 10%? What is 100% of Carmen's earnings?

_____

_____

_____

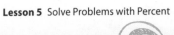

Solve.

4 Diane received 300 votes in the election for student council president. That was 60% of the students who voted in the election. How many students voted in the election? Use a double number line in your explanation.

_____

_____

5 Students sold 80% of the books donated to the used book sale. They sold 48 books in all. How many books were donated to the used book sale? Use a table in your explanation.

_____

_____

6 Omar spends $63 on souvenirs during his vacation. That is 35% of the money he brought with him. How much money does Omar have left to spend?

Show your work.

Solution: _____

Name: _____

Solve Problems with Percent

Solve the problems.

1 Jamil traveled 210 miles, which is 70% of the total distance to his grandfather's house. How many more miles does he need to travel to reach his grandfather's house?

You need to make two calculations to solve this problem.

A 90 miles **C** 300 miles

B 147 miles **D** 390 miles

Kate chose **B** as the correct answer. How did she get that answer?

_____

_____

2 Brandon plowed snow from 84 driveways in 7 days. He plowed the same number of driveways each day. Tell whether each statement is *True* or *False*.

Use the ratio of driveways to days to help you.

a. The rate is 84 driveways to 1 day. ☐ True ☐ False

b. The unit rate for driveways per day is 12. ☐ True ☐ False

c. The rate in fraction form is $\frac{12}{1}$. ☐ True ☐ False

d. If Brandon continues at the same rate, he will plow 120 driveways in 12 days. ☐ True ☐ False

3 A meteorologist said that it rained during 20% of the past 60 days. On how many days did it not rain?

Show your work.

What operation does the word "of" indicate?

Solution: _____

Solve.

4 At tryouts for the school talent show, 60% of 30 performers played a musical instrument. How many performers played a musical instrument? Use the model to find the answer.

3	3	3	3	3	3	3	3	3	3

0% 10% 20% 30% 40% 50% 60% 70% 80% 90% 100%

How many groups of 3 are in 60%?

A 3 performers   **C** 30 performers

B 18 performers   **D** 60 performers

5 Students collected 600 cans for the canned food drive. That was 80% of their goal. How many more cans do they need to collect to reach their goal?

Do you need to find the part or the whole?

Show your work.

Solution: _____

6 Megan correctly spelled 45 out of 50 words in a spelling competition. Justin spelled 27 out of 30 words correctly. Fernando spelled 82 out of 120 words correctly. Which statements are true? Select all that apply.

How can you find a percent using a ratio?

A Fernando spelled the greatest percent of words correctly.

B Megan and Justin spelled the same percent of words correctly.

C Justin spelled the least percent of words correctly.

D The percent of words that Megan spelled correctly is greater than the percent of words that Fernando spelled correctly.

Unit 1 Game

Ratio Four Squares

What you need: 2 Recording Sheets (1 for each player), number cubes (two labeled 1–6 and one labeled 4, 6, 8, 9, 10, 12)

Directions

- Your goal is to create two equivalent ratios in each Ratio Box on the Recording Sheet and find the unit rate for each set of equivalent ratios.

- Take turns. Roll all three number cubes. Pick two of them to make a ratio. You may choose to roll one, two, or all three number cubes again before picking two numbers.

- Name the ratio. You can write the ratio in any Ratio Box that has a blank space.

- If a Ratio Box already has one ratio, you can write the ratio in the blank space **if** it is equivalent to the ratio that is already in the Ratio Box.

- When you have two equivalent ratios in a Ratio Box, calculate the unit rate and write it in the space provided.

- Continue until one player has found four equivalent ratios and unit rates.

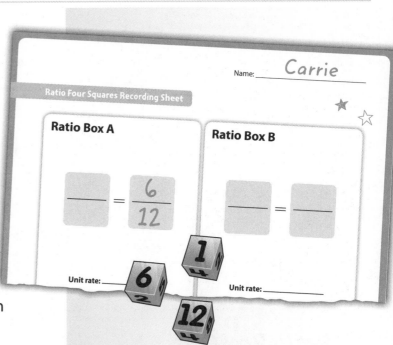

I know that $\frac{6}{12}$ is equivalent to $\frac{1}{2}$. There are a lot of ways to write ratios equivalent to $\frac{1}{2}$. Using $\frac{1}{2}$ will help me to complete the box.

Ratio Four Squares Recording Sheet

Ratio Box A

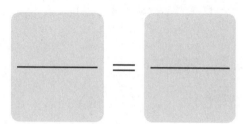

Unit rate: _____

Ratio Box B

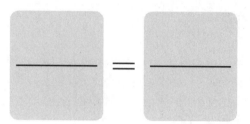

Unit rate: _____

Ratio Box C

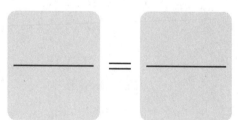

Unit rate: _____

Ratio Box D

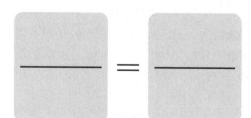

Unit rate: _____

Ratios and Proportional Relationships

In this unit you learned to:	Lesson
write a ratio to describe the relationship between two quantities.	1
find the rate and unit rate associated with a given ratio.	2
compare ratios and find equivalent ratios.	3
solve unit rate problems.	4
solve percent problems.	5

Use these skills to solve problems 1–6.

1 Hui walks at a constant speed when he walks for exercise. The table shows how many miles Hui can walk in different amounts of time. Complete the table.

Number of Miles	Number of Minutes
$\frac{1}{2}$	6
1	
	24
	42

2 Two identical boxes of softballs weigh a total of 480 ounces. Sixteen identical boxes of baseballs weigh a total of 224 pounds. Does a box of baseballs weigh more or less than a box of softballs? Explain.

_____

_____

_____

_____

Solve.

3 At basketball practice, Kyla made 60 free throws. This was 80% of her attempts. How many free throws did Kyla attempt?

   A 48 free throws   **C** 75 free throws

   B 68 free throws   **D** 80 free throws

4 Jolene can read 10 pages in 20 minutes. How fast can she read? Select all that apply.

   A 5 pages every 10 minutes   **C** 1 page every 2 minutes

   B 2 pages every 1 minute   **D** $\frac{1}{2}$ page every 1 minute

5 Philip has 5 red counters, 6 yellow counters, and 9 green counters. Tell whether each statement is *True* or *False*.

   a. The ratio of yellow counters to green counters is 2 : 3.   ☐ True   ☐ False

   b. The ratio of red counters to the total number of counters is 1 to 3.   ☐ True   ☐ False

   c. The ratio of all counters to yellow counters is $\frac{10}{3}$.   ☐ True   ☐ False

   d. Green counters make up 45% of all the counters.   ☐ True   ☐ False

6 Dawit was earning $100 per week in January. He got a raise of 10% in March, but then he had a 10% reduction in his weekly pay after changing jobs in August. Was Dawit's weekly pay after August higher, lower, or the same as it was in January? Explain.

_____

_____

_____

Name: _____

Answer the questions and show all your work on separate paper.

Your school has been awarded a $2,000 grant. You are using the money to set up an office for the science club. The items that you are considering are shown in the table. You must buy at least one of each item. You can buy more than one of any of the items as long as you stay within the $2,000 budget.

The store that sells these products has offered to give you the following discounts.
- 10% off any television over $300
- 15% off any laptop
- 5% off any printer or scanner

Television	Laptop	Printer	Scanner
32-inch $230	15-inch screen $400	Black $120	Basic scanner $120
40-inch $320	17-inch screen $460	Color $250	Scanner and color copier $300
42-inch $400	Touch screen $500		

Help the science club make a plan.
- Tell the items that you will buy.
- Calculate the total cost, including all discounts.
- Find the amount left over from the grant.

Reflect on Mathematical Practices

After you complete the task, choose one of the following questions to answer.

1 Persevere Did you use estimation to get an idea of about how many of each item you might order? Explain.

2 Make Sense of Problems How did you decide which items to buy?

Checklist

Did you . . .
- [ ] complete all the necessary calculations?
- [ ] label all the prices in your work?
- [ ] check to make sure your total is within the budget?

Performance Task Tips

Word Bank Here are some words that you might use in your answer.

percent	add	round
decimal	sum	estimate
multiply	total	subtract

Models Here are some models that you might use to find the solution.

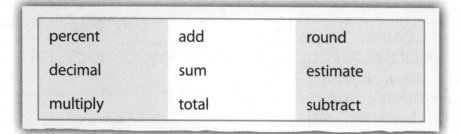

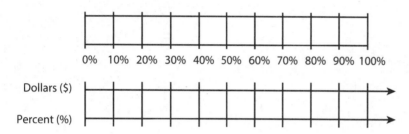

Sentence Starters Here are some sentence starters that might help you explain your work.

I chose to buy _____

To find the amount of the discount _____

The price after the discount _____

Name: _____

My Examples

corresponding terms

numbers that are in same position in two
or more related patterns

ordered pair

a pair of numbers that locate a point on a
coordinate plane

ratio

a comparison of two quantities

rate

a ratio that compares the first quantity in
a ratio to only one of the second quantity

unit rate

the numerical part of the rate, without the units; the number in a rate that is being compared to 1

equivalent ratios

two or more ratios that are equal to one another

24 : 2, 36 : 3, 48 : 4

My Words

_____

_____

_____

_____

_____

_____

_____

My Examples

Dear Family,

Your child is learning what it means to divide with fractions.

Here are some real-life situations that involve dividing with fractions.

- You want to use a 12-foot length of wood to make stakes for a garden. How many $\frac{3}{4}$-foot garden stakes can you make?

- You cut a $\frac{1}{2}$-yard length of string into 3 equal-sized pieces to make a hanging mobile. How long is each piece of string?

- You have $\frac{3}{4}$ gallon of cooking oil that you want to pour into $\frac{1}{8}$-gallon containers. How many containers will you use?

In each situation, you need to divide with fractions. In the first example, you divide a whole number by a fraction to find how many garden stakes you can make. In the second example, you divide a fraction by a whole number to find the length of each piece of string. In the last example, you divide a fraction by a fraction to find out how many containers you will use.

Consider the following situation:

Maria has an 8-gallon bag of garden soil.
Each of her planters holds $\frac{2}{3}$ gallon of soil.
How many planters can she fill with the bag
of soil?

The next page shows two different ways your child might find the number of planters that can be filled.

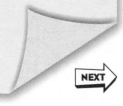

NEXT

Lesson 6 *Understand* Division with Fractions   **57**

Each planter holds $\frac{2}{3}$ gallon of soil. How can you find the number of planters Maria can fill with an 8-gallon bag of garden soil?

To find the number of planters Maria can fill, you need to divide the amount of garden soil that she has, 8 gallons, by the amount each planter can hold, $\frac{2}{3}$ gallon.

One way:
Write the division equation. $\qquad\qquad\qquad 8 \div \frac{2}{3} = ?$

Dividing by a fraction is the same as
multiplying by the reciprocal of the fraction. $\quad 8 \times \frac{3}{2} = ?$
The reciprocal of $\frac{2}{3}$ is $\frac{3}{2}$.

Solve. $\qquad\qquad\qquad\qquad\qquad\qquad 8 \times \frac{3}{2} = \frac{24}{2} = 12$

Another way:
Make a number line to show the 8 gallons of soil and divide it into thirds.

- Divide each of the 8 gallons into thirds.

- Mark groups of $\frac{2}{3}$s.

- There are 12 groups of $\frac{2}{3}$ in 8.

0 1 2 3 4 5 6 7 8

Answer: Both methods show that $8 \div \frac{2}{3} = 12$, meaning that Maria can fill 12 $\frac{2}{3}$-gallon planters with an 8-gallon bag of garden soil.

Understand
Division with Fractions

Name: _____

Prerequisite: How do you divide with unit fractions?

Study the example problem showing division of a whole number by a unit fraction. Then solve problems 1–7.

Example Problem

Karl puts $\frac{1}{2}$ cup of chopped tomatoes into each salad he makes. How many salads can he make with 3 cups of tomatoes?

The model represents the problem. You can use the model to write a division equation and a multiplication equation.

3 cups of tomatoes

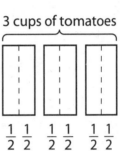

$\frac{1}{2}$ $\frac{1}{2}$ $\frac{1}{2}$ $\frac{1}{2}$ $\frac{1}{2}$ $\frac{1}{2}$

$3 \div \frac{1}{2} = 6$ $3 \times 2 = 6$

Both equations show that Karl can make 6 salads with 3 cups of tomatoes.

1 Explain how the model represents $3 \div \frac{1}{2} = 6$.

_____

_____

2 Explain how the model represents $3 \times 2 = 6$.

_____

_____

3 Suppose Karl uses 5 cups of tomatoes. How many salads can he make? Write both a division equation and a multiplication equation to show your solution.

_____

_____

Vocabulary

unit fraction a fraction with a numerator of 1.

$\frac{1}{3}, \frac{1}{8},$ and $\frac{1}{12}$ are unit fractions.

Solve.

4 Four students are sharing $\frac{1}{3}$ carton of yogurt equally. Complete the steps to find what fraction of the carton each student gets.

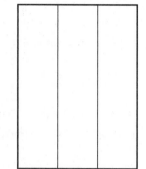

   a. The model at the right represents 1 carton. Shade the model to show $\frac{1}{3}$ carton.

   b. Divide the model into 4 equal parts by drawing horizontal lines to represent sharing among 4 students. Shade one row to show $\frac{1}{4}$.

   c. Complete the equation to show what fraction of the carton of yogurt each student gets.

      $\frac{1}{3} \div 4 =$ _____ carton of yogurt

5 Use the model in problem 4 to write a multiplication equation that can be used to solve the problem.

_____

6 Find $2 \div \frac{1}{3}$. Explain how to use the number line to find the answer.

_____

7 Ana has $\frac{1}{2}$ hour of free time. She divides the time equally between walking her dog and playing her favorite song on the piano. If she plays the song 3 times, how long is the song? Give your answer as a fraction of an hour. Write division equations to represent the problem.

Show your work.

Solution: _____

Name: _____

Divide by a Fraction

Study the example problem showing division of a fraction by a fraction. Then solve problems 1–10.

Example

Mr. Garcia has $\frac{3}{4}$ yard of ribbon to make badges for winners of the science fair. He uses $\frac{1}{8}$ yard of ribbon for each badge. How many badges can Mr. Garcia make?

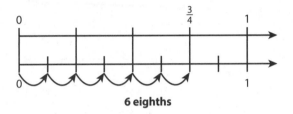

6 eighths

Find the number of eighths in $\frac{3}{4}$. Use the number lines.

$$\frac{3}{4} \div \frac{1}{8} = 6$$

Mr. Garcia can make 6 badges.

---

1 What does $\frac{3}{4}$ on the top number line represent?

_____

2 What does each equal part on the bottom number line represent?

_____

3 How many eighths are in $\frac{3}{4}$? _____

4 Suppose Mr. Garcia is making badges using $\frac{3}{8}$ yard of ribbon for each badge. He starts with the same amount of ribbon, $\frac{3}{4}$ yard. How many badges can he make? Write a division equation that supports your answer.

_____

Lesson 6 *Understand* Division with Fractions

Solve.

Use the following situation to solve problems 5–9.

> Rosa puts $\frac{2}{3}$ cup of vegetable mixture in 1 tortilla. She has 8 cups of vegetable mixture.

5 Rosa says that to find how many tortillas she can fill, she first finds find how many $\frac{1}{3}$ cups are in 8 cups. What else must Rosa do to find how many tortillas she can fill?

_____

_____

6 Do you expect the number of tortillas Rosa can fill to be less than or greater than 8? Explain.

_____

_____

7 The rectangles represent 8 cups of vegetable mixture. Draw lines to divide each rectangle into thirds.

8 Circle groups of $\frac{2}{3}$ rectangle. How many groups are there? _____

9 Complete the division equation to show how many tortillas Rosa can fill.

$8 \div \frac{2}{3} =$ _____ tortillas

10 Mike pours $\frac{12}{8}$ cups of orange juice into serving glasses. Each glass holds $\frac{3}{4}$ cup. How many glasses can he fill? Use a common denominator to divide.
Show your work.

Solution: _____

Name: _____

Reason and Write

Study the example. Underline two parts that you think make it a particularly good answer and a helpful example.

Example

Steve said that $\frac{4}{3} \div \frac{1}{6}$ equals $\frac{4}{6}$. How do you know without dividing whether Steve's statement is reasonable? Justify your answer by showing how to find the quotient.

Show your work. Use numbers, words, and models to explain your answer.

Steve's statement is not reasonable. The division $\frac{4}{3} \div \frac{1}{6}$ asks how many sixths are in $\frac{4}{3}$. $\frac{4}{3}$ is greater than 1, and there are 6 sixths in 1. So I know there are more than 6 sixths in $\frac{4}{3}$. That means the quotient must be greater than 1. It could not be a fraction less than 1, such as $\frac{4}{6}$.

I drew a number line model to find the quotient. The top number line is divided into thirds and shows $\frac{4}{3}$. The bottom number line is divided into sixths and shows that there are 8 sixths in $\frac{4}{3}$. So $\frac{4}{3} \div \frac{1}{6} = 8$.

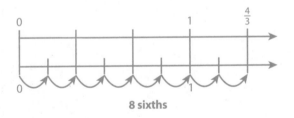

Where does the example . . .

- use numbers to explain?
- use words to explain?
- use models to explain?
- give details?

Lesson 6 *Understand* Division with Fractions

Solve the problem. Use what you learned from the model.

Brenda said that $\frac{5}{2} \div \frac{1}{4}$ equals 10. How do you know without dividing whether Brenda's statement is reasonable? Justify your answer by showing how to find the quotient.

Show your work. Use numbers, words, and models to explain your answer.

Did you . . .

• use numbers to explain?

• use words to explain?

• use models to explain?

• give details?

Dear Family,

Your child is learning about how to divide with fractions.

Problems that involve dividing with fractions include dividing a whole number by a fraction $\left(\text{for example, } 3 \div \frac{2}{5}\right)$, dividing a fraction by a fraction $\left(\text{for example, } \frac{3}{4} \div \frac{1}{8}\right)$, and dividing a mixed number by a fraction $\left(\text{for example, } 1\frac{4}{5} \div \frac{2}{5}\right)$.

Any division problem can be written as a multiplication problem because multiplication and division are inverse operations. This means that to divide a number by a fraction, you can multiply it by the reciprocal of the fraction. To find the reciprocal switch the positions of the numerator (the top number) and the denominator (the bottom number) in a fraction.

For example, to find $6 \div \frac{3}{4}$, multiply 6 by the reciprocal of $\frac{3}{4}$, which is $\frac{4}{3}$. In other words, you can find $6 \div \frac{3}{4}$ by finding $6 \times \frac{4}{3}$.

Consider this situation:

> Julie has $\frac{2}{3}$ yards of ribbon. She wants to cut it into $\frac{1}{6}$-yard lengths and use each length to make a bow. How many bows can Julie make?
>

On the next page you will see two ways your child may use division with fractions in order to find the number of bows.

Vocabulary

multiplicative inverse a number which when multiplied by *x* yields the multiplicative identity, 1

reciprocal the multiplicative inverse of a number; with fractions, the numerator and denominator are switched

NEXT

Lesson 7 Divide with Fractions

Divide with Fractions: Sample Solutions

How many bows can Julie make if she cuts $\frac{2}{3}$ yard of ribbon into $\frac{1}{6}$-yard lengths to make each bow?

One way:
Use a double number line to show thirds and sixths.

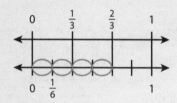

- Mark the top number line with thirds to show $\frac{2}{3}$ yard of ribbon.
- Mark the bottom number line to show $\frac{1}{6}$s.
- Count the number of $\frac{1}{6}$s that are in $\frac{2}{3}$.
- There are four $\frac{1}{6}$s in $\frac{2}{3}$.

Another way:
Write a division equation to represent the problem.

Divide $\frac{2}{3}$ by $\frac{1}{6}$ to find the number of bows.

$$\frac{2}{3} \div \frac{1}{6} = ?$$

Dividing by $\frac{1}{6}$ is the same as multiplying by its reciprocal, $\frac{6}{1}$.

$$\frac{2}{3} \times \frac{6}{1} = \frac{12}{3} = 4$$

Answer: Both methods show that $\frac{2}{3} \div \frac{1}{6} = 4$, meaning that Julie can make 4 bows using $\frac{2}{3}$ yards of ribbon that is cut into $\frac{1}{6}$-yard lengths.

Divide with Fractions

Name: _____

Prerequisite: Divide with Unit Fractions

Study the example problem showing how to solve a word problem that involves dividing with unit fractions. Then solve problems 1–6.

Example

The students in Mrs. Marco's art class use 5 jars of paint altogether. Each student uses $\frac{1}{3}$ jar of paint. How many students are in the class?

To answer this question, you need to find how many $\frac{1}{3}$s are in 5. You can draw a model to understand the problem.

$5 \div \frac{1}{3} = 15$

There are 15 students in Mrs. Marco's art class.

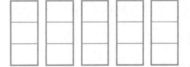

1 Explain how the model represents $5 \div \frac{1}{3} = 15$.

_____

_____

2 Complete the equation. Explain how the model also shows this equation.

_____ × _____ = 15

_____

3 Andy divided his $\frac{1}{3}$ jar of paint equally between 2 projects. What fraction of a jar of paint did Andy use for each project? Explain how to draw a model to find the answer.

_____

_____

_____

_____

Solve.

4 Judi is making a rope ladder. She uses $\frac{1}{2}$ yard of rope for each step. How many steps can she make with 6 yards of rope?

Show your work.

Solution: _____

5 Harry has $\frac{1}{4}$ of an apple pie that he wants to cut into 3 equal slices. What fraction of the whole pie is each slice?

Show your work.

Solution: _____

6 Ryan wants to plant $\frac{1}{5}$ packet of seeds in each row of his garden. He has 4 packets of seeds. Ryan used the expression $\frac{1}{5} \div 4$ to find the number of rows he can plant. Explain what is wrong with his expression. Then write an equation to show the correct number of rows.

_____

_____

_____

Name: _____

Divide a Whole Number by a Fraction

Study the example problem showing how to divide a whole number by a fraction. Then solve problems 1–6.

Example

On a field trip, students ate $\frac{3}{10}$ of a box of oranges. Altogether they ate 6 pounds of oranges. How many pounds of oranges were in the full box?

You can draw a model to represent the problem.

6 lb

| 2 lb | 2 lb | 2 lb | | | | | | | |

?

You can also use an equation to represent that $\frac{3}{10}$ of the full box is 6 pounds: $\frac{3}{10} \times ? = 6$. To solve a missing factor problem, divide: $6 \div \frac{3}{10} = ?$.

To divide by a fraction, multiply by its reciproal.

$$6 \div \frac{3}{10} = 6 \times \frac{10}{3} = 20$$

There were 20 pounds of oranges in the full box.

1. Look at the model. Explain why each tenth of the model is 2 pounds.

_____

_____

2. How can you use the model in the example to find how many pounds of oranges were in the box?

_____

_____

_____

_____

3. Suppose $\frac{4}{5}$ of a different box of oranges weighs 8 pounds. How many pounds of oranges are in the full box?

_____

Vocabulary

multiplicative inverse a number is the multiplicative inverse of another number if their product is 1.

$$9 \times \frac{1}{9} = 1$$

The fraction $\frac{1}{9}$ is the multiplicative inverse of 9.

reciprocal the multiplicative inverse of a number; with fractions, the numerator and denominator are switched.

$\frac{8}{5}$ is the reciprocal of $\frac{5}{8}$.

Solve.

4 Ling walks $\frac{3}{8}$ of the distance home from school in 9 minutes. She wants to know how long it will take her to walk the entire distance at the same speed. Ling uses the expressions $9 \div \frac{3}{8}$ and $9 \times \frac{3}{8}$ to find the answer. Explain what is wrong with Ling's expressions and then write the correct solution.

_____

_____

_____

5 Daniel has 20 quarts of water. How many $2\frac{1}{2}$-quart containers can he fill?

Show your work.

Solution: _____

6 Write a word problem that you can represent with the expression $8 \div \frac{2}{3}$. Draw a model and use equations to show the solution.

_____

_____

_____

Name: _____

Divide a Fraction by a Fraction

Study the example problem showing how to divide a fraction by a fraction. Then solve problems 1–7.

Example

A construction company is building a fence that is $\frac{2}{3}$ mile long. They can build $\frac{1}{6}$ mile of the fence every hour. How many hours will it take them to complete the fence?

You can draw a picture to represent the problem.

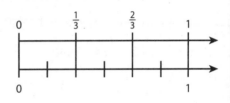

You can also use a division equation: $\frac{2}{3} \div \frac{1}{6}$. Think: How many $\frac{1}{6}$s are in $\frac{2}{3}$?

$$\frac{2}{3} \div \frac{1}{6} = \frac{2}{3} \times \frac{6}{1} = 4$$

It will take 4 hours for the company to build the fence.

1 How can you use the number lines to find how many hours it will take the company to build the fence?

_____

_____

2 Suppose you were told that the company built the fence in 4 hours and that they completed $\frac{1}{6}$ mile of the fence each hour. How would you use the double number line to help you find the length of the fence?

_____

_____

3 Suppose the length of the fence was $1\frac{1}{3}$ mile. How would you change the number lines to solve the problem?

_____

_____

Solve.

4 A chef cooks $\frac{5}{6}$ of a pound of pasta. She plans to serve $\frac{1}{12}$ of a pound to each customer. How many customers can she serve? Explain.

_____

5 Carla wants to know how many batches of birdseed she can make with $\frac{1}{2}$ cup of sunflower seeds. She puts $\frac{1}{6}$ cup of sunflower seeds in every batch. Carla divides $\frac{1}{2}$ by $\frac{1}{6}$ to find the answer. She says this is the same as multiplying $\frac{1}{6}$ by 2. Explain what Carla did wrong and show the correct solution.

_____

_____

_____

6 Jared ate $\frac{1}{4}$ of a loaf of bread. He cut the rest of the loaf into $\frac{1}{8}$-loaf slices. How many slices of bread did he cut? **Show your work.**

Solution: _____

7 A running track at a school is shaped like oval. The track is $\frac{1}{2}$ mile long. Mr. Perez puts a marker down every $\frac{1}{8}$ mile. How many markers does he need? Show how you found your answer.

_____

Divide a Mixed Number by a Fraction

Study the example problem showing how to divide a mixed number by a fraction. Then solve problems 1–6.

Example

Mali has $2\frac{1}{3}$ cups of fruit to make smoothies. She puts $\frac{2}{3}$ cup of fruit in each smoothie. How many smoothies can she make?

You can draw a model to represent the problem.

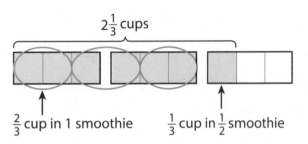

$2\frac{1}{3}$ cups

$\frac{2}{3}$ cup in 1 smoothie $\frac{1}{3}$ cup in $\frac{1}{2}$ smoothie

You can also use equations.

Think about how many $\frac{2}{3}$s are in $2\frac{1}{3}$.

$$2\frac{1}{3} \div \frac{2}{3} = \frac{7}{3} \div \frac{2}{3}$$

$$\frac{7}{3} \div \frac{2}{3} = \frac{7}{3} \times \frac{3}{2} = 3\frac{1}{2}$$

Mali can make $3\frac{1}{2}$ smoothies.

1 Explain why there is $\frac{1}{3}$ cup of fruit in half a smoothie.

_____

_____

2 Look at the equations. Explain how you know that $2\frac{1}{3}$ is equal to $\frac{7}{3}$.

_____

3 Explain how the model shows that $2\frac{1}{3}$ is equal to $\frac{7}{3}$.

_____

_____

Solve.

4 Otis made $1\frac{3}{5}$ cups of oatmeal. He put $\frac{2}{5}$ cup of oatmeal into each bowl. How many bowls of oatmeal did Otis make? Use equations to solve the problem.
Show your work.

Solution: _____

5 Juan wants to know how many $\frac{1}{4}$-cup servings are in $1\frac{3}{8}$ cups of juice. She uses the expression $\frac{12}{8} \div \frac{1}{4}$ to find the answer. Explain what is wrong with Juan's expression and find the correct solution.

_____

_____

_____

_____

6 Carmela mixes $\frac{3}{4}$ kilogram of walnuts, $\frac{1}{2}$ kilogram of almonds, and $\frac{1}{4}$ kilogram of pecans together. She divides the mixed nuts into $\frac{3}{10}$-kilogram bags. How many bags of mixed nuts does she have?
Show your work.

Solution: _____

Name: _____

Divide with Fractions

Solve the problems.

1 Dario divides $\frac{4}{6}$ yard of rope equally into $\frac{1}{12}$-yard pieces for a craft project. How many pieces of rope does Dario have? Use the number lines to solve the problem.

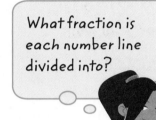

What fraction is each number line divided into?

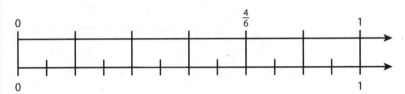

A 4 pieces

B 6 pieces

C 8 pieces

D 12 pieces

2 Check a box in each row to show whether the quotient of each expression is less than, greater than, or equal to 1.

Read each expression as a question. For example: How many $\frac{3}{10}$s are in $\frac{3}{5}$?

	quotient is less than 1	quotient is equal to than 1	quotient is greater than 1
$\frac{3}{5} \div \frac{3}{10}$			
$\frac{3}{10} \div \frac{3}{5}$			
$6 \div \frac{2}{5}$			
$2\frac{3}{4} \div \frac{3}{4}$			
$3\frac{2}{3} \div \frac{11}{3}$			
$\frac{9}{8} \div \frac{3}{2}$			

Solve.

3 Omar jogged a total of $3\frac{3}{5}$ miles last week. Each day that he jogged, he went $\frac{9}{10}$ mile. On how many days did he jog?

Show your work.

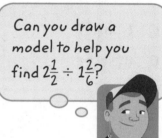

Think: How many $\frac{9}{10}$s are in $3\frac{3}{5}$?

Solution: _____

4 Choose all of the expressions that are equivalent to $2\frac{1}{2} \div 1\frac{2}{6}$.

   A $\frac{5}{2} \times \frac{6}{8}$

   B $\frac{2}{5} \times \frac{6}{8}$

   C $1\frac{2}{6} \div 2\frac{1}{2}$

   D $\frac{5}{2} \div \frac{8}{6}$

Can you draw a model to help you find $2\frac{1}{2} \div 1\frac{2}{6}$?

5 What is the value of the expression $3 \div \frac{3}{4}$?

   A $\frac{1}{4}$

   B $2\frac{1}{4}$

   C 4

   D 12

How can you use multiplication to divide a number by $\frac{3}{4}$?

Jane chose **B** as the correct answer. How did she get that answer?

_____

_____

_____

Dear Family,

Your child is learning about partial quotients and the division algorithm.

The partial quotient method is a step-by-step method that can be used to divide two numbers. At each step, you find a partial answer. After all the steps are taken, you add the partial answers together to find the quotient.

The division algorithm is also a series of steps that can be used to find a quotient. Your child is familiar with the standard algorithms for addition, subtraction, and multiplication. These algorithms are based on place value. The division algorithm is also based on place value.

Your child has learned to first estimate a quotient. You can use an estimated quotient to begin dividing when you use the division algorithm. You can also use the estimated quotient to check whether the quotient that you calculate is a reasonable answer to the division problem.

Consider the following example:

Sonya and her college friends biked 645 miles to visit a national park on summer vacation. They planned the trip so that they would bike the same number of miles each day. How many days did the trip take if they biked 43 miles each day?

The next page shows two different ways your child may divide to find the number of days it took the group of friends to bike the distance to the national park.

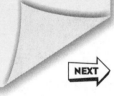
NEXT

Sonya and her friends biked 43 miles each day on a bike trip to a national park. How many days did it take them to bike the entire distance of 645 miles?

One way:
Use partial quotients to divide 645 by 43.

- First, estimate the quotient. 645 is about 650 and 43 is about 50. $650 ÷ 50 = 13$, so the quotient will be about 13.

- To find partial quotients, choose numbers that are easy to work with. For example, you know 43 goes into 645 at least 10 times, so start with 10. Divide again to find the partial quotient 5.

- Add the partial quotients: $10 + 5 = 15$. The quotient is 15.

```
        15   ← quotient
         5  ⎤ partial
        10  ⎦ quotients
   43)645
     −430   ← 10 × 43
      215
     −215   ← 5 × 43
        0
```

Another way:
Use the division algorithm to divide 645 by 43.

Show the place values with **H** for hundreds, **T** for tens, and **O** for ones.

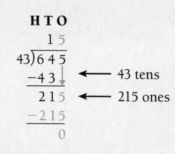

```
   H T O
     1 5
 43)6 4 5
   −4 3↓    ← 43 tens
    2 1 5   ← 215 ones
   −2 1 5
        0
```

645 is 64 tens and 5 ones.
There is 1 group of 43 in 64.
1 ten × 43 = 43 tens
64 tens − 43 tens = 21 tens

Bring down the 5.

There are 5 groups of 43 in 215.
5 ones × 43 = 215 ones
215 ones − 215 ones = 0 ones

Answer: Both methods show that $645 ÷ 43 = 15$, meaning that it took Sonya and her friends 15 days to bike the distance of 645 miles.

Divide Multi-Digit Numbers

Name: _____

Prerequisite: Dividing by a 2-Digit Divisor

Study the example problem showing division with a 2-digit divisor. Then solve problems 1–6.

Example

A farmer sells milk in crates that hold 18 bottles. She has 612 bottles of milk. How many crates can the farmer fill?

To solve, divide 612 by 18. Use the partial-quotients model.

```
    34  ← quotient
     4  ← partial quotient
    30  ← partial quotient
18)612
  −540  ← 18 × 30
    72
  − 72  ← 18 × 4
     0
```

The farmer can fill 34 crates.

1 In the example problem, why is the first partial quotient 30 and not 3?

_____

_____

_____

2 Why is the second partial quotient 4 and not 40?

_____

_____

_____

3 How do you use the partial quotients to find the quotient?

_____

Vocabulary

partial quotient a strategy used to divide multi-digit numbers. The quotients you get in each step are called "partial quotients."

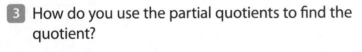

Solve.

4 A school collected 1,204 cans of food during a food drive that lasted 28 days. How many cans were collected on average each day?

Show your work.

Solution: _____

5 Tracey is trying to figure out how many rows of chairs are needed to seat 888 students, with 24 chairs in each row. She writes the equation $24 \times \boxed{} = 888$.

  a. What related division equation could Tracey use?

  _____

  b. How many rows of chairs are needed? _____

6 Ricardo used partial quotients to divide 1,862 by 38 and got 13.

  a. How could Ricardo decide whether his answer is reasonable? Is his answer reasonable?

  _____

  _____

  b. Is Ricardo's quotient correct? If not, explain and correct his error. If so, show that he is correct.

  _____

  _____

  _____

Name: _____

Using the Division Algorithm

Study the example problem showing how to use the division algorithm. Then solve problems 1–6.

> **Example**
>
> There are 896 people at the school's basketball game. The stands are divided into 16 equal sections. If each section has the same number of people, how many people are in each section?
>
> First, estimate the quotient: $900 \div 20 = 45$.
>
> You can use the division algorithm to divide 896 by 16.
>
> $$
> \begin{array}{r}
> 56 \\
> 16\overline{)896} \\
> -80\downarrow \\
> \hline
> 96 \\
> -96 \\
> \hline
> 0
> \end{array}
> $$
>
> There are 56 people in each section.

1 Why is the 5 in the quotient written above the 9 in the dividend? What does the 5 mean in the quotient?

_____

_____

2 Divide 896 by 16 using partial quotients. Compare the methods. For example, how is the 80 in the standard algorithm expressed in the partial-quotients method?

_____

_____

_____

_____

Lesson 8 Divide Multi-Digit Numbers

Solve.

3 A train traveled 936 miles at a constant speed in 12 hours.

a. How can you find the number of miles the train traveled each hour?

_____

b. What is a reasonable estimate for the quotient?

_____

c. How many miles did the train travel each hour?

_____

4 Zachary is reading a book that has 420 pages. The book is divided into 28 chapters. What is the average number of pages per chapter?

_____

5 An art teacher has 816 toothpicks to distribute equally among 16 students. How many toothpicks does each student get?

_____

6 A local theater charges $26 for each adult ticket and $17 for each student ticket. For one show, the theater took in $988 from adults and $731 from students. How many people attended the performance?

Show your work.

Solution: _____

Name: _____

Dividing with 5-Digit Dividends

Study the example problem showing how to divide with a 5-digit dividend. Then solve problems 1–7.

Example

A company is going to divide $77,024 evenly among its 32 employees for bonuses this year. What will each person get for a bonus?

First, estimate the quotient: $75,000 \div 30 = 2,500$.

You can use the division algorithm to find $77,024 \div 32$.

```
      2407
32)77,024
  -64
   130
  -128
    22
  -  0
    224
  -224
      0
```

Each person will get $2,407.

1 What does the 64 mean in the standard algorithm?

_____

2 Why is there a 0 in the quotient?

_____

_____

3 How can you use multiplication to check your answer?

_____

Solve.

4 A sporting goods company ships their baseballs in cartons that hold 48 balls. How many cartons will they need to ship 1,400 baseballs?

   a. How can you find the number of cartons?

   _____

   b. What is the quotient? What does the remainder mean?

   _____

   c. How many cartons will the company need? _____

5 Henry has a length of string that is 2,850 centimeters long. He needs some pieces that are 78 centimeters long for an art project. What is the greatest number of pieces that Henry can cut? _____

6 One of the buses in a bus company's fleet recorded 46,736 miles traveled. This was after a total of 92 trips. What was the average distance traveled on each trip?

   _____

7 A citrus grower harvested 2,419 grapefruit and 4,395 oranges last season. He packaged the grapefruit in boxes of 18 and the oranges in boxes of 30. After packing as many boxes as possible, how many pieces of fruit did the grower have left over?

   Show your work.

   Solution: _____

Name: _____

Divide Multi-Digit Numbers

Solve the problems.

1 A farmer is packing 2,205 pounds of potatoes into boxes. Each box can hold 49 pounds. How many boxes can the farmer fill?

How are the numbers in the problem related?

A   10

B   20

C   45

D   46

2 What is the quotient of 6,135 and 15?

How can estimation help me answer this question?

A   40 R9

B   49

C   409

D   6,120

Olivia chose **B** as the correct answer. How did she get that answer?

_____

3 A recipe for fruit punch calls for 2 cans of pineapple juice and 3 cans of orange juice. Hiri is making a large batch of juice for a community function and uses 72 cans of orange juice. How many cans of pineapple juice should he use?

What two numbers can you divide to help you solve this problem?

Show your work.

Solution: _____

Solve.

4   Tell whether each quotient has a remainder. Select *Yes* or *No*.

    a.   782 ÷ 17   ☐ Yes   ☐ No

    b.   1,296 ÷ 22   ☐ Yes   ☐ No

    c.   4,256 ÷ 38   ☐ Yes   ☐ No

When will you have a remainder in dividing two numbers?

5   Which of these have the quotient 128? Select all that apply.

    A   2,048 ÷ 16   **C**   5,760 ÷ 45

    B   2,986 ÷ 24   **D**   6,576 ÷ 67

Could estimation help me to eliminate any of the answer choices?

6   East High School had a total of 12,510 people in attendance during their 15-game soccer season. West High School had a total of 14,310 people for 18 games. On average, which school had a greater number of people watching per game? How much greater?

Show your work.

How can you find the average number of people who watched each game?

Solution: _____

7   A lightbulb manufacturer produces 20,000 lightbulbs each week. They ship the lightbulbs to stores in cartons of 75. How many cartons are needed to ship 20,000 lightbulbs?

    A   50 cartons   **C**   266 cartons

    B   250 cartons   **D**   267 cartons

Do you need to round up or down because of the remainder?

Dear Family,

Your child is learning about adding and subtracting decimals to the thousandths.

Your child has previously learned that adding and subtracting decimals is the same as adding and subtracting whole numbers. You line up the place values and then add or subtract as usual. With decimals, you must remember to bring down the decimal point and place it correctly in the sum or difference.

There are a few things to keep in mind when you add and subtract decimals.

- Start by estimating the sum or difference before you add or subtract. Then you can use the estimate to help you find the answer or check that your answer is reasonable.

- When decimals have different numbers of decimal places, such as 14.7 and 1.259, you can use zeros to write the decimals to the same number of decimal places. For example, 14.7 is the same as 14.700, which has the same number of decimal places as 1.259. This can help you keep the place values lined up.

$$14.7 \longrightarrow 14.700$$
$$+\ 1.259 \longrightarrow +\ 01.259$$

Consider the following example:

Karl plans to ship a box containing three gifts to his nephews. There is one shipping cost for any box that weighs up to 5 pounds. The cost increases for boxes heavier than 5 pounds.
Karl plans to ship gifts weighing 1.19 pounds, 2.3 pounds, and 1.726 pounds. What is the total weight of the gifts?

On the next page you will see two ways your child may add decimals to find the total weight of the gifts.

NEXT

Add and Subtract Decimals: Sample Solution

Three gifts weigh 1.19 pounds, 2.3 pounds, and 1.726 pounds. What is the total weight of the gifts?

You can find the total weight by adding. Start by estimating the sum by rounding each decimal up or down.

1.19 is close to 1	2.3 is close to 2	1.726 is close to 2

Then add: $1 + 2 + 2 = 5$. The weight of the gifts is about 5 pounds.

One way:
Use a place-value chart to add.

Ones	.	Tenths $\frac{1}{10}$	Hundredths $\frac{1}{100}$	Thousandths $\frac{1}{1,000}$
1	.	1	9	
+2	.	3		
+1	.	7	2	6
5	.	**2**	**1**	**6**

Another way:
Line up the decimal points to add.

$$\begin{array}{r} 1.19 \\ 2.3 \\ + \ 1.726 \end{array}$$

Place zeros to make sure that you add the same place values.

$$\begin{array}{r} 1.190 \\ 2.300 \\ + \ 1.726 \end{array}$$

Add.

$$\begin{array}{r} 1\ 1 \\ 1.190 \\ 2.300 \\ + \ 1.726 \\ \hline 5.216 \end{array}$$

Answer: Both methods show that the sum is 5.216, which means that the total weight of the three gifts is 5.216 pounds. Notice that 5.215 is close to the estimate of 5 pounds, so it is a reasonable answer.

Add and Subtract Decimals

Name: _____

Prerequisite: Adding and Subtracting Decimals

Study the example problem showing how to subtract decimals. Then solve problems 1–5.

Example

Charlie collected 3.8 pounds of shells at the beach. Sebal collected 1.55 pounds of shells. How many more pounds did Charlie collect than Sebal?

To solve, subtract 1.55 from 3.8. Use a place-value chart to help. Regroup as needed to subtract.

	ones	.	tenths	hundredths
Charlie's shells	3	.	8	0
regroup as	3	.	7	10
Sebal's shells	1	.	5	5

3 ones − 1 one = 2 ones
7 tenths − 5 tenths = 2 tenths
10 hundredths − 5 hundredths = 5 hundredths

Difference = 2 ones + 2 tenths + 5 hundredths

Charlie collected 2.25 pounds more than Sebal.

1 Explain why you have to use regrouping in the example problem?

_____

_____

2 You can also subtract decimals by writing the problem vertically, lining up the decimal points to keep track of the place values.

$$\begin{array}{r} {\scriptstyle 7\ 10} \\ 3.\cancel{8}\cancel{0} \\ -\ 1.55 \\ \hline \end{array}$$

The problem to the right is partially completed.

How does the regrouping shown relate to the place-value method used in the example?

_____

_____

Solve.

3 At a diving competition, Allison scored 78.5 on her first dive. Hannah's score on her first dive was 74.65. How many more points did Allison score on her first dive than Hannah?

Show your work.

Solution: _____

4 Franklin hiked 1.38 kilometers from the nature center to the waterfall. Then he hiked 2.6 kilometers to the bridge. Finally, he hiked 3.45 kilometers to return to the nature center. How many kilometers did Franklin hike in all?

Show your work.

Solution: _____

5 Dharma and Jorge are looking at cell phone plans. A group plan will cost an average of $135.95 per month. An individual plan will cost an average of $72.75 per month. Should Dharma and Jorge purchase a group plan or two individual plans? How much money could they save?

Show your work.

Solution: _____

90 **Lesson 9** Add and Subtract Decimals

Name: _____

Adding Decimals to Thousandths

Study the example problem showing how to add decimals to thousandths. Then solve problems 1–6.

Example

Colin found three small rocks. He measured the mass of each. One rock was 3.56 grams, another was 1.742 grams, and the third rock was 2.4 grams. What was the total mass of the three rocks?

Line up the decimal points and write 0s as needed to help you keep the place values aligned. Then add.

$$\begin{array}{r} \overset{1\ \ 1}{3.560} \\ 1.742 \\ +\ 2.400 \\ \hline 7.702 \end{array}$$

The total mass of the rocks is 7.702 grams.

1 Estimate the sum in the example problem.

_____

2 How does estimating the answer help you to know that you placed the decimal point in the sum correctly?

_____

_____

3 How does adding with decimals compare to adding whole numbers?

_____

_____

Solve.

4 Xavier has three objects in his bag. One object weighs 4.05 ounces, another weighs 2.7 ounces, and the third object weighs 1.985 ounces. What is the total weight of the objects in Xavier's bag?

Show your work.

Solution: _____

5 To qualify for the long jump competition, an athlete must jump a combined distance of more than 16 meters in 3 jumps. Jackie jumped 4.86 meters, 5.428 meters, and 5.9 meters. Did Jackie qualify for the competition?

Show your work.

Solution: _____

6 The lengths of the sides of a triangle are shown. What is the perimeter of the triangle?

Show your work.

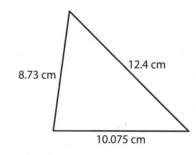

8.73 cm

12.4 cm

10.075 cm

Solution: _____

Name: _____

Subtracting Decimals to Thousandths

Study the example problem showing how to subtract decimals to thousandths. Then solve problems 1–8.

Example

A carpenter has a board that is 6.52 feet long and 1.748 feet wide. How much longer is the length than the width?

To solve, find 6.52 − 1.748. Align the decimal points and subtract.

$$\begin{array}{r} {\scriptstyle 5\ \ 14\ 11\ 10} \\ \cancel{6.52 0} \\ -\ 1.748 \\ \hline 4.772 \end{array}$$

The board is 4.772 inches longer than it is wide.

1 Why is it useful to write 6.52 as 6.520?

_____

_____

2 How could you estimate the difference?

_____

3 How do you know that the answer to a decimal subtraction problem is reasonable? How can you check that the answer is correct? Explain.

_____

_____

4 A gymnast earned a score of 9.438 on the uneven bars and a score of 8.75 on the balance beam. How much greater was her score on the uneven bars?

_____

Solve.

5 Alphonso's notecard is 7.4 inches wide. Oscar's notecard is 5.872 inches wide. Which notecard is wider, and by how much?

_____

6 Ichiro's batting average in baseball is 0.342. This is 0.08 higher than Giancarlo's batting average. What is Giancarlo's batting average?

Show your work.

Solution: _____

7 Sheila is running in a race that is 5 kilometers long. After 10 minutes, she has run 1.875 kilometers. How much farther does Sheila have to run to finish the race?

Show your work.

Solution: _____

8 In a library, bookcases A, B, C, and D are lined up in order. Bookcase A is 1.38 meters from bookcase B and 6.8 meters from bookcase C. Bookcase D is 0.925 meters farther from bookcase C than the distance between bookcases B and C. How far apart are bookcases C and D?

Show your work.

Solution: _____

Name: _____

Add and Subtract Decimals

Solve the problems.

---

1 On the floor exercise, Nadia scored 9.85. Mary Lou scored 8.975. How much higher was Nadia's score on the floor exercise?

Show your work.

You can write 0s to help you keep the place values aligned.

Solution: _____

---

2 Jeremy has three pencils. One pencil is 9.36 inches long. The second pencil is 6.7 inches long. The third pencil is 8.025 inches long. Will placing the pencils end to end make a total length greater than 2 feet?

Show your work.

How many inches are there in 2 feet?

Solution: _____

---

3 Terri walked 3.825 miles yesterday. Today she walked 5.5 miles. How many more miles did Terri walk today than yesterday?

Which number is the greater number?

A 1.675 miles   **C** 1.785 miles

B 1.725 miles   **D** 2.325 miles

Brenda chose **B** as the correct answer. How did she get that answer?

_____

_____

Solve.

4 Hal's backpack weighs 3.54 pounds. Sarah's pack weighs 2.129 pounds. Frank's pack weighs 2.8 pounds. Select *True* or *False* for each statement.

Be sure that you choose the correct operation to evaluate each statement.

a. Hal's backpack weighs 1.429 pounds more than Sarah's. ☐ True ☐ False

b. The combined weight of the backpacks is more than 8.5 pounds. ☐ True ☐ False

c. Frank's backpack is 0.671 pound heavier than Sarah's. ☐ True ☐ False

d. Hal's backpack is less than 1 pound heavier than Frank's. ☐ True ☐ False

5 Which of these equals 2.427? Select all that apply.

A $1.34 + 1.087$

B $1.4 + 1.027$

C $8.35 - 5.923$

D $6 - 3.573$

Be sure that you add or subtract digits with the same place value.

6 Kristin weighs three kittens at a vet's clinic. The heaviest one weighs 3.28 pounds. The heaviest kitten is 1.056 pounds heavier than the medium-weight one. The lightest kitten is 1.2 pounds lighter than the medium-weight kitten. What is the total weight of the kittens?

How can you find the weights of the medium-weight and lightest kittens?

Show your work.

Solution: _____

Dear Family,

Your child is learning about multiplying and dividing decimals.

You multiply decimals in the same way that you multiply whole numbers, but you have to place the decimal point in the product correctly. You can count the number of decimal places in each number that you are multiplying and then add the number of decimal places to find out how many decimal places are in the product.

$$16.4 \longleftarrow \text{1 decimal place}$$
$$\underline{\times\ 0.13} \longleftarrow \underline{\text{+ 2 decimal places}}$$
$$2.132 \longleftarrow \text{3 decimal places in the product}$$

When dividing with decimals, you can think of the decimals as fractions. You can write an equivalent fraction that has whole numbers and then divide.

$$15.25 \div 0.25 = \frac{15.25}{0.25} \longrightarrow \frac{15.25}{0.25} \times \frac{100}{100} = \frac{1{,}525}{25}$$

$15.25 \div 0.25$ is equivalent to $1{,}525 \div 25$.

$$0.25)\overline{15.25} \longrightarrow \begin{array}{r} 61 \\ 025)\overline{1525} \\ -150 \\ \hline 25 \\ -25 \\ \hline 0 \end{array}$$

Consider the following example:

A gas company measures the amount of natural gas used in units called *therms*. A home used 39.3 therms in one month. If each therm costs $0.4544, how much will the gas company charge for that month?

The next page shows two different ways your child may multiply to find the amount of the bill.

Lesson 10 Multiply and Divide Decimals   **97**

Multiply and Divide Decimals: Sample Solution

A gas company charges $0.4544 for each therm. A home used 39.3 therms in a month. How much will the gas company charge for that month?

You can find the answer by multiplying. First, estimate the product. $0.4544 is close to $0.50 and 39.3 therms is close to 40 therms.

$0.50 × 40 = 20$

The gas company will charge about $20.00.

One way:

- Write each decimal as a fraction and multiply. Use the fractions to think about the placement of the decimal in the product.

$$0.4544 = \frac{4,544}{1,000} \qquad 39.3 = 39\frac{3}{10} \text{ or } \frac{393}{10}$$

- Multiply the fractions.

$$\frac{4,544}{1,000} \times \frac{393}{10} = \frac{1,785,792}{10,000}$$

- Write the product as a decimal.

$$\frac{1,785,792}{10,000} = 17.85792$$

Another way:
Use an algorithm to multiply.

```
    0.4544   ←  4 decimal places
  ×  39.3    ←  1 decimal place
    13632
    40896
 +  13632
   17.85792  ←  5 decimal places
```

Answer: Both methods show that the product is 17.85792, meaning that the gas company will charge $17.86, rounded to the nearest cent, for the month. This is close to the estimate of $20.00.

Multiply and Divide Decimals

Name: _____

Prerequisite: Multiply Decimals to Hundredths

Study the example showing how to multiply a decimal by a decimal. Then solve problems 1–7.

Example

Find 1.5×0.4.

You can use an area model to multiply tenths by tenths.

$1 \longrightarrow 1 \times 0.4 = 0.4$

$0.5 \longrightarrow 0.5 \times 0.4 = 0.20 = 0.2$

$1.5 \times 0.4 = 0.4 + 0.2 = 0.6$

1 Explain why the factor 1.5 is broken into two numbers in the model.

_____

2 What does each small square in the model represent?

_____

3 How would the area model change if the factor 0.4 were changed to 1.4?

_____

_____

Lesson 10 Multiply and Divide Decimals

Solve.

Use the situation below to solve problems 4–5.

Lisa walks at a speed of 3.25 miles per hour for 1.5 hours. How many miles does she walk in all?

4 Complete the area model that represents 1.5 × 3.25.

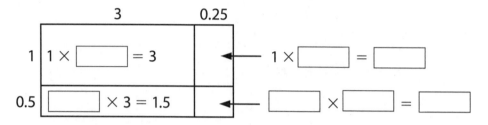

5 Explain how you can use the area model to find the number of miles that Lisa walks.

_____

6 Moira multiplies 1.8 by 2.4 and writes the product as 0.432. Tom says that her product is incorrect. How could Tom know this without multiplying the two numbers?

_____

7 Andrew lives 1.7 kilometers from the soccer field. He rode his bike 0.9 of the distance to the field. How much farther does Andrew need to ride to reach the soccer field? Include an area model in your answer.

Show your work.

Solution: _____

Name: _____

Multiply Decimals to Thousandths

Study the example problem showing how to multiply decimals to thousandths. Then solve problems 1–7.

Example

A scientist used 4.317 liters of a chemical for one experiment. She uses 1.75 times that amount for another experiment. How much of the chemical does the scientist use for the second experiment?

First, estimate. Because 4.317 is about 4 and 1.75 is about 2, the product will be about 4(2) = 8.

Multiply decimals as you would multiply whole numbers. Remember to place the decimal point in the product.

$$
\begin{array}{r}
4.317 \\
\times\ 1.75 \\
\hline
21585 \\
302190 \\
+\ 431700 \\
\hline
7.55475
\end{array}
$$

The scientist uses 7.55475 liters of the chemical for the second experiment.

1 How does your estimate help you place the decimal point in the product?

_____

2 How can you use fractions to place the decimal point in the product?

_____

_____

3 How does the number of decimal places in the factors relate to the number of decimal places in the product of the example?

_____

_____

_____

Lesson 10 Multiply and Divide Decimals   **101**

Solve.

4 Without multiplying, tell whether the product 0.644 × 0.25 will be greater than 1 or less than 1? Explain how you know. Then find the product.

_____

_____

5 Selena drove at an average speed of 50.55 miles per hour for 1.75 hours. She stopped at a rest stop and then drove at an average speed of 45.2 miles per hour for 2.25 hours. Did Selena drive more miles before or after the rest stop? How many more miles?

Show your work.

Solution: _____

6 Estimate the product of 23.725 × 6.25. Then find the product. Why is it a good idea to estimate first?

_____

_____

7 Ellen walks dogs on weekends. She gets paid $8.50 per hour. Each day she works 5 hours and 45 minutes. Does she earn more or less than $85 in one weekend? How much more or less? Explain.

_____

_____

Name: _____

Divide by Decimals

Study the example problem showing how to divide by decimals. Then solve problems 1–7.

Example

Jamie has 4.2 pounds of dried fruit to put into bags. She puts 0.35 pound of fruit in each bag. How many bags of dried fruit does she have?

First, estimate. Because 4.2 is about 4 and 0.35 is about 0.4, the quotient is about 4 divided by 4 tenths, or 10.

Next, write the divisor as a whole number by multiplying it by a power of 10. Multiply the dividend by that same power. Then divide as you would with whole numbers.

$$0.35\overline{)4.20} \longrightarrow \begin{array}{r} 12 \\ 35\overline{)420} \\ -35 \\ \hline 70 \\ -70 \\ \hline 0 \end{array}$$

Jamie has 12 bags of dried fruit.

1 Why was the divisor changed to a whole number?

_____

2 How do you change 0.35 to a whole number?

_____

3 Why must you multiply the dividend by the same power of 10 that you multiplied the divisor by to write it as a whole number?

_____

_____

4 Complete the equation to show that 4.2 ÷ 0.35 is equivalent to 420 ÷ 35.

$$4.2 \div 0.35 = \frac{\boxed{}}{\boxed{}} \times \frac{\boxed{}}{\boxed{}} = \frac{\boxed{}}{\boxed{}} = 420 \div 35$$

Solve.

5 Emma made a mistake when she divided 6.4 by 0.02. Describe her mistake and show the correct division.

$$0.02\overline{)6.4} \longrightarrow \begin{array}{r} 32 \\ 2\overline{)64} \\ -6 \\ \hline 4 \\ -4 \\ \hline 0 \end{array}$$

_____

_____

_____

6 Aaron paid $9.75 for markers that cost $0.75 each. He bought 4 times as many pencils for $0.35 each. How much did Aaron pay for the pencils?

Show your work.

Solution: _____

7 Mei spent $66 buying fabric that costs $7.50 per yard. How many yards of fabric did Mei buy? How do you know that your answer is reasonable?

_____

_____

Name: _____

Divide Decimals

Study the example problem showing how to divide decimals by using an algorithm. Then solve problems 1–6.

Example

Tanisha rode her bike 19.625 miles in 2.5 hours. What was her average speed?

First, estimate. Because 19.625 is about 20, the quotient is about 20 divided by 2.5, or 8. Next divide 19.625 by 2.5.

$$2.5\overline{)19.625} \longrightarrow \begin{array}{r} 7.85 \\ 25\overline{)196.25} \\ -\ 175 \\ \hline 212 \\ -\ 200 \\ \hline 125 \\ -\ 125 \\ \hline 0 \end{array}$$

Tanisha's average speed was 7.85 miles per hour.

1 In the example, the dividend and divisor were multiplied by what power of 10? Explain why they were multiplied by this power of 10.

_____

2 Complete the equation to show that 19.625 ÷ 2.5 is equivalent to 196.25 ÷ 25.

$$19.625 \div 2.5 = \frac{\boxed{}}{\boxed{}} \times \frac{\boxed{}}{\boxed{}} = \frac{\boxed{}}{\boxed{}} = 196.25 \div 25$$

3 Would the quotient be the same if you multiplied the numerator and the denominator by 100? Explain.

_____

_____

Lesson 10 Multiply and Divide Decimals   **105**

Solve.

Use the information below to solve problems 4–5.

Jake bought 14.5 pounds of dried navy beans for $25.52.

4 Explain how to estimate the price per pound.

_____

_____

5 What is the price per pound of the beans? Explain
how you know that your answer is reasonable.

Show your work.

Solution: _____

_____

6 Jeff is training for a walkathon. He walked 8.84 miles
at an average speed of 3.4 miles per hour. Then he
walked for an additional 1.6 hours at the same speed.
How many hours did Jeff walk in all?

Show your work.

Solution: _____

Name: _____

Multiply and Divide Decimals

Solve the problems.

1 A total of 6.825 inches of snow fell during a storm. The snow fell at an average rate of 1.3 inches per hour. For how many hours did the snow fall?

Show your work.

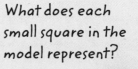

How many decimal places are in the divisor?

Solution: _____

2 Which expressions represent the model? Select all that apply.

What does each small square in the model represent?

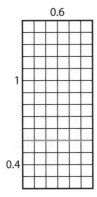

0.6

1

0.4

A 0.84

B 0.6 + 0.4

C 0.6 + 0.24

D 1.4 × 0.6

Solve.

3 Is each expression equivalent to 23.6 ÷ 4.02? Select *Yes* or *No*.

a. 2.36 ÷ 40.2   ☐ Yes   ☐ No

b. 2360 ÷ 402   ☐ Yes   ☐ No

c. 2.36 ÷ 0.402   ☐ Yes   ☐ No

d. 236 ÷ 4020   ☐ Yes   ☐ No

How can you tell whether each quotient is equivalent to the original problem?

4 Isabel's car gets 33.5 miles per gallon. Her gas tank holds 15.1 gallons of gas. How many miles can Isabel drive on a full tank of gas?

A   2.22 miles   C   505.85 miles

B   22.2 miles   D   5,058.5 miles

John chose **D** as the correct answer. How did he get that answer?

_____

_____

How can you use estimation to determine whether your answer makes sense?

5 Hillary earned $17.92 weeding gardens for 3.2 hours. She was paid the same hourly rate to mow lawns. Hillary mowed lawns for 2.75 hours. How much did Hillary earn mowing lawns?

Show your work.

Do you multiply or divide to find the hourly rate?

Solution: _____

Dear Family,

Your child is learning about common factors and multiples.

A factor is a number that is multiplied by another number. For example, the factors of 12 are 1, 2, 3, 4, 6, and 12 because $1 \times 12 = 12$, $2 \times 6 = 12$, and $3 \times 4 = 12$. You can list the factors of two numbers to find their common factors, the factors the numbers have in common.

Factors of 12: 1, 2, 3, 4, **6**, 12   **Factors of 18: 1**, **2**, **3**, **6**, 9, 18

- The common factors of 12 and 18 are 1, 2, 3, and 6.
- The greatest common factor is 6.

Multiples are the products of a number and any other whole number. You can list multiples of two numbers to find common multiples.

Multiples of 2: 2, **4**, 6, **8**, 10, …   **Multiples of 4: 4**, **8**, 12, 16, 20, …

- Some common multiples of 2 and 4 are 4 and 8.
- The least common multiple is 4.

Finding the greatest common factor and least common multiple of two numbers can be useful in everyday situations.

Consider the following example:

Tasha is making snack bags for a group hike. She has 16 juice pouches and 24 energy bars. She wants each snack bag to have the same number of juice pouches and the same number of energy bars. What is the greatest number of snack bags that Tasha can make using all the juice pouches and energy bars?

On the next page you will see two ways your child may find the greatest common factor to determine the number of snack bags.

Common Factors and Multiples: Sample Solution

> Tasha has 16 juice pouches and 24 energy bars. What is the greatest number of snack bags she can make so that each snack bag has an equal number of juice pouches and an equal number of energy bars?

One way:

List the factors of 16 and 24 and circle the common factors.

Factors of 16: ① ② ④ ⑧ 16

Factors of 24: ① ② 3 ④ 6 ⑧ 12 24

The greatest common factor of 16 and 24 is 8. The greatest common factor is the greatest number of snack bags that can be made. If you make 8 snack bags, each will have 2 juice pouches because $8 \times 2 = 16$ and 3 energy bars because $8 \times 3 = 24$.

Another way:

Make tables to show all the factors of 16 and 24.

Juice Pouches	Factors of 16				
Number of Snack Bags	1	**2**	**4**	**8**	16
Number of Juice Pouches	16	**8**	**4**	**2**	1

Energy Bars	Factors of 24						
Number of Snack Bags	1	**2**	3	**4**	6	**8**	12	24
Number of Energy Bars	24	**12**	8	**6**	4	**3**	2	1

Look at the factors in the top row of each table. The greatest common factor is 8. If you make 8 snack bags, each will have 2 juice pouches because $8 \times 2 = 16$ and 3 energy bars because $8 \times 3 = 24$.

Answer: Both methods show that the greatest common factor of 16 and 24 is 8, meaning that the greatest number of snack bags Tasha can make is 8. Each snack bag will have 2 juice pouches and 3 energy bars.

Common Factors and Multiples

Name: _____

Prerequisite: Factor Pairs

Study the example problem about factors and factor pairs. Then solve problems 1–9.

Example

Nancy has 10 movie posters. She wants to hang them on a wall in equal rows. Find all the ways that she can arrange the posters.

Nancy can arrange the posters in 4 ways.

1 row of 10 posters   2 rows of 5 posters   5 rows of 2 posters   10 rows of 1 poster

1. The equation $1 \times 10 = 10$ represents the first way that Nancy can arrange the posters. Write three more equations to represent all of the ways that Nancy can arrange the posters.

_____

2. List the four factors of 10.

_____

3. Write the two factor pairs of 10.

_____

4. What do the factor pairs represent in this situation?

_____

5. How would the factor pairs change if Nancy had only 5 posters to arrange? Explain.

_____

_____

_____

Vocabulary

factor a number you multiply.

factor pair two numbers that are multiplied together to give a product.

multiple the product of a number and any other whole number.

$2 \times 4 = 8$
2 is a factor of 8.
2 and 4 are a factor pair.
8 is a multiple of 2.

Lesson 11 Common Factors and Multiples   **111**

Solve.

6 Tell whether each statement about the factors of 24 is *True* or *False*.

    a. An arrangement of 24 objects could be 4 equal rows of 6.   ☐ True   ☐ False

    b. 2 and 12 is a factor pair.   ☐ True   ☐ False

    c. 24 is not a factor because a number cannot be a factor of itself.   ☐ True   ☐ False

    d. All of the factors of 24 are 1, 2, 6, 12, and 24.   ☐ True   ☐ False

7 Mina baked 50 muffins. She is arranging the muffins on plates. She wants the same number of muffins on each plate. Complete the table to show the different ways that Mina can arrange the muffins. Then list the factor pairs of 50.

Number of Plates						
Number of Muffins on Each Plate						

Factor pairs of 50: _____

8 Jill arranged her baseball cards in 4 rows of 9 cards. Then she arranged the cards in 2 rows of 18 cards. How many other ways can Jill arrange her baseball cards in equal rows?

Show your work.

Solution: _____

9 Look at problem 8. Sam has fewer baseball cards than Jill. There are only three ways that he can arrange his cards in equal rows. Write all the possible numbers of baseball cards that Sam could have.

_____

Name: _____

Greatest Common Factor

Study the example showing how to solve a problem using the greatest common factor (GCF). Then solve problems 1–6.

Example

Alice is making balloon bunches from 6 red balloons and 15 blue balloons. She wants the same number of red balloons and the same number of blue balloons in each bunch. What is the greatest number of balloon bunches that Alice can make using all the balloons?

You can make a table to show all the factors of 6 and all the factors of 15.

Red Balloons

Number of Bunches	1	2	3	6
Number of Red Balloons	6	3	2	1

Blue Balloons

Number of Bunches	1	3	5	15
Number of Blue Balloons	15	5	3	1

The common factors in the number of bunches are 1 and 3.
The GCF is 3.

The greatest number of balloon bunches that
Alice can make is 3.

---

1 What does the greatest common factor represent in this situation?

_____

_____

2 Alice decides to use all of the balloons to make 3 balloon bunches. How many red balloons and how many blue balloons are in each bunch?

_____

3 Alice makes 2 bunches of balloons. There are the same number of red balloons and the same number of blue balloons in each bunch. Did Alice use all of the balloons?

_____

Solve.

4 A dentist is making packages of toothbrushes and toothpaste for his patients. He has 12 toothbrushes and 18 tubes of toothpaste. Each package will have the same number of toothbrushes and the same number of tubes of toothpaste.

    a. What is the greatest number of packages that the dentist can make using all the toothbrushes and tubes of toothpaste?

    Show your work.

    Solution: _____

    b. How many toothbrushes and how many tubes of toothpaste will be in each package?

    _____

5 Luis has 8 petunias, 16 carnations, and 20 pansies to plant in flowerpots. If he plants the same number of each type of flower in the flowerpots, how many flowerpots will he use? How many of each type of flower will be in each flowerpot?

    _____

    _____

6 Use the GCF and the distributive property to write $24 + 40$ as a product.

    _____

    _____

Name: _____

Least Common Multiple

Study the example problem showing how to find the least common multiple (LCM) to solve problems. Then solve problems 1–8.

Example

Miriam is buying plates and cups for a party. She wants the same number of each. Plates are sold in packs of 8. Cups are sold in packs of 12. What is the least number of plates and cups that Miriam can buy?

You can list the multiples of each number.

8: 8, 16, **24**, 32, 40, 48, 56, 64, 72 …

12: 12, **24**, 36, 48, 60, 72, 84, 96 …

The least common multiple is 24, so the least number of plates Miriam can buy is 24, and the least number of cups she can buy is 24.

1 John says that this means that Miriam needs to buy 24 packs of plates and 24 packs of cups. Is John correct? Explain your answer.

_____

_____

2 What is the least number of packs of plates and cups that Miriam can buy?

_____

3 Name three other common multiples of 8 and 12.

_____

4 Could Miriam buy exactly 40 plates and 40 cups? Explain.

_____

_____

Solve.

5 Pizza is served in the school cafeteria every fourth school day. Tacos are served every third school day. Both pizza and tacos were served today. In how many school days will pizza and tacos be served on the same day again?

Show your work.

Solution: _____

6 Look at problem 5. If the pattern continues, will pizza and tacos be served on the same day in 21 school days? Explain why or why not.

_____

7 Every ninth person in line at a movie theater gets free popcorn. Every sixth person gets free apple juice. Shani says that the thirty-sixth customer will be the first customer to get both free popcorn and free apple juice. Is she right? If not, describe her mistake.

_____

_____

_____

8 Gary has guitar lessons every 5 days and band practice every 4 days. His first band practice is in 4 days and his first guitar lesson is in 5 days. In 100 days, how many times will Gary have had guitar lessons and band practice on the same day? Explain how you know.

_____

_____

Name: _____

Common Factors and Multiples

Solve the problems.

1. Rafael wants to buy the same number of gift bags and bows. Gift bags are sold in packs of 6. Bows are sold in packs of 9. What is the least number of gift bags and bows that Rafael can buy?

   Show your work.

   How do you find the least common multiple of two numbers?

   Solution: _____

2. While at school, Brian has a math quiz every 6 days and a science quiz every 4 days. On February 15, he had both tests. Assuming no school days off, when will he have both tests on the same day again?

   Do you need to find the greatest common factor or the least common multiple?

February						
S	M	T	W	T	F	S
			1	2	3	4
5	6	7	8	9	10	11
12	13	14	15	16	17	18
19	20	21	22	23	24	25
26	27	28	29			

March						
S	M	T	W	T	F	S
				1	2	3
4	5	6	7	8	9	10
11	12	13	14	15	16	17
18	19	20	21	22	23	24
25	26	27	28	29	30	31

   A February 27   **C** March 2

   B February 29   **D** March 16

3. Which expression uses the greatest common factor and the distributive property to write $16 + 36$ as a product?

   How can you be sure you found the greatest common factor?

   A $2(8 + 18)$

   B $6(10 + 30)$

   C $2(8) + 2(18)$

   D $4(4 + 9)$

Lesson 11 Common Factors and Multiples   **117**

Solve.

4 Tell whether each statement about the factors of 20 and 30 is *True* or *False*.

    a. The greatest common factor is 5.   ☐ True   ☐ False

    b. 2 is a common factor.   ☐ True   ☐ False

    c. 15 and 3 are a factor pair of 30.   ☐ True   ☐ False

    d. 10 is a factor of 20.   ☐ True   ☐ False

Can making a list of the factors for each number help?

5 Sally is arranging her books on shelves. She has 16 adventure books, 32 mysteries, and 12 biographies. She wants each shelf to have the same number of each type of book. What is the greatest number of shelves that Sally will use if she puts all the books on shelves? How many of each type of book will be on each shelf?

How can you use the GCF to solve the problem?

Show your work.

Solution: _____

_____

6 What is the least common multiple of 12 and 10?

    A 2   **C** 60

    B 50   **D** 120

Rachel chose **D** as the correct answer. How did she get that answer?

What is a common multiple? What is the least common multiple?

_____

_____

Dear Family,

Your child is learning about positive and negative numbers.

Positive numbers are greater than zero and negative numbers are less than zero. Here are some real-world situations that involve positive and negative numbers.

• The outdoor temperature is recorded as the number of degrees above or below zero.

• A bank account shows an amount of money deposited with a plus sign (+) and an amount of money withdrawn with a minus sign (−).

• A daily change in a stock market index is reported as "rising" or "falling" a certain number of points.

A positive number and a negative number that are the same distance from 0 are called *opposites*. For example, 3 and −3 are opposites.

Consider the following example:

Louise checks the temperature on a thermometer on two days in different months. One day the temperature was 10 degrees Celsius above zero. The second day the temperature was the opposite of the temperature on the first day. How can you represents the two temperatures with positive and negative numbers?

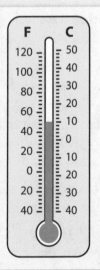

The next page shows two different ways your child may explain how the two temperatures represent a positive number and a negative number.

Lesson 12 *Understand* Positive and Negative Numbers

How can you represent 10 degrees Celsius and its opposite using positive and negative numbers?

One way:
Use a picture of a thermometer to understand the numbers.

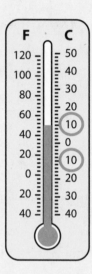

- Look at 0°C on the thermometer.

- 10 degrees Celsius is above zero so it represented by a positive number. It can be represented as 10°C, and you can think of it as +10.

- The opposite of 10°C is −10°C. It is below zero, so it is a negative number. You can think of it as −10.

Another way:
Use a number line to understand positive and negative numbers.

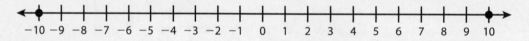

- On a number line, a positive number tells how far above or to the right of zero the number is, and a negative number tells how far below or to the left of zero a number is.

- 10 degrees Celsius is above zero, so it will be to the right of 0 on the number line.

- −10 is the opposite of 10. Both numbers are the same distance from zero but in opposite directions.

Answer: Both methods show that 10 degrees Celsius can be represented using a positive number as +10 and its opposite can be represented using as a negative number as −10.

Prerequisite: How can you graph points on the coordinate plane?

Study the example showing how to name ordered pairs on the coordinate plane. Then solve problems 1–9.

Example

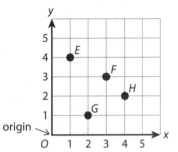

An ordered pair (*x*, *y*) describes the location of a point on the coordinate plane.

The first number in the ordered pair is the *x*-coordinate. It tells how many units the point is from the origin on the *x*-axis.

The second number is the *y*-coordinate. It tells how many units the point is from the origin on the *y*-axis.

The ordered pair for point *E* is (1, 4).

The ordered pair (0, 0) names the origin.

1. The *x*-coordinate of point *F* is _____ because it is _____ unit(s) to the right of the origin. The *y*-coordinate of point *F* is _____ because it is _____ unit(s) up from the origin. The ordered pair for point *F* is (_____, _____).

2. Ray says that the ordered pair for point *G* is (1, 2). Is Ray correct? Why or why not?

_____

_____

3. Write the ordered pair for point *H*. Explain how you got your answer.

_____

_____

_____

4. Plot and label point *J* at (1, 2) on the coordinate plane.

Vocabulary

coordinate plane a two-dimensional space formed by two perpendicular number lines called axes.

origin the point (0, 0) where the *x*-axis and *y*-axis intersect.

ordered pair a pair of numbers (*x*, *y*) that describe the location of a point on the coordinate plane.

Use the coordinate plane to solve problems 5–7.

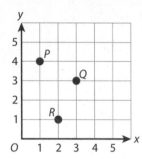

5 Write the ordered pairs for points *P*, *Q*, and *R*.

_____

6 Use the ordered pairs in the table to plot and label points *S*, *T*, and *U* on the coordinate plane.

Point	S	T	U
x-coordinate	1	3	2
y-coordinate	3	1	5

7 Choose a point on the coordinate plane. Describe its location in relation to the origin.

_____

_____

Use the following situation to solve problems 8–9.

Max drew a map of his neighborhood with his house located at the origin.

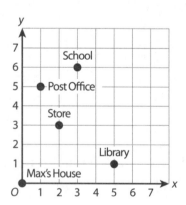

8 Which ordered pair describes the location of the library?

A (1, 1)   **C** (5, 1)

B (1, 5)   **D** (5, 5)

9 The park is located at (7, 5). Plot and label the location of the park on the map. Describe the location of the park in relation to the location of the school.

_____

_____

Name: _____

Identify Positive and Negative Numbers

Study the example showing positive and negative numbers on a number line. Then solve problems 1–10.

Example

Gareth is graphing some numbers and their opposites on the number line below. He has partially completed the number line as shown.

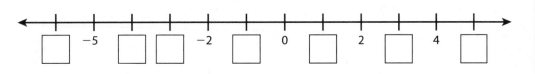

$\boxed{}$ −5 $\boxed{}$ $\boxed{}$ −2 $\boxed{}$ 0 $\boxed{}$ 2 $\boxed{}$ 4 $\boxed{}$

1 Fill in the missing numbers on Gareth's number line.

2 Choose a pair of numbers from the number line that you know are opposites. Explain how you know that the numbers are opposites.

_____

_____

3 Graph a point at 4 and at the opposite of 4 on the number line.

4 Mary says that the opposite of 0 is 0. Is she correct?

_____

_____

5 Name two numbers that are not integers but that are opposites. Explain how you know.

_____

_____

_____

Vocabulary

opposites numbers that are the same distance from 0 but on opposite sides of 0.

integers the set of whole numbers and their opposites.

Solve.

6 Use the number line below to graph and label each number and its opposite.

$1\frac{1}{2}$ −3.5   2.5

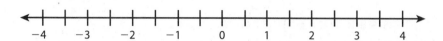

7 Pavel said that he could graph −5 by counting 5 units to the left of 5. Is he correct? Explain.

_____

_____

_____

8 Write a positive or a negative number to represent each situation.

a.   3 degrees below 0°F _____

b.   6 feet above sea level _____

c.   lost 5 pounds _____

d.   found $4 _____

9 A family wants to save $100 each month. They record their progress toward this goal at the end of each month. In January they saved $120 and recorded +$20 at the end of the month. What should they record for the month of February if they only saved $80 that month? Explain.

_____

10 When would you use a negative number to describe a real-world amount? Give an example.

_____

_____

_____

Name: _____

Reason and Write

Study the example. Underline two parts that you think make it a particularly good answer and a helpful example.

Example

The thermometer shows the temperature outdoors at noon. The temperature at midnight was the opposite of the temperature at noon. Beth says that the temperature at midnight was −40°F. Is Beth correct? Explain your reasoning.

Show your work. Use a model, positive and negative numbers, and words to explain your answer.

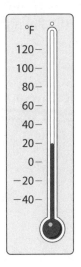

The thermometer shows that the temperature at noon was 20°F.

I can draw a number line to model the temperature.

I know that the opposite of a number is the number that is the same distance from 0 in the opposite direction on a number line. So I can use the number line to see that the opposite of 20 is −20.

20 is 20 units to the right of 0 on the number line, and −20 is 20 units to the left of 0 on the number line.

So the temperature at midnight was −20°F. Beth was not correct. The temperature was not −40°F.

Where does the example . . .

- answer the question?

- use a model to explain?

- use positive and negative numbers to explain?

- use words to explain?

Solve the problem. Use what you learned from the model.

Alex is practicing his dives at a pool. He dives from a diving board that is 15 feet above the surface of the water. His dive takes him 15 feet below the surface of the water. Alex says that the two distances are opposites, so his total dive distance is $15 + (-15) = 0$ feet. Are the two distances opposites? Is Alex's total dive distance correct? Explain your reasoning.

Show your work. Use models, positive and negative numbers, and words to explain your answer.

Did you . . .

• answer the question?

• use a model to explain ?

• use positive and negative numbers to explain?

• use words to explain?

Dear Family,

Your child is learning about absolute value and ordering numbers.

The absolute value of a number tells how far the number is from 0 on a number line. The number line at the right shows that the absolute value of −3 is 3 because −3 is 3 units from 0.

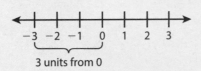

3 units from 0

A special symbol is used for absolute value: $|-3|$ means the absolute value of −3.

Absolute value is used often in the real world. For example, the height at which a helicopter flies might be described as 9,000 feet above sea level. The depth at which a submarine travels might be described as 400 feet below sea level. In these examples, you can think of the numbers 9,000 and 400 as absolute values because they both tell the distance from sea level, or 0.

Your child is also learning to compare positive and negative numbers and to order positive and negative numbers.

Consider the following example:

Players of a board game earn a positive number of points for correct answers and a negative number of points for incorrect answers. The final scores of four players are 1.5, −2.5, −1, and 3. What is the highest score? What is the lowest score?

On the next page you will see two ways your child may compare and order the numbers to find the highest and lowest scores.

Vocabulary

absolute value a number's distance from 0 on the number line.

NEXT

Four players earned scores of 1.5, −2.5, −1, and 3 in a board game. What are the highest and lowest scores?

You can graph the numbers on a number line to see the relationships between the numbers.

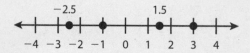

One way:
Compare the positions of the numbers on the number line from *least* to *greatest*.

−2.5 is to the left of −1, so −2.5 < −1.

−1 is to the left of 1.5, so −1 < 1.5.

1.5 is to the left of 3, so 1.5 < 3.

From least to greatest, the order of the numbers is −2.5, −1, 1.5, and 3.

Another way:
Compare the positions of the numbers on the number line from *greatest* to *least*.

3 is to the right of 1.5, so 3 > 1.5.

1.5 is to the right of −1, so 1.5 > −1.

−1 is to the right of −2.5, so −1 > −2.5.

From greatest to least, the order of the numbers is 3, 1.5, −1, and −2.5.

Answer: Both methods show that the greatest number is 3 and the least number is −2.5. This means that the highest game score is 3 and the lowest game score is −2.5.

Absolute Value and Ordering Numbers

Name: _____

Prerequisite: Understanding Integers

Study the example problem showing how to use positive and negative integers. Then solve problems 1–7.

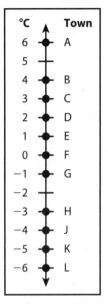

°C	Town
6	A
5	
4	B
3	C
2	D
1	E
0	F
−1	G
−2	
−3	H
−4	J
−5	K
−6	L

Example

The model shows the temperatures in 11 towns one winter morning. Which town has a temperature that is the opposite of the temperature in Town C?

The temperature in Town C is 3°C. The opposite of 3 is the same distance from 0 but in the opposite direction. The temperature in Town H is −3°C. So Town H has the opposite temperature of Town C.

1 Which town has a temperature of −4°C?

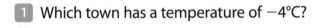

_____

2 How can you find the town with a temperature that is the opposite of −4°C? Name the town with that temperature.

_____

_____

_____

_____

3 Barry pairs each town with another town that has the opposite temperature. Which town(s) cannot be paired? Explain.

_____

_____

_____

_____

_____

Vocabulary

positive number
a number greater than 0.

negative number
a number less than 0.

opposite two numbers are opposites if they are the same distance from 0 on the number line but on opposite sides of 0.

2 is a positive number.
−2 is a negative number.
2 and −2 are opposites.

Solve.

4 Graph and label the numbers 1.75, −2.5, and 0.2 on the number line. Then graph and label their opposites.

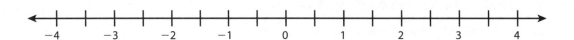

5 Graph and label the numbers $-3\frac{1}{2}$, $2\frac{1}{4}$, and $\frac{1}{2}$ on the number line. Then graph and label their opposites.

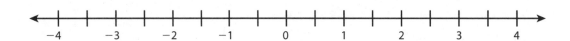

6 Write two numbers that fit each description.

a. a positive number and a negative number between 1 and −1

_____

b. a whole number and its opposite between −0.5 and 0.9

_____

c. a decimal and a fraction between −4 and −3

_____

7 Write your own problem about money or elevation that uses a number and its opposite. Solve the problem. Then explain what 0 means in your problem.

_____

_____

_____

_____

Name: _____

Compare Positive and Negative Numbers

Study the example problem showing how to compare numbers. Then solve problems 1–6.

Example

Phil and Lorena are playing golf. Phil's score after the first round is −1. Lorena's score is −4. The player with the lower score is the winner. Who wins?

Graph the two scores on a number line.

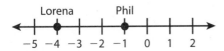

Numbers increase from left to right along a number line. Use an inequality to compare the scores.

−4 < −1

Lorena's score is the lower score, so Lorena wins.

1 Write another inequality to compare the scores.

_____

2 Rory joins the game for the second round and wins that round. What can you say about where his score would appear on the number line? Explain.

_____

_____

_____

3 Rory, Lorena, and Phil play a third round of golf. Lorena's score is 1 in the third round. Phil ties Rory's score at −3. Write an inequality that shows why Lorena lost that round.

_____

Solve.

4 When asked to compare −9 and 2, Joshua wrote
−9 > 2. Is Joshua correct? If not, explain and correct
his error.

_____

5 Tom is thinking of two numbers, *a* and *b*, where *a* is
a positive number and *b* is a negative number.

    a. Write two inequalities that Tom can use to compare
a and *b*. Explain how you know.

_____

_____

_____

_____

    b. Choose two numbers for *a* and *b*, and then use
them to write two inequalities.

_____

6 Juanita was given this information about three
integers, *n*, *m*, and *p*:

$n < 0, m < n, n < p$

    a. Graph three points on a number line that could
represent *n*, *m*, and *p*. Explain your choices.

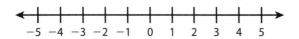

_____

_____

    b. Write two inequalities comparing *m* and *p*. Explain.

_____

Name: _____

Ordering Positive and Negative Numbers

Study the example problem showing how to order positive and negative numbers. Then solve problems 1–7.

Example

Five students draw number cards at random and make a human number line. The table shows the number that each student drew.

Student	Number
Ina	−1.5
Joe	2.1
Kit	−3.2
Larry	1.7
Mai	−0.4

From left to right, how did the students arrange themselves to form the number line?

Plot each number on a number line.

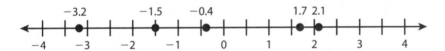

1. Which student has the least number? Explain how you know.

_____

_____

2. Which student has the greatest number? Explain how you know.

_____

_____

3. Order the students from least to greatest.

_____

4. Ned draws a number card with a −1. Where should Ned stand along the line of students?

_____

Solve.

5 Abey made a table showing the lowest temperature for five towns during one week in winter.

Town	Temperature (°C)
J	−5.4
K	1.8
L	−2.3
M	4
P	−5.7

a. Order the towns from coldest to warmest.

_____

b. The lowest temperature in Town Q that week was 0.6°C. If Abey wants to include Town Q in the ordered list, where should he put it?

_____

6 The table shows the position of four fish relative to the surface of the water. Name all the fish swimming deeper than the carp.

Fish	Position (ft)
Bass	$-15\frac{1}{2}$
Trout	$-9\frac{7}{8}$
Pike	$-20\frac{1}{5}$
Carp	$-15\frac{3}{4}$

_____

7 Plot points A, B, C, and D on a number line so that each statement is true: $B < 0$, $A < C$, $D > 0$, $B > C$.

Name: _____

Absolute Value and Ordering Numbers

Solve the problems.

1 A bird is flying at an elevation of 14 feet above the surface of the water. A fish is swimming the same distance below the surface of the water.

How can you represent a location below the surface of the water?

a. What number represents the position of the fish relative to the surface of the water? _____

b. How does the absolute value of the number you wrote show that the distances are the same? Explain.

_____

_____

_____

_____

2 If $x > y$, which statement must be true?

A On a number line, y is to the left of 0.

B On a number line, x is to the right of 0.

C On a number line, both x and y are positive.

D On a number line, y is to the left of x.

Read the inequality carefully. What does the symbol $>$ mean?

3 Ganesa wanted to write numerical examples for the inequality $a < b$, with the conditions described in the table. One of the conditions cannot be met. Complete the table. Indicate which condition cannot be met.

Be sure that you understand each condition in the table.

Condition	Numerical Example for $a < b$
$a < 0$ and $b < 0$	
$a < 0$ and $b > 0$	
$a > 0$ and $b < 0$	
$a > 0$ and $b > 0$	

Solve.

4 The table shows the temperatures for five towns.

Town	Z	Y	X	W	V
Temperature (°C)	−1.9	7.4	−12.2	6	−5.7

What is the correct order from warmest to coldest?

A X, V, Z, W, Y   **C** X, Y, W, V, Z

B Z, V, X, W, Y   **D** Y, W, Z, V, X

Reyhan chose **C** as the correct answer. How did she get that answer?

_____

Can a number line help you find the answer?

5 Look at the number line below. Select whether each statement is *True* or *False*.

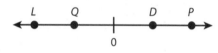

a. $L > P$ ☐ True ☐ False

b. $Q < D$ ☐ True ☐ False

c. $L < Q$ ☐ True ☐ False

How do the positions of numbers on a number line help you compare their values?

6 A teacher poses this problem: I am thinking of four numbers, *a, b, c,* and *d,* where $a < 0, b < 0, c > 0,$ and $d > 0$. What else do you need to know to plot the four numbers in the correct order on a number line? What two questions should you ask? Explain how the answers would help you plot the numbers on a number line.

_____

_____

_____

Think about how to locate positive and negative numbers on a number line.

Dear Family,

Your child is learning about the coordinate plane.

The coordinate plane is formed by the intersection of a horizontal number line and a vertical number line. The horizontal number line is called the *x*-axis. The vertical number line is called the *y*-axis. You can graph points on the coordinate plane and describe the location of a point with a pair of numbers called an *ordered pair*. An ordered pair gives the *x*- and *y*-coordinates of a point.

Coordinate Plane

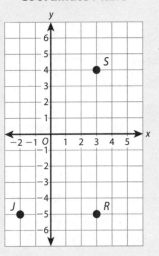

Point	x-coordinate	y-coordinate	Ordered Pair
S	3	4	(3, 4)
R	3	−5	(3, −5)
J	−2	−5	(−2, −5)

Point *S* is located at (3, 4). Point *R* is located at (3, −5). Point *J* is located at (−2, −5).

One way you can use the coordinate plane is to find the distance between two points. In the real world, the coordinate plane is used as the basis for GPS programs and for paper maps.

Consider the following example:

The points on the coordinate plane above represent the location of a school and the homes of two students. The school is at point *S*. Rudi's house is at point *R* and Jake's house is at point *J*. Each unit on the coordinate plane represents one block. How many blocks does Rudi walk to get to school? How many blocks does Jake walk to get to Rudi's house?

The next page shows two different ways your child may find the distance between two points that have the same *x*- or *y*-coordinate.

NEXT ➡

Each unit on the coordinate plane below represents one block. How many blocks does Rudi walk from his house at point *R* to get to school at point *S*? How many blocks does Jake walk from his house at point *J* to get to Rudi's house at point *R*?

One way: Count the units between the points.

Rudi's house to school:

- Point *R* is Rudi's house. Point *S* is the school.
- Both *x*-coordinates are the same, 3, so count the units between the *y*-coordinates. Count from −5 to 4, which is 9 units.

Jake's house to Rudi's house:

- Point *J* is Jake's house. Point *R* is Rudi's house.
- Both *y*-coordinates are the same, −5, so count the units between the *x*-coordinates. Count from −2 to 3, which is 5 units.

Another way: Use absolute value.

Rudi's house to school:

- Both points have the same *x*-coordinates, so find their distances to the *x*-axis. The distance from $(3, -5)$ to the *x*-axis is $|-5|$. The distance from $(3, 4)$ to the *x*-axis is $|4|$. Now add the distances.
$|-5| + |4| = 5 + 4 = 9$

Jake's house to Rudi's house:

- Both points have the same *y*-coordinates, so find their distances to the *y*-axis. The distance from $(-2, -5)$ to the *y*-axis is $|-2|$. The distance from $(3, -5)$ to the *y*-axis is $|3|$. Now add the distances.
$|-2| + |3| = 2 + 3 = 5$

Answer: Both methods show that the distance from point *R* to point *S* is 9 units and the distance from point *J* to point *R* is 5 units, meaning that Rudi walks 9 blocks to get from his house to school and that Jake walks 5 blocks to get from his house to Rudi's house.

Coordinate Plane

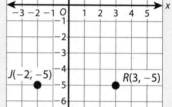

The Coordinate Plane

Name: _____

Prerequisite: Graph Points

Study the example showing how to plot points on a coordinate grid. Then solve problems 1–11.

Example

The location of a point is named with an *x*-coordinate and a *y*-coordinate. The coordinates are written as an ordered pair, (*x*-coordinate, *y*-coordinate). Follow these steps to plot point *A* at (3, 4).

- Start at the origin.

- Move 3 units to the right.

- Move 4 units up.

- Label the point *A*.

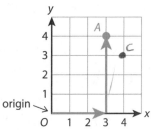

1 What ordered pair describes the origin? __0,0__

2 What are the coordinates of point *A*?

   x-coordinate: __34__   *y*-coordinate: __4__

3 Along which axis do you count each number of units in order to plot point *A*?

   3 units to the right: __x__-axis   4 units up: __y__-axis

4 Plot a new point at (4, 3). Label the point *C*.

5 Zachary says that point *C* has the same location as point *A* because both points have the same coordinates. Is Zachary right? Explain why or why not.

   __No, because the coordinates go in__

   __differents place in the x and__

   __y coordinates.__

Vocabulary

x-coordinate a point's horizontal distance from the origin along the *x*-axis.

y-coordinate a point's vertical distance from the origin along the *y*-axis.

Solve.

Use the coordinate plane at the right to solve problems 6–9.

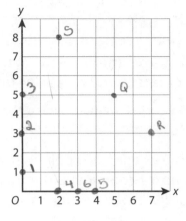

6 Plot and label the following points.

Q(5, 5)   R(7, 3)   S(2, 8)

7 Choose one point from problem 6. Complete the following statements to describe how you plotted the point.

a. Start at (__0__ , __0__).

b. Move __7__ units to the right. Move __3__ units up.

c. Label the point __R__ .

8 Plot points at (0, 3), (0, 1), and (0, 5). What is true about all points with an *x*-coordinate of 0?

They all lie on the y axis line.

9 Plot points at (2, 0), (4, 0), and (3, 0). What is true about all points with a *y*-coordinate of 0?

They all lie on the x axis line.

Use the coordinate plane at the right to solve problems 10–11.

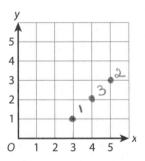

10 Write ordered pairs for four points that you can plot on the coordinate plane. Each ordered pair must have a *y*-coordinate that is 2 units less than its *x*-coordinate. Plot the points.

_1. (3,1)   2. (5,3)   3.(4,2)_

11 Describe a pattern for the points you plotted in problem 10.

They all

Name: _____

Graphing on the Coordinate Plane

Study the example showing how to graph on the coordinate plane. Then solve problems 1–7.

Example

The table shows the locations of exhibits at a science museum. Graph each exhibit on the coordinate plane.

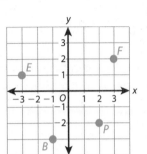

Exhibit	Fossils	Birds	Planets	Energy
Coordinates	(3, 2)	(−1, −3)	(2, −2)	(−3, 1)

For each ordered pair in the table, start at the origin, move left or right according to the x-coordinate, and then move up or down according to the y-coordinate.

---

1 Which exhibit is located at point E on the coordinate plane?

   Energy

2 What are the x- and the y-coordinates of point E?

   _(-3,1)_

3 How are the x-coordinate and the y-coordinate in an ordered pair related to the origin?

   They all start the ⟨ORIGIN⟩

   _____

4 Complete the table below to describe the location of each exhibit.

Exhibit	Location from the Origin
Fossils	3 → 2 ↑
Birds	1 ← 3 ↓
Planets	2 → 2 ↓
Energy	3 ← 1 ↑

Solve.

Use this information for problems 5–6.

You can use a coordinate plane to represent the locations of different activities at a summer camp. The ordered pairs in the table show the location of each activity.

Activity	Canoeing	Swimming	Hiking	Art	Fishing
Coordinates	(−6, 5)	(2, −2)	(−3, −3)	(4, 6)	(−4, 0)

(handwritten above columns: 1, 2, 3, 4, 5)

5 Graph each activity as a point on the coordinate plane. Label each point with the first letter of the activity.

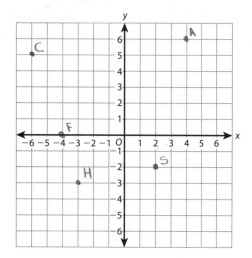

6 Describe the location from the origin of each point in problem 5.

1. II   2. IV   3. III   4. I   5. II

7 What are the signs of the coordinates of a point in each of the four quadrants?

1. (+ , +)   2. II   3. III   4. IV

(−,+)   (−,−)   (−,+)

Name: _____

Reflect Points

Study the example problem showing how to reflect points across the x-axis. Then solve problems 1–9.

Example

Rectangle *LMNK* is reflected across the x-axis to get rectangle *PQRS*. How do the coordinates of point *L* change when it is reflected across the x-axis?

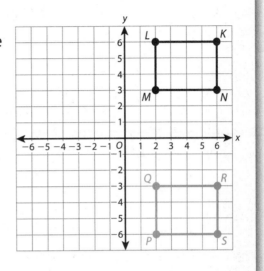

The coordinates of point *L* are (2, 6). The reflection of point *L* across the x-axis is point *P*. The coordinates of point *P* are (2, −6).

The x-coordinate of the reflection of point *L* is the same as point *L*, but the y-coordinate has the opposite sign.

1 What points are the reflections of points *M*, *N*, and *K* across the x-axis?

M:P   N:S   K:R

2 List the coordinates of the other points of rectangle *LMNK* and rectangle *PQRS*.

Point *M*: (2 , 3)   Point *Q*: (2 , -3)

Point *N*: (6 , 3)   Point *R*: (6 , -3)

Point *K*: (6 , 6)   Point *S*: (6 , -6)

3 How are the coordinates of points *M* and *Q*, points *N* and *R*, and points *K* and *S* the same? How are they different?

_____

4 How do the coordinates of a point compare with the coordinates of its reflection across the x-axis?

_____

Solve.

Use the information for problems 5–7.

The points *L*, *M*, and *N* are reflected across the *y*-axis to get the points *F*, *G*, and *H* on the coordinate plane at the right.

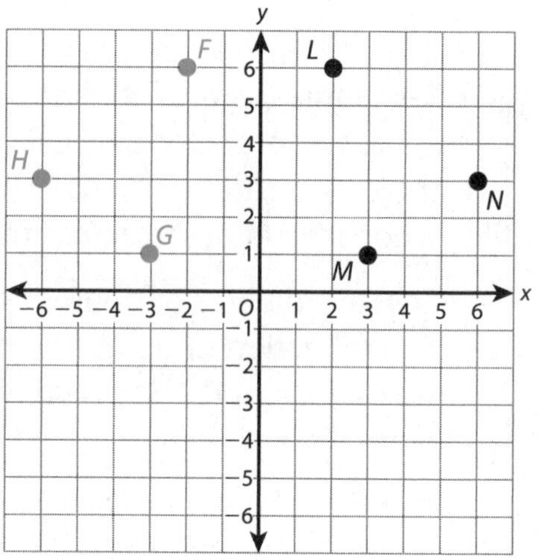

5 List the coordinates of the points shown in the graph.

Point *L*: (_____)   Point *F*: (_____)

Point *M*: (_____)   Point *G*: (_____)

Point *N*: (_____)   Point *H*: (_____)

6 How are the coordinates of each point and its reflection the same? How are they different?

_____

_____

7 How do the coordinates of a point compare with the coordinates of its reflection across the *y*-axis?

_____

_____

8 Becky reflects point *Q* at (−5, −4) across the *x*-axis to get point *Z*. What are the coordinates of point *Z*? Explain how you know.

_____

_____

9 Kanika plots point *A* at (1, −2). Next she plots a reflection of point *A* at point *W*. Finally, Kanika plots a reflection of point *W* at point *T*, which is located at (−1, 2). Describe how Kanika could have reflected each of the points to arrive at point *T*.

_____

_____

_____

Name: _____

Distance Between Points

Study the example showing how to find the distance between points in different quadrants. Then solve problems 1–9.

Example

The locations of different stores are shown on the map. There is a sports store at point S and a clothing store at point C. Each unit on the coordinate plane represents 1 mile. How many miles is the clothing store from the sports store?

Notice that the stores have the same x-coordinates, but they are in different quadrants. To find the distance between them, find the distances of both points from the x-axis and add them.

$$|5| + |-6| = 5 + 6 = 11$$

The clothing store is 11 miles from the sports store.

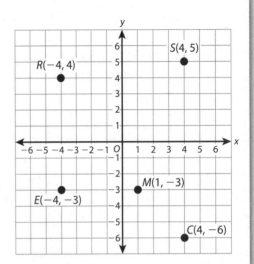

1 What are the y-coordinates of the sports store and the clothing store?

_____

2 What do $|5|$ and $|-6|$ represent in the example?

_____

_____

3 What is the relationship between the distance of the sports store and the clothing store from the x-axis and the y-coordinate of each point?

_____

_____

4 Explain how to count units to check the answer.

_____

_____

Solve.

Use the situation below and the coordinate plane to solve problems 5–8.

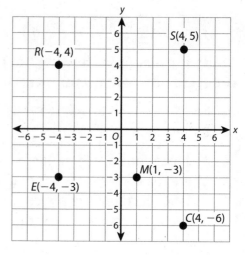

A music store is at point *M* on the coordinate plane. An electronics store is at point *E*, and a restaurant is located at point *R*. Each unit represents 1 mile.

5 What are two ways you can find the distance between the electronics store and the music store?

_____

_____

6 What is the distance between the electronics store and the music store? Count units to find the answer.

_____

7 Use absolute value to find the distance between the music store and the electronics store.

Show your work.

Solution: _____

8 Helen drove from the restaurant to the toy store, which is not shown on the map. She made a right turn at the toy store and drove to the music store. She drove a total distance of 12 miles. What are the coordinates of the toy store?

_____

9 Point *A* is located at $(-3, y)$, and point *B* is located at $(-6, y)$. How can you find the distance between these points using absolute values?

_____

_____

Name: _____

The Coordinate Plane

Solve the problems.

1 Which statements are true about the coordinate plane? Choose all that apply.

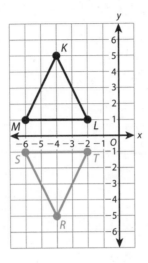

Which axis are the triangles reflected across?

A $\triangle KLM$ is reflected across the y-axis to get $\triangle RTS$.

B The x-coordinates of points K and R are the same.

C The y-coordinates of points K and R have opposite signs.

D The y-coordinates of points L and T are the same.

2 In the coordinate plane in problem 1, how can you find the distance from point R to the x-axis? Choose all that apply.

What are the x- and y-coordinates of point R?

A Find the absolute value of the x-coordinate in $(-4, -5)$.

B Add the absolute values of the x- and y-coordinates.

C Count the number of units down from the x-axis.

D Find the absolute value of the y-coordinate in $(-4, -5)$.

Julio chose **A** as a correct answer. How did he get that answer?

_____

_____

Solve.

3 Four points representing the corners of a square are D(−4, 5), E(3, 5), F(3, −2), and G(−4, −2). Graph and label the points on the coordinate plane.

What do the coordinates of a point tell you about its location from the origin?

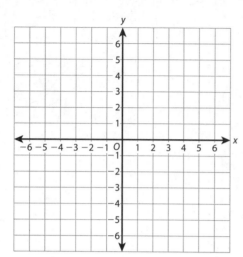

4 How could you move the square in problem 3 so that each corner point is a reflection of another corner point across the x- and y-axes? Explain your answer and graph the new square.

Show your work.

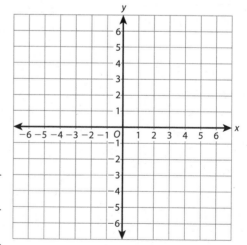
How do you find the distance between points?

Solution: _____

_____

_____

Name: _____

Decimal Scramble

What you need: Recording Sheet, 3 number cubes labeled as follows: cube 1 has 0, 1, 2, 3, 4, 5; cube 2 has 4, 5, 6, 7, 8, 9; cube 3 has 1, 2, 3, 6, 7, 8

Directions

- Your goal is to create two numbers and multiply or divide them to get as close as possible to the Target Number.

- One player rolls the number cubes. Both players use the three digits to make a number. Each player decides how to order the digits and where to put the decimal point in his or her number.

- Roll again and both players generate another number.

- Players multiply or divide their numbers and record the operation on the Recording Sheet.

- The target numbers are different for each round and as shown on the Recording Sheet.

- The player whose product or quotient is closest to the target number for the round scores 1 point.

- The player with the most points at the end of Round 4 wins. It is OK to have a tie.

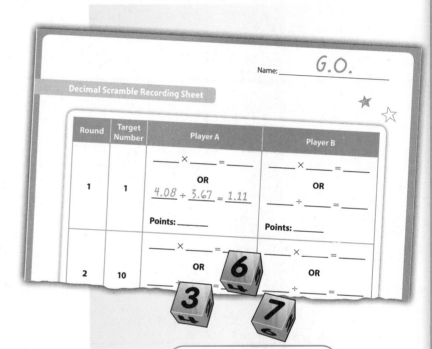

Name: G.O.

Decimal Scramble Recording Sheet

Round	Target Number	Player A	Player B
1	1	___ × ___ = ___ OR 4.08 ÷ 3.67 = 1.11 Points: ___	___ × ___ = ___ OR ___ ÷ ___ = ___ Points: ___
2	10	___ × ___ = ___ OR ___ ÷ ___ = ___	___ × ___ = ___ OR ___ ÷ ___ = ___

I think about what digit to use for the greatest place value in each number. What is their product? What is their quotient? Then I think about where to put the decimal point.

Name: _____

Decimal Scramble Recording Sheet

Round	Target Number	Player A	Player B
1	1	_____ × _____ = _____ **OR** _____ ÷ _____ = _____ **Points:** _____	_____ × _____ = _____ **OR** _____ ÷ _____ = _____ **Points:** _____
2	10	_____ × _____ = _____ **OR** _____ ÷ _____ = _____ **Points:** _____	_____ × _____ = _____ **OR** _____ ÷ _____ = _____ **Points:** _____
3	100	_____ × _____ = _____ **OR** _____ ÷ _____ = _____ **Points:** _____	_____ × _____ = _____ **OR** _____ ÷ _____ = _____ **Points:** _____
4	1,000	_____ × _____ = _____ **OR** _____ ÷ _____ = _____ **Points:** _____	_____ × _____ = _____ **OR** _____ ÷ _____ = _____ **Points:** _____

Name: _____

The Number System

In this unit you learned to:	Lesson
explain how to divide fractions, for example: explain why $\frac{2}{3} \div \frac{3}{4} = \frac{8}{9}$.	6, 7
divide multi-digit whole numbers, for example: 26,304 ÷ 24 = 1,096.	8
add and subtract multi-digit decimals, for example: 3.1 − 1.534 = 1.566.	9
multiply and divide decimals, for example: 32.5 ÷ 0.25 = 130.	10
find common factors and common multiples, for example: common factors of 4 and 6 are 1 and 2, and common multiples are 12 and 24.	11
recognize real-world uses for negative numbers and locate them on a number line.	12
order integers and find absolute value, for example: −7 < −5 and −5 < 2.	13
plot points in the four quadrants of the coordinate plane.	14

Use these skills to solve problems 1–8.

1. Which expression is equivalent to 25.85 ÷ 1.5?

   A 2,585 ÷ 15

   B 258.5 ÷ 15

   C 258.5 ÷ 0.15

   D 25.85 ÷ 15

2. How many decimal places are in the product 4.45 × 7.3?

   A 1

   B 2

   C 3

   D 4

3. A principal orders 2,592 pencils. She gives an equal number to each of 24 teachers. How many pencils does each teacher get?

   _____

4. Greta reads $1\frac{1}{2}$ pages per minute when she reads her English homework assignment. At this rate, how long does it take Greta to read 60 pages?

   _____

Solve.

5 Which statement is true? Select all that apply.

A $-5\frac{1}{4} > 2\frac{3}{4}$

B $-7.1 > -7.8$

C $2\frac{1}{2} < -9$

D $-6\frac{3}{5} < 6\frac{2}{5}$

6 The area of one rectangle is 36 square feet. The area of a second rectangle is 21 square feet. The rectangles have the same width and the dimensions are whole numbers. What is the width of both rectangles?

A 3 feet   C 7 feet

B 6 feet   D 12 feet

7 Mary walked 23.61 miles this month. That is 8.625 more miles than she walked last month. What is the total number of miles that she walked in both months?

Show your work.

Solution: _____

8 Rectangle *ABCD* is formed by connecting four points. Point *A* is located at (−3, 5). Point *B* is a reflection of point *A* across the *y*-axis. Point *D* is a reflection of point *A* across the *x*-axis. Point *C* is a reflection of point *D* across the *y*-axis.

Part A

Draw the rectangle and label the points.

Part B

What is the perimeter of the rectangle?

_____

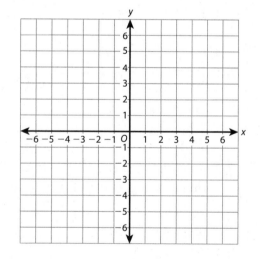

Name: _____

Answer the questions and show all your work on separate paper.

You are in charge of concessions for the upcoming school dance. You are buying the items listed in the table to sell at the dance. The table includes prices for multi-packs of each item.

Item	Package Description	Package Price
Apples	10 lb bag (about 20–22 apples)	$8.90
String cheese	Package of 24	$6.49
Peanut butter crackers	Box of 30 packs	$6.75
Granola bars	Box of 18 bars	$10.89
Cheese pizza	1 pizza (8 slices)	$6.75
Assorted juice boxes	Package of 8 juice boxes	$2.99
Bottled water	Package of 24 bottles	$5.99

Checklist

Did you . . .

☐ make a table to organize your work?

☐ explain your reasoning?

☐ check that your prices are reasonable?

You need to decide the selling price for each item. Here is what you know.
- The selling price should be about 2 or 3 times the cost of the item.
- Concession stand workers don't want to count a lot of change to give back to customers.

Here is what you need to do.
- Find your cost to buy 1 of each item.
- Decide on a selling price for each item. Show all your work and make a list of the prices.
- Explain the reasoning for each price.

Reflect on Mathematical Practices

After you complete the task, choose one of the following questions to answer.

1 Be Precise How did you use rounding to find the cost per item? Explain.

2 Use Structure How did you use coin and dollar values to help you decide on appropriate selling prices?

Performance Task Tips

Word Bank Here are some words that you might use in your answer.

multiply	divide	quotient
factor	dividend	unit rate
product	divisor	

Model Here is a model that you might use to organize your work.

Item	Cost per Item	Selling Price

Sentence Starters Here are some sentence starters that might help you explain your work.

To find the price per item _____

To find the selling price _____

I used prices that _____

Name: _____

My Examples

unit fraction

a fraction with a numerator of 1

$\frac{1}{3}$, $\frac{1}{8}$, and $\frac{1}{12}$ are unit fractions.

multiplicative inverse

reciprocal; when you multiply a number by its multiplicative inverse the product is 1.

$$9 \times \frac{1}{9} = 1$$

The fraction $\frac{1}{9}$ is the multiplicative inverse of 9.

reciprocal

the multiplicative inverse of a number; with fractions, the numerator and denominator are switched

$$\frac{5}{8} \times \frac{8}{5} = 1$$

$\frac{8}{5}$ is the reciprocal of $\frac{5}{8}$.

partial quotient

a strategy used to divide multi-digit numbers; the quotients you get in each step are called: "partial quotients"

factor

a number you multiply

$2 \times 4 = 8$

2 is a factor of 8.

4 is a factor of 8.

factor pair

two numbers that are multiplied together to give a product

$2 \times 4 = 8$

2 and 4 are a factor pair.

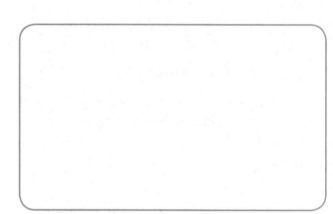

multiple

the product of a number and any whole number

$2 \times 4 = 8$

8 is a multiple of 2.

8 is a multiple of 4.

coordinate plane

a two-dimensional space formed by two perpendicular number lines called axes

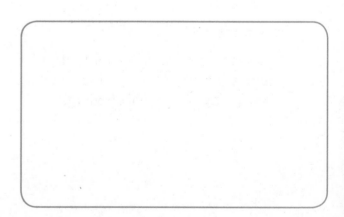

My Examples

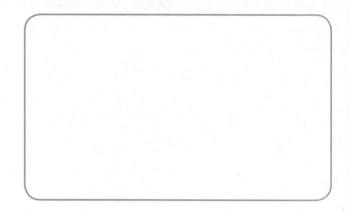

origin

the point (0, 0) where the *x*-axis and
y-axis intersect

ordered pair

a pair of numbers (*x*, *y*) that describe
the location of a point on the
coordinate plane

opposites

two numbers are opposites if they are the
same distance from 0 on the number line
but on opposite sides of 0.

2 is a positive number.

−2 is a negative number.

2 and −2 are opposites.

integers

the set of whole numbers and their
opposites

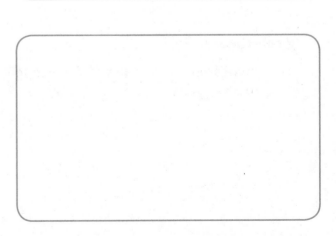

My Examples

positive number

a number greater than 0

negative number

a number less than 0

x-coordinate

a point's horizontal distance from the
origin along the *x*-axis

y-coordinate

a point's vertical distance from the origin
along the *y*-axis

Dear Family,

Your child is learning about numerical expressions with exponents.

A numerical expression shows a mathematical relationship using numbers and symbols, but it does not have an equal sign. You can evaluate any numerical expression to find its value. Here are some examples of numerical expressions:

$$1,095 \qquad 3.6 + 8 \qquad 0.75 \times 24 \qquad 6^2 \qquad \frac{7}{8} \div \frac{5}{6} \qquad 9(5 + 2) - 6 \cdot 8$$

The expression 6^2 is an *exponential expression* because it contains an exponent. You can read 6^2 as "six squared" or "6 to the second power."

$$6 \text{ is the } base. \longrightarrow 6^2 \longleftarrow 2 \text{ is the } exponent.$$

To find the value of an exponential expression, multiply the base by itself the number of times indicated by the exponent. For example, to find the value of 6^2, multiply 6 by itself two times: 6×6. The value of 6^2 is 36.

Consider this situation:

Art students created a mural using tiles. They placed 3 tiles during the first class as they established their design. During each of the next 4 classes, the students tripled the number of tiles placed in the previous class. How many tiles did the students place during the fifth class?

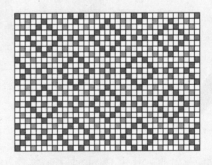

On the next page you will see two ways your child may write and evaluate a numerical expressions to find the number of tiles placed in the fifth class.

Numerical Expressions with Exponents: Sample Solution

> Students placed 3 tiles in a mural during one class. For each of the next 4 classes, the students tripled the number of tiles they had placed in the previous class. How many tiles did the students place during the fifth class?

One way: Use multiplication to represent the problem.

Find the number of tiles that the students placed during each class. Because the students tripled the number of tiles placed in the previous class each time, multiply the number of tiles in each previous class by 3.

First Class	Second Class	Third Class	Fourth Class	Fifth Class
3	$3 \cdot 3 = 9$	$9 \cdot 3 = 27$	$27 \cdot 3 = 81$	$81 \cdot 3 = 243$

The number of tiles placed during the fifth class is 243.

Another way: Represent the problem with repeated multiplication.

The expression in each row of the table shows the expression from the previous row multiplied by 3.

Class	Number of Tiles Placed
First	$3 = 3^1$
Second	$3 \cdot 3 = 3^2$
Third	$3 \cdot 3 \cdot 3 = 3^3$
Fourth	$3 \cdot 3 \cdot 3 \cdot 3 = 3^4$
Fifth	$3 \cdot 3 \cdot 3 \cdot 3 \cdot 3 = 3^5$

The expression in the last row of the table shows that the number of tiles placed during the fifth class is $3 \cdot 3 \cdot 3 \cdot 3 \cdot 3$, which can be written as the exponential expression 3^5. Evaluate the expression. 3^5 has a value of 243.

Answer: The methods show that the numerical expressions $81 \cdot 3$, $3 \cdot 3 \cdot 3 \cdot 3 \cdot 3$, and 3^5 all represent the number of tiles the students placed during the fifth class. The expressions all have a value of 243, so the students placed 243 mosaic tiles during the fifth class.

Numerical Expressions with Exponents

Name: _____

Study the example showing how to multiply by a power of 10. Then solve problems 1–7.

Example

Find $10^2 \times 0.008$.

Break 10^2 into a product of 10s and multiply.

$$10^2 \times 0.008 = 100 \times 0.008$$
$$= 10 \times \mathbf{10} \times \mathbf{0.008}$$
$$= 10 \times \mathbf{0.08}$$
$$= 0.8$$

This means that $10^2 \times 0.008 = 0.8$.

1 By how many factors of 10 did you multiply 0.008? Why?

_____

_____

2 Consider the expression $10^3 \times 0.006$.

   a. What is the exponent in the power of 10?

   _____

   b. How many factors of 10 are in 10^3?

   _____

   c. How do your answers to the last two questions relate to one another?

   _____

   _____

   _____

   d. What is the value of $10^3 \times 0.006$?

   _____

Vocabulary

power of ten a number that can be written as a product of tens.

100 and 10^2 are powers of ten.

exponent the number in a power that shows how many times to multiply the base by itself.

In the expression 10^2, the exponent is 2 and the base is 10.

Solve.

3 Complete the equations showing powers of 10 using exponents.

 a. $3 \times 1{,}000 = 3 \times$ _____ = _____

 b. $0.07 \times 100 = 0.07 \times$ _____ = _____

 c. $0.009 \times$ _____ $= 0.009 \times 10^2 =$ _____

4 Find each product. Explain how the place value of the digit 6 changes as the exponent changes.

 a. What is 0.006×10^1? _____

 b. What is 0.006×10^2? _____

 c. What is 0.006×10^3? _____

 _____

 _____

5 Describe the similarities and differences between 0.008×100 and 0.008×10^2.

 _____

 _____

 _____

6 What power of 10 can you multipy 0.02 by to get a product of 20? Explain your answer.

 _____

 _____

 _____

7 What is the product $4 \times 1{,}000$? Explain how you know.

 _____

 _____

Name: _____

Write and Evaluate Expressions with Exponents

Study the example problem showing how to write and evaluate expressions with exponents. Then solve problems 1–9.

Example

Adrian wants to buy a skateboard that costs $85. After 1 month, he has $4 in savings and plans to quadruple the amount he has saved each month for 4 months. Will Adrian have enough money to buy the skateboard in 4 months?

Month 1	Month 2	Month 3	Month 4
4	$4 \cdot 4 = 16$	$16 \cdot 4 = 64$	$64 \cdot 4 = 256$

Adrian will have enough money to buy the skateboard in 4 months. He will have $171 more than he needs.

1 What does it mean to say that the amount of money from the previous month is quadrupled?

_____

2 Represent the problem with repeated multiplication.

Month	Amount Saved (in dollars)
1	4
2	$4 \cdot \underline{} = 16$
3	_____
4	_____

3 Write an expression using an exponent to represent the amount of money Adrian will have saved by month 4.

_____

4 What is the value of the expression you wrote in problem 3?

_____

Solve.

Use the following situation to solve problems 5–7.

Five students received the same text message at 9:00 AM. Each of them sent the message to 5 more students at 10:00 AM. Each of those students sent the message to 5 more students at 11:00 AM.

5 Represent the situation with exponential expressions. Simplify the expressions.

Time That Message Is Received	Number of Students Receiving Text Message
9:00 AM	$5^1 = 5$
10:00 AM	
11:00 AM	

6 If the pattern continues, how many students will receive the text message at noon? Explain how to use the pattern to find the answer.

_____

_____

_____

7 If the pattern continues, at what time will 15,625 students receive the text message? Explain how you know.

_____

_____

_____

8 Write and simplify an expression to represent 6^3.

_____

9 Chin says that the value of 2^5 is 10. Explain what Chin did wrong and find the correct value.

_____

_____

Name: _____

Evaluate Expressions with Exponents

Study the example problem showing how to evaluate expressions with exponents. Then solve problems 1–9.

Example

Follow the order of operations to simplify $12 - 3^2$.

First find 3^2.

$$3^2 = 3 \cdot 3$$
$$= 9$$

Then subtract 9 from 12. $12 - 9 = 3$

This means that:

$$12 - 3^2 = 12 - 9$$
$$= 3$$

The value of the expression is 3.

1 Explain why you must simplify 3^2 first.

_____

_____

2 Diallo says that the value of $12 - 3^2$ is 81. How did he get that answer?

_____

_____

3 Maggie says that if the expression was $12 \div 3^2$, you would divide before simplifying 3^2. Is she right? Explain.

_____

_____

4 Suppose the expression was $(12 - 3)^2$. Would you still simplify 3^2 first? Explain.

_____

_____

Solve.

5 What is the value of $4 + 2^3 \cdot 3$?

Show your work.

Solution: _____

6 What is the value of $\frac{4^2}{2}$? Describe the steps you took to find your answer.

_____

_____

7 Darren and Barb each tried to evaluate $6^2 + 4 \div 2$.

Darren

$6^2 + 4 \div 2$
$= 36 + 4 \div 2$
$= 40 \div 2$
$= 20$

Barb

$6^2 + 4 \div 2$
$= 36 + 4 \div 2$
$= 36 + 2$
$= 38$

Who evaluated the expression correctly? Explain what the other student did wrong.

_____

_____

8 Use the numbers 8, 6, and 2 and one operation to write an expression that includes an exponent and has a value of 8. Use each number only once.

_____

9 Show where to place parentheses in the expression $4 + 3^2 \cdot 5 - 2$ so that the value of the expression is 31.

$4 + 3^2 \cdot 5 - 2$

Name: _____

Numerical Expressions with Exponents

Solve the problems.

1 What is the value of $0.9 \cdot 10^2$?

A 0.09

B 0.9

C 9

D 90

How many factors of 10 are in 10^2?

2 Look at the expression.

$4 \cdot (12 - 8) + 2^3$

Tell whether each statement about the expression is *True* or *False*.

What does the order of operations tell you?

a. The last step in evaluating the expression is to simplify 2^3. ☐ True ☐ False

b. The value of 2^3 is 6. ☐ True ☐ False

c. The first step in evaluating the expression is to subtract $12 - 8$. ☐ True ☐ False

d. The value of the expression is 48. ☐ True ☐ False

3 Beth is making a beanbag seat in the shape of a cube. Each side of the seat is 2 feet long. Beth needs to find the volume of the seat so that she can buy the correct amount of beans. Beans are sold in bags that hold 2 cubic feet of beans. How many bags of beans should Beth buy?

How do you find the volume of a cube?

Show your work.

Solution: _____

Solve.

4 Which expression shows the first step in evaluating

$2 + 7 \cdot \dfrac{12}{6} - 3^2$?

A $2 + \dfrac{84}{6} - 3^2$

B $9 \cdot \dfrac{12}{6} - 3^2$

C $2 + 7 \cdot \dfrac{12}{6} - 9$

D $2 + 7 \cdot 2 - 3^2$

What operation is done first in the order of operations?

5 Students at a cooking school made a supersized rectangular pizza for a class party. Lupita cut the pizza into 3 equal pieces. Then she cut each piece into 3 equal parts two more times. Lupita needs 27 pieces of pizza. Does she have enough pieces yet? Explain how you know.

How can you use exponents to help you solve this problem?

_____

6 Students are getting signatures for a petition to increase sports activities at the community center. The number of signatures they get each day is 3 times as many as the day before. The expression 3^6 represents the number of signatures they got on the sixth day. How many signatures did they get on the first day?

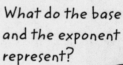

What do the base and the exponent represent?

A 3

B 6

C 18

D 729

Betsy chose **B** as the correct answer. How did she get that answer?

_____

Dear Family,

Your child is learning about algebraic expressions.

Algebraic expressions use variables. A *variable* is a letter that stands for an unknown number. Here are some examples of algebraic expressions:

$$6m \qquad 8b - 2 \qquad 75 + 9p \qquad x + (4 \cdot 5) \qquad 72 \div 3s \qquad \frac{1}{3}(5r + 2)$$

The letters m, b, p, x, s, and r in the expressions above are variables.

Algebraic expressions can be used to represent situations in which an amount is unknown. Here are some examples.

Expression	Situation
6m	the number of granola bars in m boxes, if each box has 6 granola bars
75 + 9p	the number of miles biked when 75 miles are biked in 1 week and p miles are biked in each of the following 9 weeks.

Consider the following example:

A local food pantry has 1 box of plain yogurt with 18 yogurt cups in it. It also has 4 boxes of fruit yogurt each with the same number of yogurt cups, c. Write an expression to show the total number of yogurt cups at the food pantry. If each box of fruit yogurt has 8 yogurt cups, what is the total number of yogurt containers at the food pantry?

On the next page you will see two ways your child may write and evaluate an expression with variables.

Vocabulary

variable a letter that stands for an unknown number.

Algebraic Expressions: Sample Solution

There is 1 box of plain yogurt with 18 yogurt cups. There are 4 boxes of fruit yogurt each with *c* yogurt cups. Write an expression to show the total number of yogurt cups. If each box of fruit yogurt has 8 yogurt cups, what is the total number of yogurt cups?

One way: Draw a picture to understand the problem.

18 containers   *c* containers   *c* containers   *c* containers   *c* containers

- Use the picture to write an expression to show the total number of yogurt cups, *c*.

    $18 + 4c$

- Evaluate the expression for $c = 8$.

    $18 + 4(8) = 18 + 32 = 40$

Another way: Use words to understand the problem.

- Write a sentence that describes the total number of yogurt containers.

    The total number of yogurt cups is the sum of the number of cups in 1 box of plain yogurt and the number of cups, *c*, in 4 boxes of fruit yogurt.

- You can think of the expression as: First amount + Second amount
  An expression for the total number of yogurt cups is $18 + 4c$.

- Evaluate the expression for $c = 8$.

    $18 + 4(8) = 18 + 32 = 40$

Answer: Both methods show that an expression representing the total number of yogurt cups is $18 + 4c$, where "18" is the number of plain yogurt cups and "4c" represents the number of fruit yogurt cups. If each box of fruit yogurt has 8 cups the total number of yogurt cups is 40.

Algebraic Expressions

Name: _____

Prerequisite: Write Numerical Expressions

Study the example showing how to write numerical expressions. Then solve problems 1–6.

Example

Write a numerical expression for this phrase: 12 minus the product of 3 and 2.

Think about what the words mean.

12 minus   the product of 3 and 2

↑   ↑

Minus means   A product is the result
to subtract.   of multiplication.

Before you can subtract the product from 12, you need to multiply 3 by 2 to find the product. Use parentheses to show that first you need to multiply.

The numerical expression is $12 - (3 \times 2)$.

---

1 Jennifer says that you can also write $(12 - 3) \times 2$ for the phrase in the example. Is Jennifer correct? Explain why or why not.

No b/c you can only do this when the operation
is the same when you change the parenthases

2 Write a numerical expression for the phrase "16 times the difference of 9 and 3." What operation should you perform first? Explain.

16(9-3) : You would do the
subtraction inside in parenthases
according to pemdas.

Vocabulary

parentheses the symbols ( ) that can be used to group numbers and operations in an expression.

$24 - (3 \times 5)$

$(5 + 7) \times 3$

Solve.

3 To evaluate the expression "10 minus the sum of 2 and 3," should you subtract or add first? Explain how you know.

10 − (2 + 3) : you would do the addition first b/c it is in the parenthases and parenthases always come first

4 Write a numerical expression for each word phrase. Then evaluate the expression.

a. 5 times the sum of 3 and 4

5 (3 + 4) = 35

b. 24 divided by the sum of 6 and 2

24 ÷ (6 + 2) = 3

c. Divide the difference of 18 and 3 by the sum of 1 and 2.

(18 − 3) ÷ (1 + 2) = 5

d. the sum of 4 and 3 multiplied by the quotient of 4 and 2

(4 + 3) × (4 ÷ 2) = 14

5 Write a word phrase for the expression 12 ÷ (7 − 3).

12 divided by the difference of 7 and 3

6 Marisa made a fruit salad. She used 1 cup of green grapes and 3 cups of red grapes. She used twice as many cups of blueberries as cups of grapes.

Write an expression for the number of cups of blueberries that Marisa used. Then evaluate the expression. Explain your reasoning.

(3 + 1) × 2 = 8 : I did this b/c

Name: _____

Write Expressions with Variables

Study the example showing how to write an expression from words. Then solve problems 1–10.

Example

Write an expression with the same meaning as "add a number times 2 to 5."

Find operation words to help you write the expression. *Add* a number times 2 to 5. This expression will be an addition of two terms.

| First term | + | Second term |

The first term is 5. The second term is 2*x*. So the expression is 5 + 2*x*.

---

1 What does the variable *x* in the example represent?

It represents the 2nd term

2 The number 2 in the expression 5 + 2*x* is called the coefficient of *x*. How does changing the coefficient to 6 change the meaning of the expression?

That means that 2 would be the constants

3 In the expression, 5 + 2*x*, how is the first term different from the second term?

The first term is not multiplied by anything (constant) while the 2nd term is multiplied by the value of x.

4 Write an expression for each word phrase.

a. Multiply 4 by a number and then subtract 5.

4x - 5

b. 15 more than half a number

x/2 + 15

Vocabulary

variable a letter that stands for an unknown number.

constant a term that is a known number without variables.

coefficient a factor of a variable term that is a known number. The coefficient of the term 4*x* is 4.

Solve.

5 Connie says an expression for the phrase "10 more than the square of a number" is $x^2 + 10$. Sharon says it is $10x^2$. Who is correct? Explain.

Connie is correct b/c Sharon's expression means you do 10 time x to the 2nd power

6 Write an expression for each word phrase.

a. 5 less than the quotient of a number and 2

x l 2 -5

b. 5 minus the quotient of a number and 2

5 - x l 2

7 How are the expressions that you wrote in problem 6 similar? How are they different?

They are similar b/c they both have the same operation but one of them is subtracted from and one is subtracted by

8 Write a word phrase for the expression $16 \div (x + 4)$.

16 divided by x plus 4.

9 Write an expression with two terms. One term should have a coefficient with a variable and the other term should be a constant. Name the coefficient, the variable, and the constant in the expression. Then write a word phrase for your expression.

4x + 2y : 4 times a number added to 2 times a number.

10 Mario says that the expression $4 + 3n^2$ has four terms: 4, 3, n, and 2. Is he correct? Explain.

Name: _____

Write and Evaluate Expressions

Study the example showing how to write and evaluate expressions. Then solve problems 1–7.

Example

Lina is making jewelry. She has 7 beads and buys 4 additional packets of beads that each have the same number of beads. Write an expression to show the total number of beads that Lina uses.

Draw the beads she starts with and the packets she buys, and label the number of beads in each. You don't know how many beads are in each packet, so use a variable like *b* to label the number of beads in each packet.

Amount Lina Starts With	Additional Amount Lina Buys

7 beads	*b* beads *b* beads *b* beads *b* beads

1 Write an expression for each word or phrase.

    a. the number of beads Lina starts with

    _____

    b. the total number of beads in the four packets

    _____

    c. the total number of beads Lina has

    _____

2 Laura wrote and solved the following expression to find the total number of beads Lina has if there are 6 beads in each packet. Find and correct Laura's mistake.

$$7 + 4b = 11b$$
$$= 11(6)$$
$$= 66$$

_____

_____

Solve.

3 Blake and three friends meet for lunch. His friends all get the same thing, but Blake gets a different lunch that costs $6. Write an expression to show the total amount that Blake and his friends spend. Then find the total amount that Blake and his friends spend if each friend spends $8.

_____

4 Ana's age is 8 years less than 4 times her sister's age. Write an expression for Ana's age. How old is Ana if her sister is 5 years old?

_____

5 Belle put the muffins she baked on six plates, four of which are red and two of which are yellow. The four red plates each have 5 muffins. The two yellow plates each have the same number of muffins. Write an expression for the total number of muffins Belle baked. If each yellow plate has 8 muffins, find how many muffins Belle baked in all. Explain.

_____

_____

6 Adam says that the expression $52 - 3y$ is equal to 20 when $y = 2$. Explain why Adam's answer is incorrect.

_____

_____

7 A blue suitcase weighs 10 pounds less than three-fourths the weight of a green suitcase. Write an expression that you can use to find the weight of the blue suitcase. Then explain how you can find the total weight of both suitcases if the green suitcase weighs 36 pounds.

_____

_____

_____

Name: _____

Write and Evaluate More Expressions

Study the example showing how to write and evaluate more expressions. Then solve problems 1–5.

Example

Last week Juan mowed lawns and walked his neighbor's dog to earn money. For mowing lawns, he earned $6 less than twice as much as he did for walking dogs. Juan saves one-third of the money he earns and spends the rest.

Write an expression to show how much money Juan earned last week.

Draw a picture to help you understand the problem.

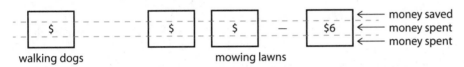

Let w be the amount Juan earned walking dogs. Then $(2w - 6)$ is the amount Juan earned mowing lawns. The total amount Juan earned is $w + (2w - 6)$, or $3w - 6$.

---

1 Emma wrote the expression $2(3w - 6)$ to represent the amount of money that Juan spent. Is she correct? Explain.

_____

_____

2 Explain how you can find the amount of money Juan saved if he earned $12 walking dogs.

_____

_____

_____

_____

Solve.

3 The price *p* of a gallon of gas goes up $0.05 cents on Friday. On Saturday the price goes down $0.03. Write an expression with three terms to show the price of a gallon of gas on Saturday.

_____

4 Look at problem 3. If the price of a gallon of gas was $2.59 on Friday morning before the change in price, what was the price of a gallon of gas on Saturday? Explain how you know.

_____

_____

5 Katie gives Maggie half of her pencils. Maggie keeps 5 pencils and gives the rest to Jamil.

a. Write an expression for the number of pencils Maggie gives to Jamil.

_____

b. If Katie had 16 pencils, how many pencils does Maggie give to Jamil?

   Show your work.

   Solution: _____

c. How many pencils did Katie have if Maggie gave Jamil 1 pencil? Explain how you can use the expression to help you answer the question.

   Show your work.

   Solution: _____

   _____

Name: _____

Algebraic Expressions

Solve the problems.

1. Lewa's hiking backpack weighs 5 pounds less than $\frac{1}{2}$ the weight of Alani's hiking backpack. Write an expression to describe the weight of Lewa's backpack. How many pounds does Lewa's backpack weigh if Alani's backpack weighs 36 pounds?

   Show your work.

   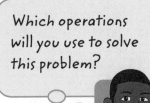

   Finding $\frac{1}{2}$ of an amount is the same as dividing that amount by 2.

   Solution: _____

2. A bookcase has two shelves. The top shelf has 10 more than $\frac{1}{3}$ the number of books on the bottom shelf. There are 12 books on the bottom shelf. How many books are on the top shelf?

   A 4   **C** 40

   B 14   **D** 46

   Cohen chose **D** as the correct answer. How did he get that answer?

   Which operations will you use to solve this problem?

   _____

   _____

3. Which expression equals 6 when $a = 5$ and $b = \frac{1}{3}$? Circle all that apply.

   A $9b^2 + 3a - 10$

   B $a^2 - 20 - 3b$

   C $3(a - 2) - a + 6b$

   D $9b + ab$

   Remember to use the order of operations when evaluating expressions.

Solve.

---

4 Martin used some apples to make muffins. Omar used some apples to make applesauce. Omar used 5 fewer than half as many apples as Martin used.

After you find the solution, read the problem again and check to be sure that your solution makes sense.

a. Write an expression to show the number of apples that Martin and Omar used in all. What does your variable represent?

_____

_____

b. Could Martin have used 10 apples? Why or why not? Use the expression to help you decide.

Show your work.

Solution: _____

_____

_____

_____

---

5 Lilla read $\frac{1}{5}$ of her book last week. This week she read 3 times as much as she read last week.

What should the variable in your expression represent?

a. Write an expression to show how much of her book Lilla has left to read. Then simplify the expression.

_____

_____

b. There are 75 pages in Lilla's book. How many pages does she have left to read?

Show your work.

Solution: _____

Dear Family,

Your child is learning about equivalent expressions.

Equivalent expressions are expressions that have the same value. To find an equivalent expression, you can use properties of operations to:

- reorder the terms (Commutative property of addition).
  For example, $5 + 3k + 18 = 3k + 5 + 18$.

- regroup the terms (Associative property of addition).
  For example, $(2m + 1) + 3 = 2m + (1 + 3)$.

- distribute a factor to the terms (Distributive property).
  For example, $7 + 4(x + 3) = 7 + 4x + 12$.

- factor a common factor out of the terms (Distributive property).
  For example, $9x + 15 = 3(3x + 5)$.

Consider the following example:

Diego and Sally are building a fence. Diego has 2 boxes of nails, and Sally has 3 boxes of nails. Each box contains the same number of nails. Write an expression for the total number of nails. Then simplify the expression to create an equivalent expression.

On the next page you will see two ways your child may use properties of operations to write equivalent expressions with variables.

Vocabulary

like terms two or more terms in a variable expression that have the same variable factors.

NEXT

Equivalent Expressions: Sample Solution

Diego has 2 boxes of nails, and Sally has 3 boxes of nails. Each box contains the same number of nails.

Write an expression for the total number of nails. Then simplify the expression to create an equivalent expression.

One way: Draw a picture of the boxes of nails.

* Write an expression for the number of nails Diego has: $2x$
* Write an expression for the number of nails Sally has: $3x$
* Write an expression for the total number of nails: $2x + 3x$
* Because both terms have the same variable, x, they are like terms. Use the distributive property to simplify the expression:
  $(2x) + (3x) = x(2 + 3) = 5x$

Another way: Model the boxes of nails with math tiles.

Diego: | x | | x |

Sally: | x | | x | | x |

* Write expressions for the number of nails each person has:
  Diego: $2x$ Sally: $3x$
* Write an expression for the total number of nails: $2x + 3x$
* Factor out the common factor x: $(2x) + (3x) = x(2 + 3)$
* Simplify the expression: $x(2 + 3) = 5x$

Answer: Both methods show that the expression $2x + 3x$ represents the total number of nails Diego and Sally have. You can simplify $2x + 3x$ to the equivalent expression $5x$.

Equivalent Expressions

Name: _____

Study the example showing how to write and evaluate expressions with variables. Then solve problems 1–7.

Example

The number of runners on a marathon team this year is 6 more than 4 times the number of runners on last year's team. Half of the runners this year are female and half are male. What expression represents the number of female runners on the team this year?

You can draw a model to represent the situation.

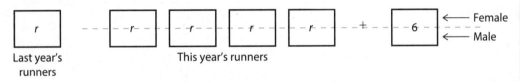

Last year's runners · · · This year's runners · · · + 6 ← Female ← Male

The model shows that the number of female runners can be represented by the expression $\frac{1}{2}(4r + 6)$.

1 What does $4r + 6$ represent in the expression?

   This years runners   times   last   year   plus   6

2 Does the expression $\frac{(4r + 6)}{2}$ also represent the number of females on the team this year? Explain.

   Yes (+6)

3 If there were only 9 runners on the team last year, how many female runners are on the team this year? Explain how you found the answer.

   There   are   21   because   9 × 4 = 36 + 6 = 42
   ÷ 2 = 21.

Vocabulary

evaluate to find the value of an algebraic expression.

Solve.

Use the situation below to solve problems 4–6.

The temperature increased 12°F between 9 AM and noon. It decreased 9°F between noon and 6 PM.

4 Write an expression with three terms to show the change in temperature. Let the first term represent the temperature at 9 AM.

$T + 12 - 9 -$

5 If the temperature was 45°F at 9 AM, what was the temperature at 6 PM? 48°

6 Suppose the temperature at 6 PM was 30°F. What would the temperature have been at 9 AM? Explain how you can use the expression you wrote in problem 4 to find the answer.

30° +12 : You can use it by seeing what to do and the represents the temperature at 6 pm and +12 -9 represents the procedure.

7 Jill makes purses and backpacks. To make each purse, she uses 1 foot less than $\frac{1}{2}$ the amount of fabric she uses to make a backpack. Write an expression for the amount of fabric that Jill needs to make a purse. If she uses 6 feet of fabric to make a backpack, how many feet of fabric will she use to make a purse?

Show your work.

$F \div 2 - 1$
$\downarrow$
$6 \div 2 = 3 - 1 = 2$

Solution: 2 ft

Name: _____

Properties of Operations

Study the example showing how to use properties of operations to write equivalent expressions with variables. Then solve problems 1–9.

Example

Sam bought 2 granola bars and Hayley bought 5 granola bars. Each granola bar was the same price.

Write an expression for the total price of the granola bars. Then simplify the expression to create an equivalent expression. Use the model to help you.

Sam [b] [b]

Hayley [b] [b] [b] [b] [b]

$2b + 5b = b(2 + 5) = 7b$

1. What does b represent in the expressions?

   Price

2. What does $2b + 5b$ represent?

   2b: Amount times price plus other amount times price

3. Does the expression $2b + 5b$ have like terms? Explain.

   Yes, because the both have the same variable.

4. What is the common factor of each term in the expression $2b + 5b$?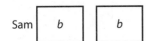

5. Explain how to use the distributive property to create an expression that is equivalent to $2b + 5b$.

   _____

   _____

Solve.

Use the situation below to solve problems 6–7.

Larry bought 12 containers of pasta salad for a school picnic. Each container held the same number of ounces of salad. Students finished the pasta salad in 8 of the containers.

6 Let p equal the number of ounces of pasta salad in one container. Write an expression with two terms to represent how many ounces of pasta salad are left.

_____

7 Simplify the expression you wrote in problem 6 to create an equivalent expression. Use the distributive property.

_____

8 A soccer coach bought 16 medium T-shirts and 9 large T-shirts. Each T-shirt was the same price. Onaje and Paula tried to write equivalent expressions to represent the total price of the T-shirts. The expressions they wrote are shown below.

Onaje: $16t + 9t = t(16 + 9) = 25t$
Paula: $16t + 9t = 16 + 9 + 2t = 25 + 2t$

Whose expression is correct? Why is the other expression incorrect?

_____

_____

9 Adem writes 18y to simplify an expression with three like terms.

   a. What could the expression be?

   _____

   b. Simplify the expression you wrote for part (a) to check your answer.

   _____

Name: _____

Properties and Equivalent Expressions

Study the example showing how to use properties of operations to write equivalent expressions with variables. Then solve problems 1–9.

Example

Four students are buying tickets to a play. The tickets cost $5 each plus a service fee. The expression $4(5 + x)$ represents the total cost. Write an expression that is equivalent to $4(5 + x)$.

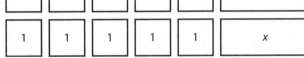

You can use math tiles to model $4(5 + x)$.

From the math tiles, you can see that the expression $4(5 + x) = (5 + 5 + 5 + 5) + (x + x + x + x)$.

---

1 Explain how the model shows $4(5 + x)$.

_____

2 Simplify the expression in the example. _____

3 What are the factors in the expression $4(5 + x)$? _____

4 Show how to use the distributive property to simplify $4(5 + x)$.

_____

_____

5 Are the expressions $(5 + 5 + 5 + 5) + (x + x + x + x)$ and $4(5 + x)$ equivalent? If so, write another expression that is equivalent to both of them. If not, explain why not.

_____

_____

Solve.

6 Use the distributive property to find two expressions that are equivalent to $7(3x - 4)$.

_____

_____

7 A rectangular play area is 8 yards long. The expression $56 + 8x$ represents the area of the play area in square yards. What expression represents the width of the play area in yards? Draw a picture to model the problem.

Show your work.

Solution: _____

8 Use the distributive property to write two expressions that are equivalent to $12 + 30x$. Describe the steps you follow to find the expressions.

_____

_____

_____

9 Are $9(4 - x)$ and $36 - 9x$ equivalent expressions? Explain how you know.

_____

_____

Name: _____

Determine Whether Expressions Are Equivalent

Study the example problem showing how to determine whether expressions are equivalent. Then solve problems 1–7.

Example

Is $2s + 3s^2$ equivalent to $5s$?

Use math tiles to model $2s + 3s^2$ and $5s$.

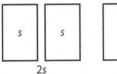

The expression $2s + 3s^2$ is not equivalent to $5s$.

---

1 Are the terms $2s$ and $3s^2$ like terms? Explain.

_____

_____

2 Explain how the tiles show that $2s + 3s^2$ is not equivalent to $5s$.

_____

_____

_____

3 Use substitution to prove that $2s + 3s^2$ is not equivalent to $5s$.

_____

_____

4 Use the distributive property to write an expression that is equivalent to $2s + 3s^2$.

_____

Solve.

5 Look at the expressions $s^2 + 2s^2$ and $3s^2$.

    a. Draw math tiles to model $s^2 + 2s^2$ and $3s^2$.
        Does your model show that they are equivalent
        expressions? Explain.

    _____

    b. Use substitution to check your answer in part (a).

    _____

    _____

    _____

    _____

6 Use the terms 4, $12a$, 6, $2a$, and 24 to make equivalent
expressions. Use each term only once. Use substitution
to prove that the expressions are equivalent.

Show your work.

Solution: _____

7 Bethany says that $3x + 6 + x$ and $3(x + 2)$ are
equivalent expressions. She used substitution to
support her answer. Explain what Bethany did wrong.

Let $x = 2$.

$3x + 6 + x = 3(2) + 6 = 6 + 6 = 12$

$3(x + 2) = 3(2 + 2) = 3(4) = 12$

$12 = 12$

_____

Name: _____

Equivalent Expressions

Solve the problems.

1 Are $5n + 9 + n$ and $3(2n + 9)$ equivalent expressions? Use substitution to check your answer.

Show your work.

What value will you substitute for n to check your answer?

Solution: _____

2 The picture shows the dimensions of a vegetable garden and a flower garden.

How do you find the area of a rectangle?

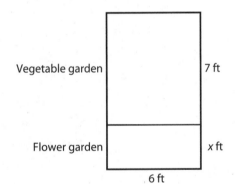

Vegetable garden   7 ft

Flower garden   x ft

6 ft

Which expression represents the combined area of the gardens in square feet? Select all that apply.

A $42 + 6x$

B $(6 \cdot 7) + (6 \cdot x)$

C $13 + 6 + x$

D $6(7 + x)$

William chose **C** as a correct answer. How did he get that answer?

_____

_____

Solve.

3 Look at the expression $\frac{1}{2}(c + 8)$. Tell whether each statement about the expression is *True* or *False*.

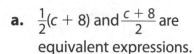
How do you know that expressions are equivalent?

a. $\frac{1}{2}(c + 8)$ and $\frac{c + 8}{2}$ are equivalent expressions. ☐ True ☐ False

b. $\frac{1}{2}(c + 8)$ and $\frac{1}{2}c + 4$ are equivalent expressions. ☐ True ☐ False

c. The only terms in $\frac{1}{2}(c + 8)$ are c and 8. ☐ True ☐ False

d. You can multiply c and 8 by $\frac{1}{2}$ in $\frac{1}{2}(c + 8)$ to find an equivalent expression. ☐ True ☐ False

4 The expressions $a(8x + 7)$ and $4x + 3.5$ are equivalent. What is the value of a?

Show your work.

Look at the expressions. Do you have to distribute a to find its value?

Solution: _____

5 Which expression is equivalent to $6 + 7n + 4 + 8n$? Select all that apply.

A $13n + 12n$

B $5(3n + 2)$

C $5(3n + 10)$

D $15n + 10$

How can you use the distributive property to find equivalent expressions?

Dear Family,

Your child is learning about how to understand solutions to equations.

Your child has already learned that equivalent expressions are expressions that have the same value. Now your child is learning that an equation is a statement that shows two equivalent expressions.

You can think of an equation as a pan balance. Placing two items with the same weight on each pan keeps the pans balanced.

In a similar way, writing two expressions that have equivalent values on each side of an equation makes an equation true.

To solve the equation $3 + x = 8$ means to find the value of x that makes the expression "$3 + x$" equivalent to the expression "8."

Because 5 added to 3 gives a result of 8, the solution to the equation is x is equal to 5.

Consider the following example:

Nick had $10.50 in his wallet. He bought lunch with some of his money. Now he has $6.00 left. Write and solve an equation to find the amount Nick spent on lunch.

The next page shows two ways your child may write and solve an equation to find the amount Nick spent on lunch.

Vocabulary

equation a statement that shows two equivalent expressions.

NEXT

Nick had $10.50. He spent some money on lunch and now has $6.00 left. Write and solve an equation to find the amount of money Nick spent on lunch.

First, you have to write an equation.

- Choose a variable, such as a, to represent the unknown amount Nick spent on lunch.

- Write an expression that shows Nick started with $10.50 and spent a dollars on lunch. You can write $10.50 as 10.5: $10.5 - a$.

- Write an expression that shows the amount Nick has left: 6.

- Write an equation by setting the expressions equal to each other: $10.5 - a = 6$.

- Now, solve the equation to find the value of a.

One way:
Use a number line to find the number that is subtracted from 10.5 to get 6.

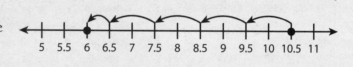

Start at 10.5. You must subtract 4.5 from 10.5 to get 6. The value of a is 4.5.

Another way:
Draw a model to find the number that is subtracted from 10.5 to get 6.

Start with a group of 10.5. To get 6, you must subtract 4.5 from 10.5. The value of a is 4.5

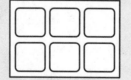
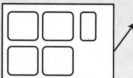

Answer: You can write the equation $10.5 - a = 6$ to represent the given situation. Both methods of solving the equation show that the value of a is 4.5, which means that Nick spent $4.50 on lunch.

Name: _____

Prerequisite: **How can you use the properties of operations to write equivalent expressions?**

Study the example problem showing how to write equivalent expressions. Then solve problems 1–8.

Example

Gail plants 3 pots of roses and 2 pots of tulips. The number of flowers in each pot is the same. Write an expression for the total number of flowers. Simplify the expression to create an equivalent expression.

You can use math tiles to represent the problem.

Roses | f | f | f

Tulips | f | f

Add to find the total number of flowers. An expression for the total number of flowers is $3f + 2f$. Then simplify.

$$3f + 2f = f(3 + 2) = 5f$$

1 Look at the example. What does f represent?

Flower _____

2 Tell what each expression below represents.

 a. $3f$ _Roses_ _____

 b. $2f$ _Tulips_ _____

 c. $3f + 2f$ _Roses + Tulips_ _____

3 How was the distributive property used to create an expression that is equivalent to $3f + 2f$?

 _$f(3 + 2)$_ _____

Vocabulary

like terms terms in an expression that have the same variable raised to the same power. Constants are like terms.

x and $-4x$

1 and 1.5

x^2 and $8x^2$

Solve.

4 David says that he can apply the commutative and distributive properties to $7s + 8 + 5s$ to get $12s + 8$. Is he correct? Explain.

Yes, b/c they both have like terms

5 Use three of the terms below to fill in the two expressions. Each term may be used only once. Both of your expressions must be equivalent to $0.5x + 1.5$.

| 0.5 | 2 | x | 0.25x | 3 | 0.75 |

$\underline{\quad 2 \quad} (\underline{\quad .25x \quad} + \underline{\quad .75 \quad})$

$\underline{\quad .5 \quad} (\underline{\quad x \quad} + \underline{\quad 3 \quad})$

6 Write a story that you could represent with the expression $8b + 4b - 2$. Then write an expression that is equivalent to $8b + 4b - 2$.

Honey Bees go in pairs of 8. Wasps come in pairs of 8.
Everyday, 2 total Bees + Wasps get killed. How many are
left at the end of the day?

7 Is $d(10 + 20)$ equivalent to $d \times 10 + 20 \times d$? Use a property, or properties, to explain.

Yes, that is the expanded form of the distributive property

8 Use the distributive property to write an expression that is equivalent to $45 + 30x$.

_5 (9 + 6x)_

196 **Lesson 18** *Understand* Solutions to Equations

Name: _____

Writing and Solving Equations

Study the example problem showing how to write and solve equations. Then solve problems 1–9.

Example

Larry mows 4 lawns and earns $24. He is paid the same amount of money for each lawn. Write and solve an equation to find how much Larry is paid to mow one lawn.

You can draw a bar model to help you write and solve an equation that represents the problem. The equation $4p = 24$ represents the problem.

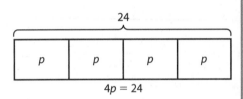

The equation is asking: What number could you multiply by 4 to get 24?

$4 \times 6 = 24$

Larry is paid $6 to mow one lawn.

---

1 What does p represent in the example?

Paid

2 What does the expression $4p$ represent?

4 lawns with unknown price

3 What is the solution to the equation $4p = 24$?

$p = $ 96

4 Bev went to the grocery store with $45. She spent d dollars and came home with $21. Write and solve an equation to find how much Bev spent at the store.

Show your work.

$45 - p = 21$

$45 - 21 = 24$

Solution: $24

Solve.

Use this situation for problems 5–9.

Yaro buys a baseball cap for $9.50. He also buys a new baseball. Yaro spends $13.50 altogether.

5 Write an equation to represent how much Yaro pays for the baseball.

$9.50 + p = 13.50$

6 Do you expect the solution to your equation to be less than or greater than $13.50? Explain.

less, b/c it was 13.50 all together

7 What is the solution to the equation you wrote in problem 5? Draw a number line. What increments did you use to label your number line? How can you use it to help you find the solution?

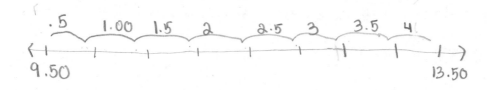

8 How much does Yaro pay for the baseball? _____

9 Write an equation using a different operation to represent how much Yaro pays for the baseball. Explain why you can use equations with different operations to represent the same problem.

©Curriculum Associates, LLC   Copying is not permitted.

Name: _____

Reason and Write

Study the example. Underline two parts that you think make it a particularly good answer and a helpful example.

Example

Ling says that the solution to $8s = 2$ is that s must be greater than 1. Does Ling's solution make sense? Explain how you know whether or not Ling's solution makes sense without solving the equation. Then draw a model of the problem and solve the equation.

Show your work. Use numbers, words, and models to explain your answer.

Ling's solution does not make sense. The expression $8s$ means to multiply 8 by s. If I multiply 8 by 1, I get 8, which is greater than 2. So the solution must be less than 1.

I can draw a bar model to help me solve the problem.

```
                         2
 ┌──────────────────────────────────────────────┐
 │  s  │  s  │  s  │  s  │  s  │  s  │  s  │  s  │
 └──────────────────────────────────────────────┘
```

The bar model shows that 8 times s gives me 2, so I can ask myself what number I could multiply by 8 to get 2. I know that the number is less than 1, so it must be a fraction.

The model shows that 8 bars represent 2, so 4 bars must represent 1. Therefore, each bar represents $\frac{1}{4}$.

The solution to $8s = 2$ is $s = \frac{1}{4}$.

> Where does the example . . .
> - use numbers to explain?
> - use words to explain?
> - use models to explain?
> - give details?

Solve the problem. Use what you learned from the model.

Jake says that the solution to $8.5 - a = 5$ is that a equals 13.5 because addition and subtraction are inverse operations and $8.5 + 5 = 13.5$. Does Jake's solution make sense? Explain how you know whether or not Jake's solution makes sense without solving the equation. Then draw a model of the problem and solve the equation.

Show your work. Use numbers, words, and models to explain your answer.

NO, that would equal in the
↓
negatives

$8.5 - 13.5 = -5$

Did you . . .

• use numbers to explain?

• use words to explain?

• use models to explain?

• give details?

Dear Family,

Your child is learning about solving equations.

An equation is a statement that shows two equivalent expressions. To solve an equation, you isolate the variable on one side by using inverse operations, or operations that "undo" each other. The equation must stay balanced so the expressions on both sides stay equivalent. This means if you perform an operation on one side of an equation, you must do the same on the other side as well.

Examples of equations:

$$x + 2 = 5$$

$$43 - t = 21$$

$$\frac{1}{2y} = 30$$

$$3s = 18$$

For example, suppose you had 2 apples and then someone gave you more apples so you have 5 apples. You can write and solve the equation $x + 2 = 5$ to find how many apples you were given.

$x + 2 = 5$ The equation involves addition, so you can use the inverse operation, subtraction.

$x + 2 - 2 = 5 - 2$ Subtract 2 from both sides of the equation to isolate x and to keep the equation balanced.

$x = 3$ The solution is 3.

The solution means that you were given 3 apples.

Consider the following example:

A theater group rehearsed for 7 weeks before the opening of the spring show. Each week the group rehearsed for the same number of hours for a total of 91 hours. How many hours did the group spend rehearsing each week?

On the next page you will see two ways your child may write and solve an equation to find the number of hours spent in rehearsals each week.

NEXT

A community theater group rehearsed for the same number of hours each week for 7 weeks. The group rehearsed for a total of 91 hours. How many hours did they rehearse each week?

To find the number of hours the group rehearsed each week, write and solve an equation that represents the situation.

One way: Create a bar model to show the situation.

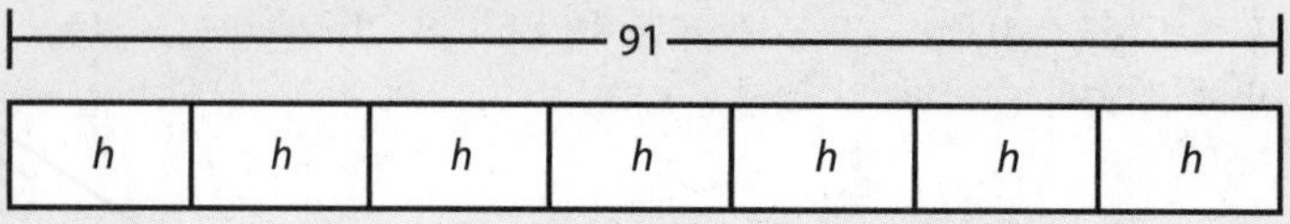

$$\begin{array}{|c|c|c|c|c|c|c|} \hline h & h & h & h & h & h & h \\ \hline \end{array}$$

(top bracket labeled 91)

- The top bar represents the total number of hours the group rehearsed.

- The bottom bar represents the number of hours h that the group rehearsed in each of 7 weeks, or $7h$.

- The bars are the same length, so $7h = 91$.

- Solve the equation: $7h = 91$

$$\frac{7h}{7} = \frac{91}{7} \quad \text{Divide both sides by 7 to isolate } h.$$

$$h = 13$$

Another way: Use words to describe the situation.

7 rehearsals times the number of hours in each rehearsal equals the total number of hours.

$$7 \qquad \times \qquad h \qquad = \qquad 91$$

- Write an equation: $7h = 91$

- Solve the equation: $7h = 91$

$$7h \div 7 = 91 \div 7 \quad \text{Divide both sides by 7 to isolate } h.$$

$$h = 13$$

Answer: Both methods show that the equation $7h = 91$ represents the situation and that the solution to the equation is $h = 13$. This means that the theater group spent 13 hours rehearsing each week.

Solve Equations

Name: _____

Prerequisite: Write an Equation

Study the example problem showing how to write and solve an equation. Then solve problems 1–8.

Example

Kanika divides a package of sunflower seeds equally among 4 flower beds. She plants 14 seeds in each bed. Write and solve an equation to find how many seeds were in the package.

You can draw a bar model to help you write and solve an equation that represents the problem. The equation $\frac{s}{4} = 14$ represents the problem.

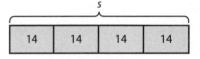

The equation is asking: What number divided by 4 equals 14? You can solve a division equation using multiplication. Since $14 \times 4 = 56$, $56 \div 4 = 14$.

There were 56 seeds in the package.

1 What does s represent in the example? What does the expression $\frac{s}{4}$ represent?

_____

_____

Vocabulary

equation a statement showing that two expressions are equivalent.

2 What is the solution to the equation $\frac{s}{4} = 14$?

$s =$ _____

3 Consider the pan balance. What would happen if you replaced the 8-ounce weight with a 10-ounce weight?

_____

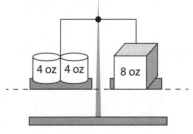

4 Suppose you change one of the 4-ounce weights to a 7-ounce weight. How much weight would you have to add on the right side to make the pans balance? Explain.

_____

_____

Solve.

5 Paulo had a rope that was 15 feet long. He cut off *n* feet of the rope to hang a bird feeder. Paulo now has $11\frac{1}{2}$ feet of rope left.

    a. Write an equation to represent the problem.

        _____

    b. Draw a number line labeled from $10\frac{1}{2}$ to $15\frac{1}{2}$ and explain how you could use it to solve the problem. How much rope did Paulo use?

6 Piper bought 5 movie tickets and 1 bottle of water. She spent $28. The water cost $3. How much did each ticket cost? Write an equation to solve the problem and answer the question.

    _____

7 Write a real-world problem that you could represent with the equation $4x + 5 = 37$. Solve the equation to find the answer to your question.

    _____

    _____

    _____

8 Without solving, explain how you can tell whether the solution to $0.5x = 10$ is less than 1 or greater than 1.

    _____

    _____

    _____

Name: _____

Solve Addition and Subtraction Equations

Study the example problem showing how to solve an addition equation. Then solve problems 1–10.

Example

Cora puts 5 blocks and a bag containing an unknown number of blocks on one pan of a balance. She puts 12 blocks on the other pan to make the pans hang evenly. How many blocks are in the bag?

Draw a picture to represent the problem.

Write an expression for the number of blocks in each pan.

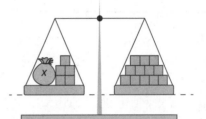

number of blocks on the left side: $x + 5$

number of blocks on the right side: 12

Write an equation to compare the expressions.

$x + 5 = 12$

---

1 What operation does the expression $x + 5$ involve?

_____

2 What is the inverse of this operation?

_____

3 How do you isolate the variable in $x + 5 = 12$?

_____

4 What must you do to keep the equation balanced?

_____

> **Vocabulary**
>
> **inverse operations**
> operations that "undo" each other.
>
> $+$ and $-$ are inverse operations.
>
> $\times$ and $\div$ are inverse operations.

5 Solve the equation $x + 5 = 12$. Show and justify each step you take to solve the equation.

$x + 5 = 12$ Write the equation.

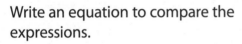

$x + 5$ ____ $= 12$ ____   _____

x ____ $=$ ____   _____

$x =$ ____   _____

Solve.

6 Write the inverse of each operation.

    a. addition   _____

    b. multiplication   _____

7 Solve each problem.
Show your work.

    a. $x + 12 = 18$ **b.** $x - 7 = 3$

8 Tim said that to solve the equation $x - 2 = 9$, he would need to subtract 2 from both sides of the equation. Is Tim correct? Explain.

_____

_____

9 Write the equations described below.

    a. an addition equation with one variable that has a solution of 3

    _____

    b. a subtraction equation with one variable that has a solution of $\frac{2}{3}$

    _____

10 Marge said that she subtracted 20 from both sides of an equation to solve it. Colin thinks that the equation she was solving could have been $6 + t = 20$. Does Colin's reasoning make sense? Explain.

_____

_____

_____

Name: _____

Solve Multiplication Equations

Study the example problem showing how to solve a multiplication equation. Then solve problems 1–10.

Example

There are 3 bags of marbles in the left-side pan of a balance. Each bag has the same number of marbles. After you put 9 marbles in the right-side pan, the pans hang evenly. How many marbles are in each bag?

Draw a picture to represent the problem.

Write an expression for the number of marbles in each pan.

number of marbles in left-side pan: $3x$

number of marbles in right-side pan: 9

Write an equation to show that the expressions are equivalent: $3x = 9$.

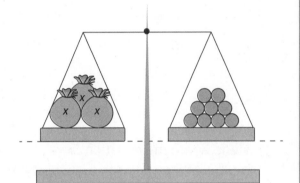

1 What operation does the expression $3x$ involve?

_____

2 What is the inverse of this operation?

_____

3 How do you isolate the variable in $3x = 9$?

_____

4 When you isolate the variable, how do you keep the equation balanced?

_____

5 Solve the equation $3x = 9$. Show and justify each step you take to solve the equation.

$3x = 9$ Write the equation.

$\dfrac{3x}{\square} = \dfrac{9}{\square}$ Divide each side by 3.

$x = \square$ _____

Solve.

6 Draw a picture that you could use to help you solve this problem.

$2x = 8$

7 Solve each problem.

Show your work.

a. $4x = 20$

b. $9x = 72$

8 Elena wrote the equation $5x = 25$. She wants to multiply 25 by 5 to solve it. Does this make sense? Explain why or why not, and then give the solution.

_____

_____

_____

9 Find the solution for $8x = 48$. Then explain how you could check your solution.

Show your work.

10 Write a multiplication equation with one variable and one fraction that has the solution 8.

_____

Name: _____

Solve Equations for Real-World Situations

Study the example problem showing how to write and solve an equation based on a real-world situation. Then solve problems 1–7.

> ### Example
>
> In 5 days, Lan jogged a total of 15 miles. She jogged the same number of miles each day. How many miles did Lan jog each day?
>
> Create a bar model to represent the 5 days that Lan jogged and the total number of miles that she jogged. Let m = the number of miles she jogged each day.
>
>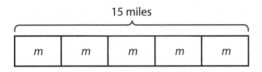

1 What does each part of the bar model represent?

_____

_____

2 What expression can you write for the bottom bar?

_____

3 Explain how the model shows that $5m = 15$.

_____

4 Solve the equation $5m = 15$ to find the number of miles that Lan jogged each day. Justify each step you take to solve the equation.

Show your work.

Solution: _____

Solve.

5 It costs Luis $5 to park his car at a parking meter for 2 hours. What is the price to park for 1 hour? Draw a bar model or write a word sentence to help you solve the problem. Then write and solve a multiplication equation.

Show your work.

Solution: _____

6 Juliana buys 7.5 meters of ribbon to make bows. She wants to use the same amount of ribbon for each bow. If she makes 5 bows, how many meters of ribbon should she use for each bow? Write and solve an equation.

Show your work.

Solution: _____

7 Henry knows that the area of a rectangle is 30 square inches. The perimeter is 22 inches. If the length is 1 inch longer than the width, what are the length and width of Henry's rectangle? Explain how you know.

_____

_____

Name: _____

Solve Equations

Solve the problems.

1 Which equation has a solution of 4? Select all that apply.

A $12x = 3$ **C** $10 + x = 14$

B $6x = 24$ **D** $x - 4 = 8$

How are inverse operations used to solve equations?

2 Elisa is saving an equal amount each week for 8 weeks to buy a video game that costs $40. How much is she saving each week?

A $4 **C** $32

B $5 **D** $48

Jesse chose **C** as the correct answer. How did he get that answer?

What operation will the equation you use to solve this problem involve?

_____

3 Hector buys a shirt and a tie. The shirt costs $34, which is $18 more than the cost of the tie. Olivia and Max each write an equation to find the cost of the tie t. Is one equation, both equations, or neither equation correct? Explain how you know. Solve each correct equation.

Olivia: $t + 18 = 34$ Max: $34 - t = 18$

How do the two equations differ?

_____

_____

_____

_____

_____

Solve.

4 Haley's exercise routine takes 12 minutes. Let *r* represent the number of times that Haley exercised, and let *T* represent the total number of minutes she exercised. Tell whether each statement is *True* or *False*.

A model might help you understand this problem.

a. The equation $r + 12 = T$ can be used to find the total number of minutes that Haley exercised. ☐ True ☐ False

b. It takes Haley 36 minutes to do her exercise routine 3 times. ☐ True ☐ False

c. If Haley spent a total of 1 hour doing her exercise routine, then she did the routine 6 times. ☐ True ☐ False

d. 12*r* represents the total number of minutes that Haley exercised. ☐ True ☐ False

5 Todd has 17 inches of rope. This is $\frac{1}{3}$ of the length of rope that he needs to tie his boat to a dock. How many inches of rope does he need to tie his boat to the dock.

How can you keep an equation balanced?

Show your work.

Solution: _____

6 Write a scenario that could be represented by this equation. $\frac{3}{4}x = 12$

What real-world scenario might use the operation used in the equation?

_____

_____

_____

Dear Family,

Your child is learning about solving inequalities.

An inequality is a way to compare two values that might not be equal. Here are some examples of inequalities:

$x < 8$ $9.5 \geq y$ $c \leq 173$ $4t > 88$

Below are examples of phrases that indicate inequalities.

Symbol	Meaning
<	less than
>	greater than
≤	less than or equal to
≥	greater than or equal to

x is greater than or equal to 3. ($x \geq 3$) x is less than or equal to 3. ($x \leq 3$)
x is at least 3. ($x \geq 3$) x is at most 3. ($x \leq 3$)
x is no less than 3. ($x \geq 3$) x is no more than 3. ($x \leq 3$)
x is a minimum of 3. ($x \geq 3$) x is a maximum of 3. ($x \leq 3$)

You can represent real-world situations with inequalities. For example, suppose a person plans to wear shorts if the temperature is 78°F or greater. You can represent this situation with the inequality $x \geq 78$, where x is the temperature in degrees Fahrenheit.

An inequality has more than one solution. The solution is values that make the inequality true. In the inequality $x \geq 78$, any number greater than or equal to 78 is a solution. So, both 79 and 85 are solutions.

Consider the following example:

A store offers reward points to customers who spend a minimum of $50. Suzanne earned reward points the last time she was at the store. Write an inequality to represent the amount of money Suzanne could have spent and give three possible amounts.

REWARD CARD

The next page shows two ways your child may write and solve an inequality for this problem.

NEXT

A store offers reward points for spending a minimum of $50. Suzanne earned reward points on her last trip to the store. Write an inequality to represent the amount of money Suzanne could have spent and give three possible amounts.

One way: Use words and symbols to write an inequality.

From the problem you know that Suzanne spent a minimum of $50. You can use this information to write an inequality. Let s be the amount of money Suzanne spent.

The amount Suzanne spent is a minimum of 50.

$$s \qquad \geq \qquad 50$$

So the inequality is $s \geq 50$. Some numbers that make this inequality true are: 68, 72, and 150.

So Suzanne could have spent $68, $72, or $150 to earn rewards points.

Another way: Write and graph an inequality.

You can write the inequality for the situation as $s \geq 50$ or as $50 \leq s$. Both inequalities say that s is 50 or more.

To graph the inequality, you use a closed circle at 50 to show that 50 is a solution. You shade the graph to the right because values greater than 50 are also solutions.

From the number line you can see that 50, 83, and 90 are all solutions, so Suzanne could have spent $50, $83, or $90 to earn rewards points.

Answer: Both methods show that the inequality $s \geq 50$ (or $50 \leq s$) represents the amount of money Suzanne spent. The methods show 50, 68, 72, 83, 90, and 150 are all solutions to the inequality. So $50, $68, $72, $83, $90, and $150 are all possible amounts Suzanne could have spent in order to earn reward points.

Solve Inequalities

Name: _____

Prerequisite: Solve Equations

Study the example problem showing how to solve an equation. Then solve problems 1–7.

Example

Taryn planted 91 tulip bulbs in 7 rows. She planted the same number of bulbs in each row. How many bulbs did she plant in each row?

Create a bar model to represent the 7 rows and the total number of bulbs that Taryn planted.

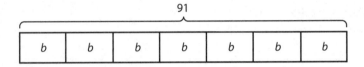

91

1 What does *b* represent in the bar model?

_____

2 What does each part of the bar model represent?

_____

_____

3 Explain how the model shows that $7b = 91$.

_____

4 What operation will you use to solve the equation $7b = 91$? Solve the equation to find the number of bulbs, and justify each step you take to solve the equation.

Show your work.

Solution: _____

Solve.

5 Milo and Audrey sold tickets to the school concert. Milo sold 14 fewer tickets than Audrey. If Milo sold 32 tickets, how many tickets did Audrey sell?

Show your work.

Solution: _____

6 Carmen buys 4 daisies and some roses to make a flower arrangement. The number of daisies is $\frac{1}{3}$ of the number of roses that she buys. How many roses does she buy?

Show your work.

Solution: _____

7 Write a multiplication equation and a subtraction equation that both involve a fraction and have the same solution. Solve your equations to show that the solutions are the same.

Name: _____

Write and Solve an Inequality

Study the example problem showing how to write and solve an inequality for a real-world problem. Then solve problems 1–9.

Example

Mr. Gomez gets a notice from the bank when the amount in his checking account drops below $20. For what amounts will Mr. Gomez receive a notice from the bank?

Use words and symbols to represent the situation. Let x represent the amount in Mr. Gomez's account. When x is less than $20, the bank will send a notice.

$x < 20$

Graph the inequality to show all of the solutions. Use an open circle shows that 20 is NOT a solution.

1 Why is the graph in the example shaded to the left?

_____

2 Is −$10 a solution? Substitute −10 into the inequality in the example to check.

_____

3 Name an amount that is NOT a solution to the inequality. Explain how you know.

_____

_____

4 Suppose the bank sent Mr. Gomez a notice whenever the amount in his account dropped to $15 or less. How would the graph in the example change?

_____

_____

Vocabulary

inequality a statement that contains the symbol $<$, $>$, $\leq$, or $\geq$. For any inequality, there are many possible solutions. These are inequalities.

$x < 5$

$x > -2$

$x \leq 15$

$x \geq 0$

Solve.

5 Write the inequality shown on each graph.

a.
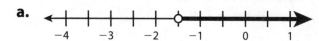

_____

b.
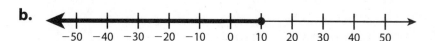

_____

6 The children at Lincoln School go outside for recess if the temperature is 3°C or higher. For what temperatures will the students go outside? Write an inequality to represent this situation. Then graph the solution.

_____

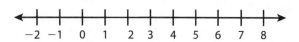

7 If your score on a computer game is less than 0, you lose your next turn. For what scores will you lose your turn? Write an inequality to represent this situation. Then graph the solution.

_____

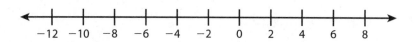

8 Write a real-world situation for this inequality: $x \geq 9$

_____

_____

9 Explain how an equation and an inequality are different. Give an example of each.

_____

_____

_____

More Inequalities

Study the example problem showing how to write and solve an inequality. Then solve problems 1–9.

Example

You need to be at least 40 inches tall to ride on the roller coaster at the amusement park. What are some possible heights for riders? Write an inequality to represent the heights, and graph the solution on a number line.

Use symbols to represent the situation. Let x be the possible heights in inches for riders.

$x \geq 40$

Graph the inequality to show all of the solutions.

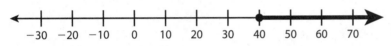

1 Leigh is 40 inches tall. Can she ride on the roller coaster?

_____

2 Brennon is 38 inches tall. Can he ride on the roller coaster? Use the graph to explain your answer.

_____

3 Joy wrote the inequality $40 \leq x$ to represent the situation. Is her inequality correct?

_____

4 Suppose this graph represents a problem about the height of people riding the roller coaster. How would the situation have changed?

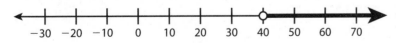

_____

_____

Solve.

Use this situation for problems 5–6.

You must spend at least $10 at the grocery store to get a free greeting card.

5 Write an inequality to represent the amount you need to spend to get a free greeting card. Then graph the solution on the number line.

_____

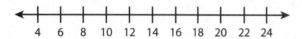

6 If you spend $9.50, will you get a free greeting card? Use the graph to explain how you know.

_____

7 Zarina is scuba diving. She will not dive below −30 meters relative to the surface of the water. Write an inequality that represents this situation. Is −20 a solution to the inequality? Explain how you know.

_____

8 Write an inequality that has the solution shown on the graph. Then write a real-world situation for the inequality.

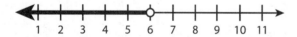

_____

_____

9 Markim looks at the graph below and says that −1 is the only possible negative solution. Do you agree or disagree? Explain.

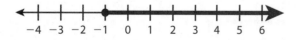

_____

_____

_____

Name: _____

Solve Inequalities

Solve the problems.

1 Write an inequality for each graph.

a.

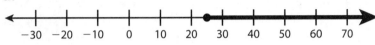

_____

b.

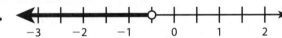

_____

What does the direction of the arrow on the shaded line tell you about the inequality?

2 Samuel wants to eat at least 15 grams of protein each day. Let x represent the amount of protein he should eat each day to meet his goal. Which inequality represents this situation?

A $x < 15$ **C** $x \le 15$

B $x > 15$ **D** $x \ge 15$

Karli chose **B** as the correct answer. How did she get that answer?

_____

Would a graph for this situation have an open circle or a closed circle?

3 The graph shows information about the low temperature in a particular city in degrees Celsius each day during one week in January. Write an inequality for this situation. Then write in words what the graph shows about the temperature readings.

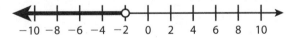

_____

_____

What are some words that describe a situation in which the shaded line on the graph points left?

Solve.

---

4 Kalista practices the piano for at least 8 hours each week. Write an inequality for this situation. Then graph the solution on the number line. _____

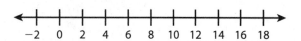

−2 0 2 4 6 8 10 12 14 16 18

Does "at least" include 8 as a solution?

---

5 Which of these values is a solution to the inequality $x - 1 \geq 6$?

7      $3\frac{1}{2}$ 2.5   10

Show your work.

Does a given value for x make the inequality true or false?

Solution: _____

6 Consider the inequality $x > -0.75$. Tell whether each statement is *True* or *False*.

a. −0.75 is a solution to the inequality.   ☐ True   ☐ False

b. There are many solutions to this inequality.   ☐ True   ☐ False

c. All of the solutions to the inequality are negative.   ☐ True   ☐ False

d. The inequality $-0.75 < x$ is equivalent to the given inequality.   ☐ True   ☐ False

e. −4.5 is a solution to the inequality.   ☐ True   ☐ False

How do you know whether a given value is a solution to the inequality?

Dear Family,

Your child is learning about dependent and independent variables.

Here are some examples of situations involving dependent and independent variables that may be familiar to you.

- A worker is paid by the hour. The amount of money earned depends on the hours worked.

- A bike shop rents bicycles by the hour. The cost of renting a bicycle depends on the number of hours the bike is rented.

- A recipe requires a certain number of cups of flour. The amount of flour you use depends on how many batches of the recipe you make.

In each situation, the value of one variable, the independent variable, *determines* the value of the other variable, the dependent variable.

Number of hours worked	*determines*	amount of money earned
Number of bike rental hours	*determines*	total cost of bike rental
Number of batches	*determines*	cups of flour you use

Consider the following example:

It costs $15.00 per hour for a family to bowl at a local bowling alley. The cost to rent their shoes is $5.00. Write an equation to represent the relationship between total cost, c, and the number of hours, h, that the family bowls.
Show the relationship in a table and a graph.

On the next page you will see two ways your child may show the relationship between the total cost of bowling and the number of games the family plays.

Dependent and Independent Variables: Sample Solution

Bowling costs $15.00 per hour plus a $5.00 shoe rental fee. Write an equation to represent the relationship between the total cost, c, and the number of hours, h, that the family bowls. Show the relationship in a table and a graph.

Equation:

To write an equation, use the words from the problem.

cost	equals	rate per hour	times	number of hours	plus	rental fee
c	$=$	15	$\cdot$	h	$+$	5

An equation is $c = 15h + 5$.

Table:

Show the relationship in a table.

The number of hours, h, is the independent variable. The total cost, c, is the dependent variable.

Number of Hours, h	$15h + 5$	Total Cost ($), c
1	$15(1) + 5$	20
2	$15(2) + 5$	35
3	$15(3) + 5$	50
4	$15(4) + 5$	65
5	$15(5) + 5$	80

Graph:

Draw a graph to show the relationship.

Write ordered pairs (h, c) from the table and graph them on a coordinate plane.

$(1, 20), (2, 35), (3, 50), (4, 65),$ and $(5, 80)$

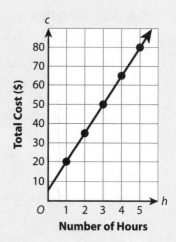

Answer: The equation $c = 15h + 5$ represents the relationship between the total cost, c, and the number of hours, h, that the family plays. Each row in the table and each point on the graph show the total cost of bowling for a given number of hours.

Dependent and Independent Variables

Name: _____

Study the example showing how to compare two patterns on a graph. Then solve problems 1–9.

Example

Suppose two patterns both start at 0. The rule for one pattern is "add 2," and the rule for the other pattern is "add 4." Compare the patterns using a graph.

Write the first four numbers of each pattern.

add 2: 0, 2, 4, 6
add 4: 0, 4, 8, 12

Use the numbers in each pattern to write ordered pairs and plot them on a graph.

(0, 0)　　(2, 4)　　(4, 8)　　(6, 12)

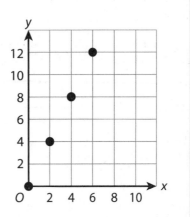

1　Explain how the terms in each pattern are related to the coordinates in the ordered pairs.

They have the same coordinates. The term is

_2x._

2　Use the ordered pairs to describe how the terms in the second pattern are related to the corresponding terms in the first pattern.

The term in the second pattern is 2

times more than pattern 1.

3　How would the graph look if you connected the points?

It would look like a linear

Vocabulary

corresponding terms the numbers that are in the same position in two or more related patterns.
Pattern 1: 0, **2**, 4, 6
Pattern 2: 0, **4**, 8, 12
The numbers 2 and 4 are corresponding terms.

ordered pairs a pair of numbers that locate a point on the coordinate plane.

Solve.

Use the following patterns for problems 4–8.

Suppose two patterns both start at 0. The rule for one pattern is "add 6," and the rule for the other pattern is "add 2."

4 Complete the table to show the first four numbers in each pattern. Use the corresponding terms in each pattern to write ordered pairs.

Add 6	Add 2	Ordered Pairs
0	0	(0,0)
6	2	(6,2)
12	4	(12,4)
18	6	

5 Graph the ordered pairs.

6 Describe the relationship between the corresponding terms of the two patterns.

_____

_____

_____

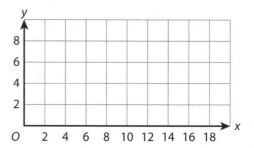

7 What directions would you give someone to get from one point to the next on the graph?

_____

8 How do the directions that you would give in problem 7 relate to the rules for the patterns?

_____

_____

9 Consider the ordered pairs.

   (0, 0)   (1.5, 4.5)   (3, 9)   (4.5, 13.5)

Write two rules, one for the x-terms of the given ordered pairs and one for the y-terms. Describe the relationship between corresponding terms.

_____

_____

Name: _____

Relationship Between Variables

Study the example showing the relationship between variables with a table and an equation. Then solve problems 1–7.

Example

A music store sells sets of headphones for $6. The table shows the relationship between the number of headphones the store sells, h, and the amount of money, m, the store earns from headphone sales. Write an equation that represents the amount of money the store earns from headphone sales.

Number of Headphones, h	0	1	2	3	4	5
Amount of Money, m ($)	0	6	12	18	24	30

Use the table to write an equation.

amount of money	equals	price of each set of headphones	times	number of headphones
m	$=$	6	$\cdot$	h

The equation is $m = 6h$.

1 Which is the dependent variable and which is the independent variable in the example? Explain.

_____

_____

_____

2 How much money does the store earn if the store sells 8 sets of headphones? Explain how to use the equation to find the answer.

_____

3 One week, the store earned $60 in headphone sales. How many sets of headphones did the store sell? Can you use the equation to find the answer? Explain.

_____

Solve.

Use the example problem to solve problems 4–7.

In the example, you explored how to represent a relationship with a table and an equation.

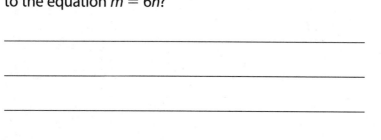

Number of Headphones, h	0	1	2	3	4	5
Amount of Money, m ($)	0	6	12	18	24	30

$m = 6h$

You can also represent the same situation with a graph.

4 Think of *h* and *m* as *x*- and *y*-coordinates, and use the values from the table to write ordered pairs (*h*, *m*).

_____

5 Graph the ordered pairs. How do they show solutions to the equation $m = 6h$?

_____

_____

_____

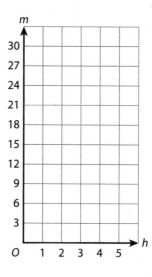

6 Which point represents the amount of money the store earns if the store sells 4 headphones? How do you know?

_____

_____

_____

7 Sonia paid $18 for headphones. How many sets of headphones did she buy? Explain how to use the graph to find the answer.

_____

_____

_____

Name: _____

Representing a Problem

Study the example showing how to represent a problem with an equation and a table. Then solve problems 1–8.

Example

Jamil pays $10.00 for a swim club membership and $1.50 for each day that he goes to the pool. Write an equation and make a table to represent the total cost c that Jamil will pay the swim club if he goes to the pool d days.

You can use the information given in the problem to write an equation.

total cost	equals	price per day	times	number of days	plus	membership fee
c	$=$	1.5	$\cdot$	d	$+$	10

The equation is $c = 1.5d + 10$. You can use the equation to make a table to find Jamil's total cost.

Days, d	1.5d + 10	Total Cost, c ($)
0	1.5(0) + 10	10
1	1.5(1) + 10	11.5
2	1.5(2) + 10	13
3	1.5(3) + 10	14.5
4	1.5(4) + 10	16

---

1 Name the dependent and independent variables in the problem. Describe the relationship between them.

_____

_____

2 What is the total cost if Jamil uses the pool on 6 days? Explain how to use the equation to find the cost.

_____

3 Lee joins the club but does not go to the pool. Is the total cost $0? Use the equation to explain your answer.

_____

_____

Lesson 21 Dependent and Independent Variables

Solve.

Use the example problem to solve problems 4–8.

In the example, you explored how to represent a relationship with an equation and a table.

$c = 1.5d + 10$

Days, d	$1.5d + 10$	Total Cost, c ($)
0	1.5(0) + 10	10
1	1.5(1) + 10	11.5
2	1.5(2) + 10	13
3	1.5(3) + 10	14.5
4	1.5(4) + 10	16

4 Use the values from the table to write ordered pairs.

_____

5 Graph the ordered pairs on the coordinate plane.

6 What is the total cost of using the pool for 6 days? Explain how to use the equation and the graph.

_____

_____

_____

_____

_____

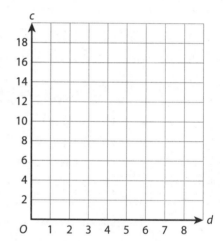

7 If a member paid $25, how many times did he or she use the pool? Explain how you found your answer. Did you use the table, equation, or graph to find your answer? Why?

_____

_____

8 Why is only the first quadrant shown in the graph of this situation?

_____

_____

Name: _____

Dependent and Independent Variables

Solve the problems.

---

1 Admission to an amusement park costs $5.00 and each ride ticket costs $1.50. The equation $c = 1.5t + 5$ represents the total cost, c, for admission with a certain numbers of ride tickets, t. Which statement about the equation is true? Select all that apply.

How can you use the equation to find the total cost?

A The variable t is the dependent variable.

B The total cost for admission with 5 ride tickets is $7.50.

C The total cost for admission with 6 ride tickets is $14.00.

D The total cost, c, depends on the number of ride tickets, t.

Colin chose **A** as a correct answer. Why did he choose that answer?

_____

_____

---

2 Which ordered pair is NOT included in the graph of $p = 3m + 6$? Select all that apply.

Which coordinate in the ordered pairs represents the values of p on the graph?

A (1, 9)   **C** (10, 36)

B (3, 12)   **D** (6, 18)

---

3 Describe a situation with two variables that you can represent with an equation that uses two operations. Write the equation. Explain the relationship between the variables.

How does knowing which variable is the dependent variable help you to write an equation?

_____

_____

_____

_____

Solve.

4 Use a graph to compare a pattern with the rule "add 4" to a pattern with the rule "add 2." Start both patterns at 0. Describe the relationship between the corresponding terms.

How do you use two patterns to locate points on a graph?

Show your work.

Solution: _____

_____

5 Some students volunteer to plant trees in a new park. They can plant 8 trees per hour. The table shows the relationship between the total number of trees they plant, *s,* and the number of hours, *h.* Tell whether each statement is *True* or *False.*

What is the relationship between h and s?

Number of Hours, *h*	2	4	6	8	10
Total Number of Trees Planted, *s*	16	32	48	64	80

a. In 7 hours, the students can plant 49 trees.　☐ True　☐ False

b. The equation *s* = 8*h* represents the relationship between *s* and *h.*　☐ True　☐ False

c. The students need 3 hours to plant 24 trees.　☐ True　☐ False

d. The number of trees is the dependent variable.　☐ True　☐ False

Name: _____

Twenty-Four

What you need: Recording Sheet, Number and Variable Cards

Directions

- Your goal is to write an expression and evaluate it to get as close as possible to 24.

- Mix up the cards and make two piles, one for numbers and one for variables. Players take turns picking two number cards and two variable cards.

- Write an expression using all of the numbers and variables on your cards. You can use any operation, as well as parentheses and exponents.

- Write an equivalent expression.

- Try to find numbers to substitute for the variables in either expression so that you get 24 when you evaluate it. Then record the value of the expression for the numbers you chose.

- Earn 1 point for making an equivalent expression and 2 more points if the evaluated expression equals 24. After 5 rounds, the player with the most points wins.

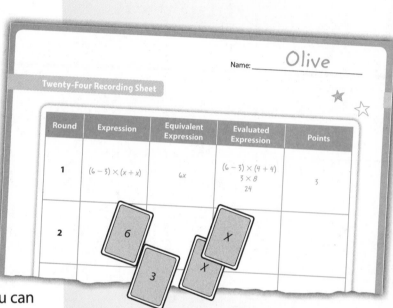

I try writing different expressions. I think about ways to make 24. And I try different ways to evaluate the expression before I write it on my recording sheet.

Name: _____

Round	Expression	Equivalent Expression	Evaluated Expression	Points
1				
2				
3				
4				
5				

Total Points: _____

Name: _____

1	1	1	2	2
2	3	3	3	4
4	4	6	6	6
8	8	8	x	x
x	x	y	y	y

Unit 3 Practice

Name: _____

Expressions and Equations

In this unit you learned to:	Lesson
evaluate numerical expressions that contain exponents, for example: $2^4 + 6 = 22$.	15
interpret and evaluate algebraic expressions, for example: $2(x + 7)$ means twice the sum of a number and 7.	16, 17
solve equations, for example: if $3 = \frac{1}{2}k$, then $k = 6$.	18, 19
solve inequalities, for example: if $3x \geq 15$, then $x \geq 5$.	20
use equations and inequalities to solve word problems.	19, 20
write equations to show the relationship between dependent and independent variables.	21

Use these skills to solve problems 1–8.

1 Which inequality is true?

A $4^2 > 2^4$

B $(5 + 2)^2 > 5^2 + 2^2$

C $4^2 > 3^3$

D $1 + 2^3 < 3^2 - 1$

2 Which equation has a solution of $n = 4$?

A $6 + n = 24$　　**C** $12 - n = 16$

B $5n = 54$　　**D** $7n = 28$

3 Bryce has 4 less than 3 times as many baseball cards as Dwight. Let x represent the number of cards that Dwight has.

Part A: Write an expression for the number of baseball cards Bryce has.

_____

Part B: How many baseball cards does Bryce have if Dwight has 25 cards?

_____

4 The perimeter of a square is at most 22 feet. Let n represent the length of one side of the square.

Part A: Write an inequality that represents the situation.

_____

Part B: Of the lengths 2.5 ft, 4.8 ft, 5.2 ft, 5.8 ft, 6 ft, which could be the side length of the square? Write all that apply.

_____

©Curriculum Associates, LLC   Copying is not permitted.

Solve.

5 The equation $c = 45h + 80$ represents the total cost, c, of a car repair that takes h hours.

Part A: Identify the dependent and independent variables.

_____

_____

Part B: Write three ordered pairs that satisfy the equation.

_____

_____

6 The length of a rectangle is 2 inches less than 5 times the width, w. What is an expression for the perimeter of the rectangle, in inches? Select all that apply.

A $2(5w - 2) + 2w$

B $w + w + 5w + 5w - 2$

C $2(6w - 2)$

D $12w - 4$

7 There are a total of 420 students at South School. This is 3 times the number of students in the sixth grade. How many students, n, are there in the sixth grade?

Show your work.

Solution: _____

8 Solve the equation for x.
$ax + bx = 14$

Show your work.

Solution: _____

Answer the questions and show all your work on separate paper.

Jayne is planning a hike with her friends. She asks each friend for her comfortable hiking pace. Their answers all fall between 2.5 and 3 miles per hour.

Jayne wants to hike one trail in the morning. When the girls get back from that hike, they will stop for lunch for about an hour. Then they will hike a different trail in the afternoon. All trails can be accessed from the same picnic area. Here is information about the trails.

Trail A – 8.5 miles

Trail B – 9.2 miles

Trail C – 9.4 miles

Trail D – 7.8 miles

Here is what you need to do.
- Pick two trails to hike.
- Decide on a pace for the hike.
- Write an equation that shows how long it will take the girls to hike a trail at this pace. Find how long it will take them to hike each of the trails you picked.
- Make a plan for the girls' day that includes the approximate times they might start and end each hike and take a lunch break in between.

Reflect on Mathematical Practices

After you complete the task, choose one of the following questions to answer.

1 **Use a Model** How do the equations that you wrote model the problem? What are the dependent and independent variables in each equation?

2 **Make an Argument** How did you decide what pace to use? Explain your reasoning.

Checklist

Did you . . .
- [ ] select an appropriate pace?
- [ ] label your work with appropriate units?
- [ ] write a detailed plan that includes all the times that the problem asks for?

Performance Task Tips

Word Bank Here are some words that you might use in your answer.

miles	independent variable	equation
hours	dependent variable	solution
time		

Model Here is a model that you might use to find the solution.

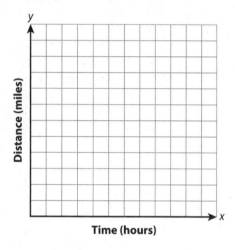

Sentence Starters Here are some sentence starters that might help you explain your work.

The girls can start the first hike _____

The first hike will take about _____

To find the time for a hike _____

Unit 3 Vocabulary

Name: _____

My Examples

power of ten

a number that can be written as a product of tens; 100 and 10^2 are powers of ten

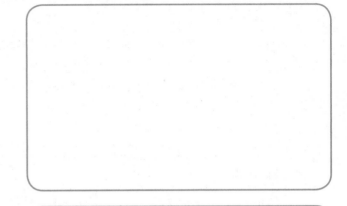

exponent

the number in a power that shows how many times the base is used as a factor

In the expression 10^2, the exponent is 2 and the base is 10.

parentheses

the symbols ( ) that can be used to group numbers and operations in an expression

$24 - (3 \times 5)$

$(5 + 7) \times 3$

variable

a letter that stands for an unknown number

My Examples

constant

a term that is a known number without variables

coefficient

a factor of a variable term that is a known number; the coefficient of the term 4x is 4

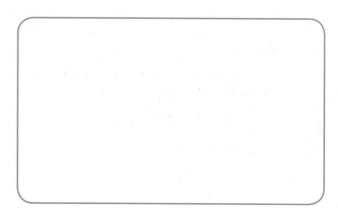

evaluate

to find the value of an algebraic expression

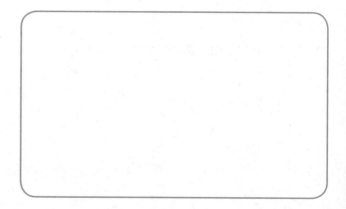

like terms

two or more terms in a variable expression that have the same variable factor; the like terms in the expression 4x + 3x + 3 are 4x and 3x

equation

a statement showing that two expressions are equivalent

Inverse operations

operations that "undo" each other

$+$ and $-$ are inverse operations

$\times$ and $\div$ are inverse operations

Inequality

a statement that contains the symbol $<$, $>$, $\leq$, or $\geq$.; for any inequality, there are many possible solutions

These are inequalities.

$x < 5$

$x > -2$

$x \leq 15$

$x \geq 0$

corresponding terms

the numbers that are in the same position in two or more related patterns

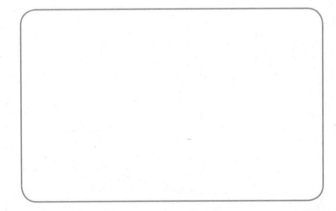

Pattern 1: 0, **2**, 4, 6

Pattern 2: 0, **4**, 8, 12

The numbers 2 and 4 are corresponding terms.

ordered pairs

a pair of numbers that locate a point on the coordinate plane

My Examples

My Words

Dear Family,

Your child is learning how to find the area of polygons.

Your child is familiar with finding the area of a rectangle from work in earlier grades. A rectangle is a type of polygon. Some other kinds of polygons are triangles, parallelograms, and trapezoids.

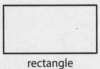   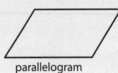

rectangle   right triangle   triangle   parallelogram   trapezoid

To find the area of a rectangle or a parallelogram, multiply the base *b* by the height *h*.

$A = bh$

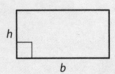 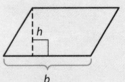

You can think of the area of a triangle as one-half of the area of a rectangle or a parallelogram. So, to find the area of a triangle, multiply the product of the base and height by $\frac{1}{2}$.

$A = \frac{1}{2}bh$

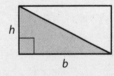 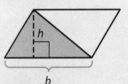

Consider the following example:

Ms. Herrera's flower bed has the shape of the trapezoid shown at the right. What is the area of the flower bed?

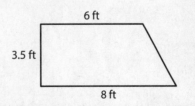

The next page shows two ways your child may find the area of the flower bed.

NEXT

What is the area of Ms. Herrera's flower bed?

One way:
You can think of a trapezoid as a rectangle and a triangle, so you can find its area by adding the areas of the rectangle and the triangle.

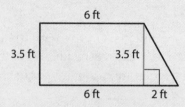

Divide the trapezoid, label the dimensions, and find each area.

Area of the rectangle $= bh$ Area of the triangle $= \frac{1}{2}bh$

$= 6(3.5)$ $= \frac{1}{2}(2)(3.5)$

$= 21$ $= 3.5$

Add the areas: 21 square feet + 3.5 square feet = 24.5 square feet.

Another way:
You can think of a trapezoid as two triangles, so you can find its area by adding the areas of the triangles.

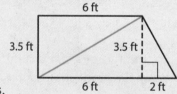

Divide the trapezoid, label the dimensions, and find each area.

Area of one triangle   Area of the other triangle

$\frac{1}{2}bh = \frac{1}{2}(6)(3.5)$ $\frac{1}{2}bh = \frac{1}{2}(6 + 2)(3.5)$

$= 10.5$ $= \frac{1}{2}(8)(3.5)$

                       $= 14$

Add the areas: 10.5 square feet + 14 square feet = 24.5 square feet.

Answer: Both methods show that the area of the trapezoid is 24.5 square feet, which means that Ms. Herrera's flower bed has an area of 24.5 square feet.

Area of Polygons

Name: _____

Study the example problem showing how to multiply fractions using an area model. Then solve problems 1–7.

Example

Ben has a piece of plywood that measures 1 yard on each side. He cuts the wood into 6 equal pieces. Each piece is $\frac{1}{3}$ yard wide and $\frac{1}{2}$ yard long. What is the area of each piece that Ben cuts?

You can use a model to help you understand the problem. Start by drawing a square that is 1 yard on each side and then divide it as described in the problem. Use your model to solve the problem.

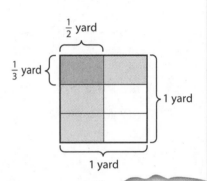

area of one piece $= \frac{1}{2} \times \frac{1}{3} = \frac{1 \times 1}{2 \times 3} = \frac{1}{6}$

The area of each piece of plywood is $\frac{1}{6}$ square yard.

---

1 Explain how the product $\frac{1}{2} \times \frac{1}{3}$ relates to the model.

_____

_____

2 How many pieces do you need to cover $\frac{1}{2}$ square yard? Explain how you know.

_____

_____

3 Suppose Ben cuts pieces that are $\frac{1}{3}$ yard wide but the area of each piece is $\frac{1}{12}$ square yard. What is the length of each piece? Explain how you know.

_____

_____

Solve.

Use the following situation to solve problems 4–5.

Isabel has a sticker that is $\frac{2}{3}$ inch wide and $\frac{1}{4}$ inch long.

4 Shade and label the area model to represent the area of the sticker.

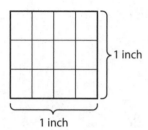

5 What is the area of the sticker?

Show your work.

Solution: _____

6 Fill in the missing numbers to make the equation true.
Then divide and shade the model to check your answer.

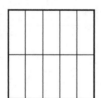

$\frac{1}{5} \times \dfrac{\boxed{}}{\boxed{}} = \frac{1}{10}$

7 A student uses this model to represent the product of two fractions. What are two possible fractions that the student could have been multiplying? Find the product of those two fractions, and shade the model to represent the product.

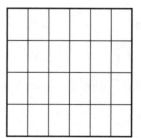

_____

Name: _____

Area of Triangles and Parallelograms

Study the example showing how to find the area of a figure by breaking it apart. Then solve problems 1–8.

Example

Karen drew the design shown at the right. How can she break apart her design in order to find its area?

Karen can break the design it into two parallelograms and one triangle as shown below. Then, she can find the area of the two parallelograms and the triangle to find the total area of the design.

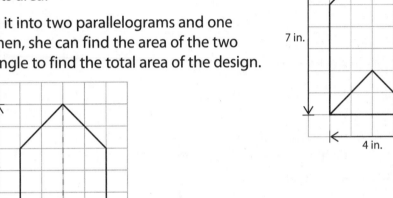

7 in.

4 in.

7 in.

4 in.

1 Label the dimensions of the triangle and one of the parallelograms from Karen's design.

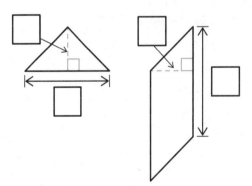

2 What is the area of one of the parallelograms? Use the formula: Area of a parallelogram = bh.

_____

3 What is the area of the triangle? Use the formula:
Area of a triangle = $\frac{1}{2}bh$.

_____

4 What is the area of the design? Explain how you know.

_____

_____

_____

Solve.

5 Brie and Lisa want to find the area of this figure. They agree to separate the figure as shown, but they disagree about what to do next. Lisa wants to add the areas of all four shapes in the figure. Brie wants to find the sum of the areas of one parallelogram and one triangle and then multiply that sum by 2. Who is correct? Explain.

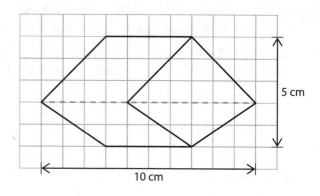

_____

_____

_____

6 Draw each parallelogram and each triangle that you need to find the area of in problem 5. Then label the dimensions on each figure.

7 What is the area of the figure?

Show your work.

Solution: _____

8 Show a different way to separate the figure into shapes. You may draw more than one line. Explain how to find the area of the figure using those shapes.

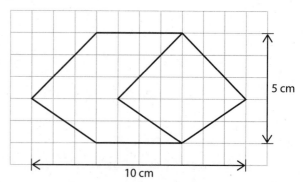

_____

_____

_____

Name: _____

Area of Trapezoids

Study the example problem showing how to find the area of a trapezoid. Then solve problems 1–7.

Example

Roberta is making a sign in the shape of the trapezoid shown. What is the area of the sign?

Separate the trapezoid into a triangle and a rectangle, and label the dimensions as shown below. Then find the combined area of the triangle and the rectangle.

Area of a triangle $= \frac{1}{2}bh = \frac{1}{2}(1)(5) = 2.5$ square feet

Area of a rectangle $= bh = (2)(5) = 10$ square feet

2.5 square feet $+$ 10 square feet $=$ 12.5 square feet

The area of the sign is 12.5 square feet.

---

1 Why is the trapezoid separated into a triangle and a rectangle?

_____

_____

2 How do you find the base of the triangle?

_____

3 Which measure do you use to find both the area of the triangle and the area of the rectangle? Explain.

_____

Solve.

Use the trapezoid at the right to solve problems 4–6.

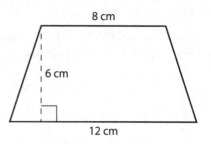

4 Draw lines to separate the trapezoid into a rectangle and two identical triangles. What are their dimensions?

_____

_____

_____

5 What is the area of the trapezoid?

Show your work.

Solution: _____

6 Nick says that if you separate the trapezoid into one parallelogram and one triangle, as shown, the area will change. Is he correct? Explain.

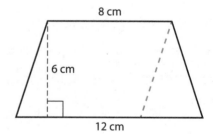

_____

_____

_____

7 The area of a trapezoid is 30 square centimeters. The height is 4 centimeters. The shorter base measures 6 centimeters. What is the measure of the longer base? Draw a picture of the problem. Explain your thinking.

_____

_____

_____

_____

_____

Name: _____

Area of Polygons

Solve the problems.

1 What is the area of the figure at the right? Explain how you found your answer.

Show your work.

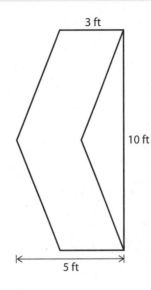

3 ft

10 ft

5 ft

How can separating the figure into smaller shapes help you?

Solution: _____

2 A kitchen floor has the shape of this trapezoid.

Tell whether each statement is *True* or *False*.

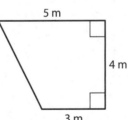

5 m

4 m

3 m

How do you find the area of a trapezoid?

a. The height of the trapezoid measures 5 meters. ☐ True ☐ False

b. You can separate the trapezoid into a triangle and a rectangle. ☐ True ☐ False

c. You can use the expression $(3 \cdot 4) + \left(\frac{1}{2} \cdot 2 \cdot 4\right)$ to find the area of the trapezoid. ☐ True ☐ False

d. The area is 12 square meters. ☐ True ☐ False

Solve.

3 The floor plan for a sports store is shown below.

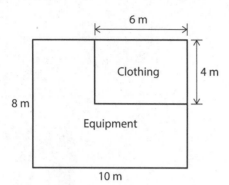

6 m

Clothing 4 m

8 m

Equipment

10 m

How can you use the area of the clothing section to find the area of the equipment section?

Which statement about the floor plan is true?
Select all that apply.

A The area of the equipment section is
80 square meters.

B The area of the clothing section is half the area of
the equipment section.

C The area of the equipment section is
56 square meters.

D The area of the equipment section is the area of
the store minus the area of the clothing section.

Peter chose **A** as a correct answer. How did he get that
answer?

_____

_____

4 Students play table tennis in a rectangular room that
is 15 feet by 25 feet. There is 8 feet of floor space from
each end of the table to the wall and 5 feet from each
side of the table to the wall. What is the area of the floor
not covered by the table?

You might want to draw a picture to help you.

A 40 square feet   **C** 170 square feet

B 45 square feet   **D** 330 square feet

Dear Family,

Your child is learning about polygons in the coordinate plane.

Polygons, such as triangles and rectangles, can be shown on the coordinate plane.

The triangle on the coordinate plane at the right has vertices, or corners, at the points (−1, 4), (2, 1), and (−4, 1). To find the area of the triangle, you can use the formula $A = \frac{1}{2}bh$.

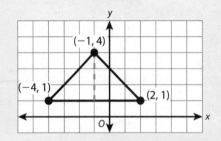

First you need to find the length of the base, *b*, and the height, *h*, of the triangle. You can count units on the coordinate plane to find the lengths.

Count units along the base of the triangle. The base, *b*, is 6 units. Count units from the base to the top vertex. The height, *h*, is 3 units. Now you can use the formula to find area of the triangle.

$$A = \frac{1}{2}bh$$

$$= \frac{1}{2}(6)(3)$$

$$= 9$$

The area of the triangle is 9 square units.

Consider the following example:

A swim club plans to replace the decorative edging around a rectangular pool. A diagram of the pool is drawn on a coordinate plane. Three corners of the pool have coordinates at (3, 4), (3, −5), and (−1, −5). Find the coordinates of the fourth corner and the perimeter of the pool.

On the next page you will see how your child can find the coordinates of the fourth corner and two ways your child may find the perimeter of the pool.

NEXT

Lesson 23 Polygons in the Coordinate Plane   **255**

A diagram of a rectangular pool drawn on a coordinate plane has coordinates (3, 4), (−5, 4), and (3, −1) for three of its corners. Find the coordinates of the fourth corner and the perimeter of the pool.

To find the fourth corner of the pool, draw a horizontal line that goes through (3, −1) and a vertical line that goes through (−5, 4). The fourth corner is at (−5, −1).

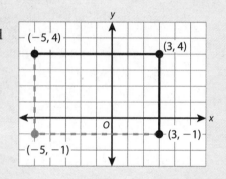

To find the perimeter of the pool, find its length and width.

One way: Find length and width by counting units.

To find the length, count the units from (−5, 4) to (3, 4): 9 units.

To find the width, count the units from (3, 4) to (3, −1): 5 units.

The perimeter is 5 + 9 + 5 + 9, or 28 units.

Another way: Find length and width using absolute value.

- To find the length, find the distance from (−5, 4) to (3, 4). The points have the same y-coordinate, so find their distances from the y-axis. Then add the distances.
  The distance from (−5, 4) to the y-axis is $|-5|$.
  The distance from (3, 4) to the y-axis is $|3|$.
  $|-5| + |3| = 5 + 3 = 9$

- To find the width, find the distance from (3, 4) to (3, −1). The points have the same x-coordinate, so find their distances from the x-axis. Then add the distances.
  The distance from (3, 4) to the x-axis is $|4|$.
  The distance from (3, −1) to the x-axis is $|-1|$.
  $|4| + |-1| = 4 + 1 = 5$

The perimeter is $2\ell + 2w$: $2(9) + 2(5) = 18 + 10 = 28$ units

Answer: The fourth corner of the pool is located at (−5, −1). Both methods show that the perimeter of the pool is 28 units.

Polygons in the Coordinate Plane

Name: _____

Prerequisite: Find Distance on a Coordinate Plane

Study the example showing how to solve a measurement problem using a shape on a coordinate plane. Then solve problems 1–9.

Example

Mr. Hiroshi plans to tile the floor of his family room. He draws a rectangle on the coordinate plane to represent the floor. What is the area of the floor in square units?

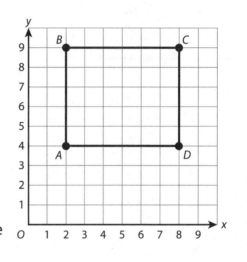

The area of a rectangle is length × width. You can count units to find the length and the width.

The length of $\overline{AB}$ is 5 units. The length of $\overline{BC}$ is 6 units. The area of rectangle ABCD is 5 × 6, or 30 square units.

You can also use ordered pairs to find the horizontal distance and the vertical distance between points on the coordinate plane.

---

1. Write the ordered pair for each point.

   A (_____) B(_____) C(_____) D(_____)

2. Explain how to use the x-coordinates of point A and point D to find the distance between the two points.

   _____

3. Explain how to use the y-coordinates of point C and point D to find the distance between the two points.

   _____

4. Find the lengths of these sides using the coordinates of their endpoints.

   $\overline{AD}$ _____ $\overline{CD}$ _____

5. What is the perimeter of rectangle ABCD? Explain how you found the perimeter.

   _____

   _____

Solve.

Use the shape on the coordinate plane to solve problems 6–8.

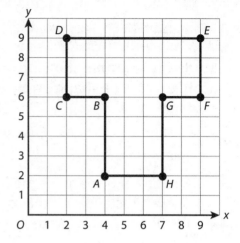

6 What are the coordinates of each point on the shape?

A(_____) B(_____) C(_____) D(_____)

E(_____) F(_____) G(_____) H(_____)

7 Find the area of the shape. Explain how you found your answer.

Show your work.

Solution: _____

8 Find the perimeter of the shape.

Show your work.

Solution: _____

9 Use the coordinate plane to draw a rectangle with an area of 24 square units. Label the corners of the rectangle *W, X, Y,* and *Z.* Explain how you know that the area of the rectangle is 24 square units.

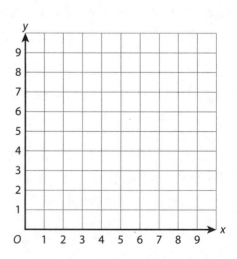

©Curriculum Associates, LLC   Copying is not permitted.

Name: _____

Find Missing Coordinates and Dimensions

Study the example problem showing how to find missing coordinates and dimensions of a rectangle. Then solve problems 1–9.

Example

Ms. Issa is planning to build a rectangular fishpond in her garden. A drawing shows three corners of the pond with coordinates (4, −2), (−2, −2), and (−2, 5). Where is the fourth corner?

You can graph the information given and then sketch the rectangle.

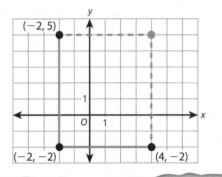

1 What are the coordinates of the fourth corner?

_____

2 How did you locate the fourth corner to sketch the rectangle?

_____

_____

_____

3 Explain how to use counting to find the distance between (−2, −2) and (4, −2).

_____

4 Explain how to use absolute value to find the distance between (−2, −2) and (−2, 5).

_____

_____

5 Explain how to find the area of the pond.

_____

_____

Solve.

Use the following situation to solve problems 6–8.

Mrs. Rockwell is buying a rectangular lot on which to build a new home. Three corners of the lot are at (5, −3), (−2, −3), and (−2, 2) on the coordinate plane.

6 Graph the three corners on the coordinate plane. What is the ordered pair for the fourth corner of the lot?

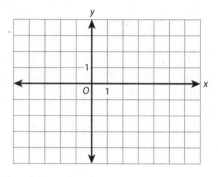

_____

7 What is the perimeter of the lot?

Show your work.

Solution: _____

8 Mr. Brown bought a lot that is half as long and twice as wide as Mrs. Rockwell's lot. How does the area of his lot compare to the area of Mrs. Rockwell's lot? Explain how you know.

_____

_____

_____

9 Nadim wants to build a square pen for his rabbits. He plots two corners on a coordinate plane at (3, −3) and (−3, 3). Abe says that he should plot another corner at (3, 3). Does this make sense? Explain why or why not.

_____

_____

_____

_____

Name: _____

Find Area on a Coordinate Plane

**Study the example problem showing how to find the
area of a polygon on a coordinate plane. Then solve
problems 1–7.**

Example

A floor plan for a building shows corners of the building at
(0, 0), (6, 0), (9, 5), and (3, 5). What is the shape of the floor
of the building? How can you find the area of the floor?

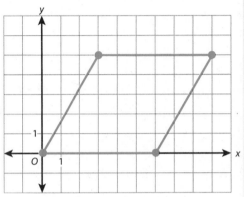

You can graph the information given and connect the
points to find the shape of the floor. The connected points
form a parallelogram, so the floor is a parallelogram.

You can find the area of the floor by multiplying its base
times its height since it is a parallelogram.

---

1 What is the base length of the parallelogram in the
example? How did you find the base length?

_____

2 What is the height of the parallelogram in the example?
How did you find the height?

_____

3 Find the area.

_____

4 Katerine divided the parallelogram into two congruent
triangles and a rectangle in order to find its area.
Does her method work? If so, show that it works.
If not, explain why not.

_____

_____

_____

_____

_____

Solve.

Use the following situation to solve problems 5–6.

Madeline plotted these points to represent the corners of a vegetable garden: (0, 0), (6, 0), (3, 7).

5 | Draw the shape on the coordinate plane. What shape is the garden? Find the area of the garden.

Show your work.

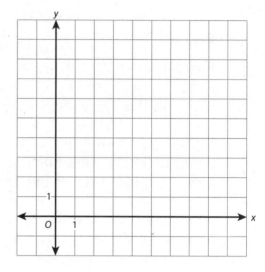

Solution: _____

_____

6 | Suppose Madeline uses (6, 7) rather than (3, 7) as the third corner for her garden. How will that change the shape of the garden? How will the areas of the two gardens compare?

_____

_____

7 | A flower garden and the lawn around it are shown on the coordinate plane. What is the area of the lawn?

Show your work.

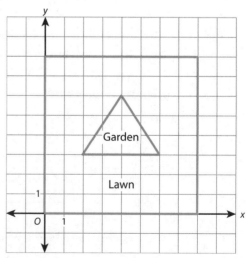

Solution: _____

©Curriculum Associates, LLC   Copying is not permitted.

Name: _____

Polygons in the Coordinate Plane

Solve the problems.

1 Find the area of the trapezoid.

Show your work.

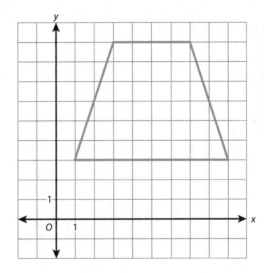

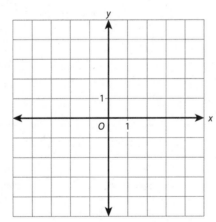

How can you separate this trapezoid into different shapes?

Solution: _____

2 Three corners of a rectangular park are located at (−3, 1), (4, 1), and (4, −2).

Part A

What are the coordinates of the fourth corner?

_____

Part B

What is the perimeter of the park? Explain how you found your answer.

_____

_____

How does plotting points for the three corners help you find the point for the fourth corner?

Solve.

3 Keaton drew a parallelogram on a coordinate plane. Two vertices of the parallelogram were located at (1, 1) and (1, 7). The area of the parallelogram is 18 square units. Tell whether each statement is *True* or *False*.

What is the formula for the area of a parallelogram?

a. The *x*-coordinate of the other two vertices of the parallelogram could be −2. ☐ True ☐ False

b. The *x*-coordinate of the other two vertices of the parallelogram could be 4. ☐ True ☐ False

c. The parallelogram must be a square. ☐ True ☐ False

d. The perimeter of this parallelogram could be 18 units. ☐ True ☐ False

4 Gianna plotted these points and then connected the points in order from *J* to *N* and then back to *J* to show the shape of her room. Draw the room on the coordinate plane. What is the area of Gianna's room?

What shapes do you see when you plot and connect the points?

J(1, 0) *K*(1, 6) *L*(9, 6) *M*(9, 3) *N*(6, 3)

Show your work.

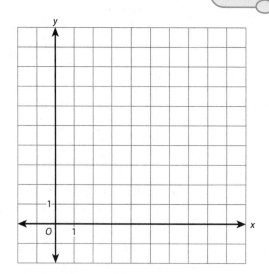

Solution: _____

Dear Family,

Your child is learning about nets and surface area.

Your child has learned how to find the area of plane figures such as rectangles and triangles. Now your child is going to use that knowledge to find the surface area of three-dimensional figures.

The surface area is the combined area of all of the "faces" of a figure. You can think of a "face" as a flat side of a three-dimensional figure. The rectangular prism below has six faces.

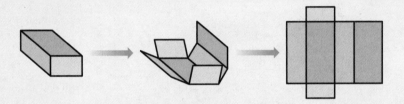

Imagine cutting a three-dimensional figure along its edges and unfolding it. The flat, unfolded model of the figure is called a *net*. You can use the net of a figure to find the surface area of the figure.

A familiar way that surface area is used in everyday life is wrapping a gift box. The surface area of the box determines the amount of wrapping paper you need.

Consider the following example:

Lorena is making pyramid-shaped gift boxes. The length of each edge of the base of the pyramid is 9 cm. The height of each triangular face of the pyramid is 8 cm. How much card stock does Lorena need to make each box?

The next page shows two ways your child may find the surface area of each pyramid-shaped box to figure out how much card stock is needed.

Lorena is making pyramid-shaped gift boxes. The length of each edge of the base of the pyramid is 9 cm. The height of each triangular face of the pyramid is 8 cm. How much card stock does Lorena need to make each box?

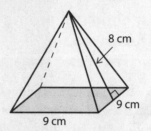

One way: Label a net of the pyramid to find its surface area.

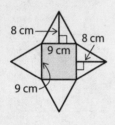

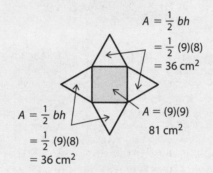

$$A = \frac{1}{2} bh$$
$$= \frac{1}{2} (9)(8)$$
$$= 36 \text{ cm}^2$$

$$A = \frac{1}{2} bh$$
$$= \frac{1}{2} (9)(8)$$
$$= 36 \text{ cm}^2$$

$$A = (9)(9)$$
$$81 \text{ cm}^2$$

Add the areas of the faces: $81 + 4(36) = 81 + 144 = 225 \text{ cm}^2$

Another way: Use a table to organize the information and find the surface area of the pyramid.

Face	Base (cm)	Height (cm)	Area (cm²)
Triangle	9	8	36
Triangle	9	8	36
Triangle	9	8	36
Triangle	9	8	36
Square	9	9	81

Add the areas of the faces: $36 + 36 + 36 + 36 + 81 = 225 \text{ cm}^2$

Answer: Both methods show that the surface area of the pyramid is 225 cm². So Lorena needs 225 square centimeters of card stock to make each box.

Nets and Surface Area

Name: _____

Study the example problem showing how to find the area of a polygon. Then solve problems 1–8.

Example

Gary drew a picture of a nameplate that he plans to make. He wants to find the area of the nameplate. How could Gary break apart the figure to find its area?

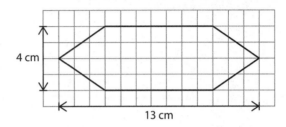

Gary separates the figure he drew into two triangles and a rectangle.

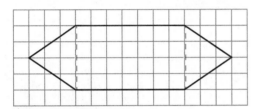

1 Label the dimensions of the rectangle and one of the triangles.

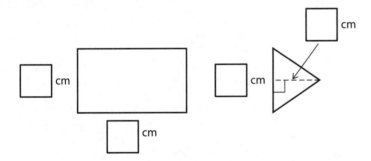

2 What is the area of the rectangle?

_____

3 What is the area of the triangle?

_____

4 What is the area of the nameplate? Write an equation to show your solution.

_____

Solve.

Use the trapezoid to solve problems 5–6.

5. Separate the trapezoid into figures whose areas you can find. Label the dimensions.

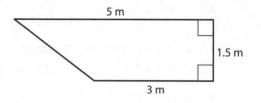

6. What is the area of the trapezoid?

Show your work.

Solution: _____

7. Hector drew three rectangles to show the letter H on his notebook. Use the rectangles to find the area of the letter he drew.

Show your work.

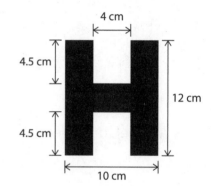

Solution: _____

8. Pat says that the parallelograms below do not have the same area. Is she correct? Explain.

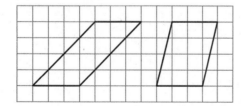

_____

_____

©Curriculum Associates, LLC   Copying is not permitted.

Name: _____

Surface Area of a Rectangular Prism

Study the example showing how to find the surface area of a rectangular prism. Then solve problems 1–8.

Example

Kanene wants to know how much wrapping paper she needs to cover this box. How much wrapping paper does she need?

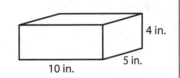

You can use a net to help you solve the problem.

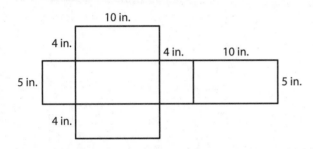

1 Complete the table to find the area of each face.

Face	Length (in.)	Width (in.)	Area (sq in.)
Top	10	5	
Bottom			
Front			
Back			
Right side			
Left side			

2 Which pairs of faces have the same areas?

_____

3 What is the surface area of the box? Use your answer to problem 2 to write an equation.

_____

4 What is the relationship between the surface area of a rectangular prism and the area of each face?

_____

Solve.

5 Carl drew this net for a wooden shed that he will build. He wants to protect the wood against the weather by using a sealant on all of the outside surfaces, including the bottom. Will a container of sealant that covers 200 square feet be enough to protect the outside surfaces?

Show your work.

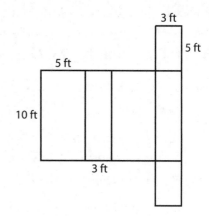

Solution: _____

6 Susana is making a small box. The 20-cm by 20-cm front of the box will be glass. The other faces will be wood. How much wood does Susana need to make the box?

Show your work.

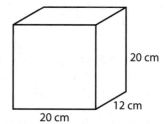

Solution: _____

7 The surface area of a cube is 216 square meters. What is the height of the cube? Explain.

_____

_____

8 Mike says that if he doubles each dimension of any rectangular prism, the surface area also doubles. Is Mike correct? Give an example to support your answer.

_____

_____

_____

_____

Name: _____

Surface Area of a Triangular Prism

Study the example showing how to find the surface area of a triangular prism. Then solve problems 1–7.

Example

What is the surface area of the triangular prism shown?

You can draw and label a net of the prism to help you.

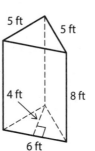

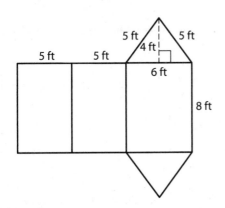

---

1 Complete the table to find the area of each face.

Face	Base (ft)	Height (ft)	Area (sq ft)
Triangle	6	4	
Triangle			
Rectangle			
Rectangle			
Rectangle			

2 Why do the rectangular faces have different areas?

_____

_____

_____

3 What is the surface area of the triangular prism? Write two equations to represent the surface area.

_____

Solve.

Use the following situation to solve problems 4–6.

Jane is decorating a paperweight in the shape of a triangular prism. The diagram shows its dimensions.

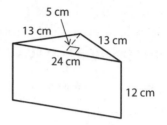

4 Label the net of the triangular prism to show the dimensions of the faces.

5 What is the surface area of the paperweight?

Show your work.

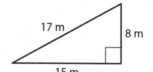

Solution: _____

6 Amad used the expression $2\left(\frac{1}{2} \cdot 24 \cdot 5\right) + 3(13 \cdot 12)$ to find the surface area of the paperweight. What is wrong with his expression? Correct Amad's mistake.

_____

_____

_____

7 The picture shows the dimensions of one base of a triangular prism. The height of the prism is 2 meters. What is the surface area of the triangular prism? Explain how to find the answer.

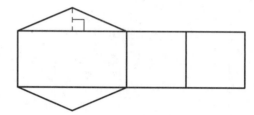

_____

_____

_____

_____

_____

_____

Name: _____

Surface Area of a Pyramid

Study the example problem showing how to find the surface area of a pyramid. Then solve problems 1–8.

Example

What is the surface area of the pyramid?

You can draw and label a net to help you.

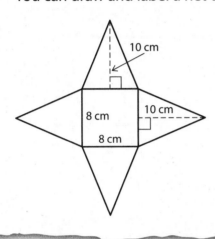

1 Complete the table to find the area of each face.

Face	Base (cm)	Height (cm)	Area (sq cm)
Triangle	8	10	
Triangle			
Triangle			
Triangle			
Square			

2 Describe the number of faces and their shapes.

_____

3 Use formulas to explain how to find the area of each face.

_____

_____

4 What is the surface area of the pyramid? Write an equation to represent the surface area.

_____

Solve.

Use the following situation to solve problems 5–7.

Marcos is making a pyramid in his wood shop class. The base of the pyramid is a rectangle.

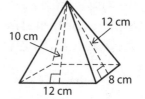

5 Label the net of the pyramid with the dimensions of the faces.

6 What is the surface area of the pyramid?

   Show your work.

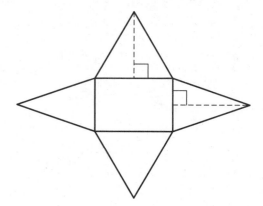

Solution: _____

7 Yolanda used the expression $\left(\frac{1}{2} \cdot 12 \cdot 10\right) + \left(\frac{1}{2} \cdot 8 \cdot 12\right) +$
   $(12 \cdot 8)$ to find the surface area of the pyramid. What is wrong with the expression? Correct Yolanda's mistake.

   _____

   _____

8 The surface area of a pyramid is 540 square inches. Its base is a square with a side length of 10 inches. What is the height of one of the triangular faces of the pyramid? Explain how to find the answer.

   _____

   _____

   _____

   _____

Name: _____

Nets and Surface Area

Solve the problems.

1 Rita keeps her craft supplies in a container without a top. The container is a triangular prism. Rita plans to cover the outside of the container with decorative paper. How much paper does she need?

Show your work.

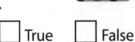

How many faces should you include in your calculations?

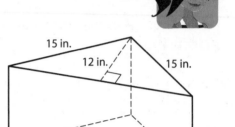

15 in. 12 in. 15 in. 10 in. 18 in.

Solution: _____

2 Look at the pyramid below.

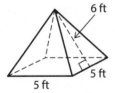

6 ft   5 ft   5 ft

What do you need to know to find the surface area of a pyramid?

Tell whether each statement about the pyramid is *True* or *False*.

a. The area of each triangular face is 30 square feet. ☐ True ☐ False

b. The surface area of the pyramid is 85 square feet. ☐ True ☐ False

c. A net of the pyramid would have three triangular faces. ☐ True ☐ False

d. The area of the base is 25 square feet. ☐ True ☐ False

Solve.

3 The net represents a rectangular prism. Which expression represents the surface area? Select all that apply.

 3 cm
 5 cm
2 cm
5 cm

A $(3 \cdot 5) + (5 \cdot 2) + (2 \cdot 3)$

B $15 + 15 + 6 + 6 + 10$

C $2(3 \cdot 5) + 2(3 \cdot 2) + 2(2 \cdot 5)$

D $2(10) + 2(6) + 2(15)$

Horus chose **A** as the correct answer. How did he get that answer?

_____

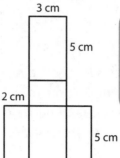

How do you find the surface area of a rectangular prism?

_____

4 Does the diagram represent the net of a triangular prism? Choose *Yes* or *No*.

a.

☐ Yes   ☐ No

How many faces on a triangular prism are triangles?

b.

☐ Yes   ☐ No

c.

☐ Yes   ☐ No

5 Design your own pyramid. Describe your pyramid, and then choose its dimensions and find its surface area.

_____

_____

276 **Lesson 24** Nets and Surface Area

©Curriculum Associates, LLC   Copying is not permitted.

Dear Family,

Your child is learning about volume.

Your child has already learned about volume as the amount of space inside a solid figure. He or she has counted cubes or used a formula to find the volume of rectangular prisms. Now your child is going to find the volume of rectangular prisms whose edges have fractional measurements.

You can use the volume formula to find the volume of the prism at the right. The length is 10 inches, the width is 10 inches, and the height is $11\frac{1}{2}$ inches.

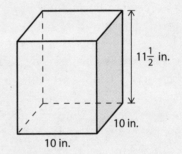

$11\frac{1}{2}$ in.

10 in.

10 in.

$$\text{Volume} = \text{length} \times \text{width} \times \text{height}$$

$$V = \ell \times w \times h$$

$$= 10 \times 10 \times 11\frac{1}{2}$$

$$= 1{,}150$$

The volume of the rectangular prism is 1,150 cubic inches.

Consider the following example:

Marissa has a rectangular fish pond in her yard. The pond is 6 feet long, 3 feet wide, and 2 feet deep. Marissa fills the pond so that the water is $1\frac{1}{2}$ feet deep. What is the volume of the water in the fish pond?

On the next page you will see two ways your child may find the volume of water in the fish pond.

NEXT ➡

Volume: Sample Solution

Marissa fills a rectangular fish pond with water to a depth of $1\frac{1}{2}$ feet. The pond is 6 feet long and 3 feet wide. What is the volume of water in the fish pond.

One way:
Model the volume of water in the pond with 1-foot unit cubes.

You can think of the water in the pond as a rectangular prism. Fill the prism with 1-foot unit cubes.

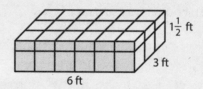

Each cube on the top layer is half the height of a 1-foot unit cube.

The bottom layer has 18 cubes. The top layer has 18 half cubes, or 9 whole cubes. The prism has $18 + 9 = 27$ one-foot unit cubes, so it has a volume of 27 cubic feet.

Another way:
Make a sketch of the water in the pond and label it with the information in the problem.

Use the volume formula to find the volume of the rectangular prism.

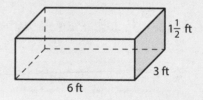

$$V = \ell \times w \times h$$

$$= 6 \times 3 \times 1\frac{1}{2}$$

$$= 18 \times 1\frac{1}{2}$$

$$= 27$$

The volume of the rectangular prism is 27 cubic feet.

Answer: Both methods show that the volume of the rectangular prism is 27 cubic feet, which means that there is 27 cubic feet of water in Marissa's fish pond.

Volume

Name: _____

Prerequisite: Use Formulas

Study the example problem showing how to use formulas to find the volume of a rectangular prism. Then solve problems 1–8.

Example

Some building supplies are stored in a container that is 4 feet long, 2 feet wide, and 3 feet high. What is the volume of the container?

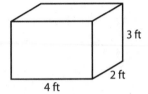
3 ft
2 ft
4 ft

Use the formula.

Volume = length × width × height

Volume = 4 × 2 × 3 = 24

The volume is 24 cubic feet.

1 What part of the formula represents the area of the base of the container?

_____

2 Use your answer to problem 1 to write another formula for finding the volume of a rectangular prism.

Volume = _____ × height

3 Use the new formula to find the volume of a container that is 6 feet long, 5 feet wide, and 7 feet high.

area of the base = _____ × _____

area of the base = _____ square feet

Volume = _____ × _____

Volume = _____ cubic feet

4 If you know the volume of a rectangular prism and the area of the base, how can you find the height?

_____

_____

_____

Solve.

5 Some sewing supplies are stored in a container that is 5 inches tall, 7 inches wide, and 12 inches long.

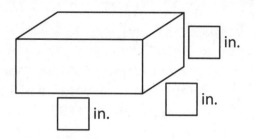

a. Label the picture of the box with its dimensions.

b. What is the volume of the box?

Show your work.

Solution: _____

6 The base of a rectangular prism is 40 centimeters long and 5 centimeters wide. The height of the prism is 2 centimeters. Write two different equations that represent the volume of the prism.

_____

7 The volume of the prism shown is 84 cubic yards. What is the height of the prism?

Show your work.

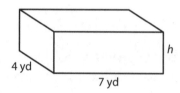

4 yd

7 yd

h

Solution: _____

8 Shawn's teacher said that the volume of a rectangular prism is 64 cubic centimeters. Shawn said that he has enough information already to find the width. Is this correct? If not, explain why not. Otherwise, give the width and explain your thinking.

_____

_____

_____

Name: _____

Fractional Dimensions

Study the example problem showing how to find the volume of a rectangular prism whose dimensions are not all whole numbers. Then solve problems 1–6.

Example

A food storage container is a rectangular prism that is 3 inches long, 2 inches wide, and 4 inches tall. The granola in the container is $3\frac{1}{2}$ inches deep. What is the volume of the granola?

You can sketch the amount of granola in the container and label its dimensions. You can also model the volume with 1-inch unit cubes.

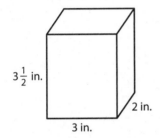

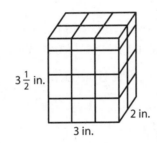

The volume of the granola is 21 cubic inches.

1. Look at the model. How many whole cubes can you make with the half cubes in the top layer? Explain.

   _____

2. Use your answer to problem 1 to explain how the model shows that the volume of the granola in the container is 21 cubic inches?

   _____

3. Use the formula $V = lwh$ to find the volume of the granola in the container.

   _____

Solve.

4 A school locker is $\frac{3}{4}$ foot wide, $1\frac{1}{2}$ feet deep, and 6 feet tall. What is the volume of the locker? Draw a picture and label the dimensions.

Show your work.

Solution: _____

5 Kylie has two full containers of trail mix, one that is red and one that is blue. The red container is 4 inches long, 5 inches wide, and $2\frac{3}{4}$ inches tall. The blue container is $2\frac{2}{3}$ inches long, 7 inches wide, and 3 inches tall. Which container holds more trail mix?

Show your work.

Solution: _____

6 The height of a rectangular prism is half its width. The width of the prism is $\frac{1}{3}$ of its length. If the width of the prism is 3 centimeters, what is the volume?

_____

Find an Unknown Dimension

Study the example problem showing how to find one dimension of a rectangular prism whose dimensions are not all whole numbers. Then solve problems 1–6.

Example

A walkway is made up of rectangular blocks. The volume of a block is 255 cubic inches. The width is 10 inches and the height is 2 inches. What is the length of a block?

You can sketch the block and label it with the given information. Then you can use the formula $V = l \times w \times h$ to find the value of l.

$V = l \times w \times h$

$255 = l \times 10 \times 2$

$255 = l \times 20$

$12\frac{3}{4} = l$

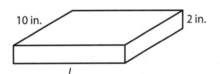

10 in.   2 in.

l

The length of a block is $12\frac{3}{4}$ inches.

---

1 What operation was used on the equation $255 = l \times 20$ to find the length l?

_____

2 Another block has a volume of 180 cubic inches. The area of the base is 72 square inches. What is the height of the block? Use the formula $V = Bh$ to find the answer.

_____

3 A third block that is 5 inches high has a volume of 165 cubic inches. The width is $5\frac{1}{2}$ inches. Is the length the smallest dimension? Explain.

_____

_____

Solve.

4 The owner of a gift shop keeps holiday decorations in a rectangular box that has a volume of 30 cubic feet. The length of the box is 4 feet and the height is 2.5 feet. What is the width of the box? Draw a picture and label the dimensions.

Show your work.

Solution: _____

5 Vicky and Jim have a lawn care business. Jim keeps equipment in a shed that has a volume of 66 cubic feet. The length of his shed is 5 feet and the width is $2\frac{1}{5}$ feet. Vicky keeps equipment in another shed that has a volume of 63 cubic feet. The length of her shed is 4 feet and the width is $2\frac{1}{4}$ feet. They want to store a new lawn mower in the taller shed. Which shed will they use?

Show your work.

Solution: _____

6 The base of a rectangular prism is a square. The height of the prism is half the length of one edge of the base. The volume of the rectangular prism is 13.5 cubic units. What are the dimensions of the prism?

_____

©Curriculum Associates, LLC   Copying is not permitted.

Name: _____

Volume

Solve the problems.

1   Is the volume of a rectangular prism with the given dimensions less than, equal to, or greater than 24 cubic meters? Mark an X in the correct column.

Dimensions	Less than	Equal to	Greater than
5 m, $1\frac{1}{2}$ m, 3 m			
3 m, 4 m, 2 m			
5 m, 2 m, $2\frac{1}{2}$ m			

What is the formula for the volume of a rectangular prism?

2   The volume of a rectangular gift box is 98 cubic inches. The height is 4 inches and the width is $3\frac{1}{2}$ inches. What is the length of the gift box?

Show your work.

Sketching the prism is a good way to organize the information.

Solution: _____

3   The volume of a cube is 125 cubic centimeters. A rectangular prism with three different whole-number dimensions has the same volume. What are the dimensions of the rectangular prism?

_____

Could finding factors of 125 help you solve the problem?

Solve.

4 Tell whether each statement about the rectangular prism is *True* or *False*.

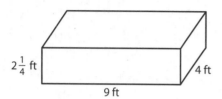

$2\frac{1}{4}$ ft   4 ft

9 ft

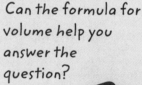
Which two dimensions identify the base of a rectangular prism?

a. The base is a square. ☐ True ☐ False

b. The volume of the rectangular prism is 81 cubic feet. ☐ True ☐ False

c. The area of the base is 36 square feet. ☐ True ☐ False

d. If you doubled the height, the volume would also double. ☐ True ☐ False

---

5 A rectangular prism has a volume of 52 cubic meters, a length of 12 meters, and a width of $2\frac{1}{6}$ meters. Which expression could you use to find the height of the rectangular prism? Select all that apply.

Can the formula for volume help you answer the question?

A $52 \div 26$

B $52 \times 12 \times 2\frac{1}{6}$

C $52 + 12 + 2\frac{1}{6}$

D $52 \div \left(12 \times 2\frac{1}{6}\right)$

---

6 The length of a rectangular prism is 5 feet. The width is 2.4 feet and the height is 8 feet. What is the volume of the rectangular prism?

What operation do you use to find volume?

A   12 cubic feet

B   15.4 cubic feet

C   40 cubic feet

D   96 cubic feet

Olivia chose **A** as the correct answer. How did she get that answer?

_____

_____

Area-Rama

What you need: Recording Sheet, 2 number cubes (one labeled 0–4 and "choice"; the other labeled 2–6 and "choice"), ruler or straightedge

Directions

- Your goal is to fill up as much space as possible on the grid.

- On your turn, roll both number cubes. Use the numbers you roll to make a two-digit number. If you roll "choice," you can choose any number 0–9.

- The two-digit number represents the area of a polygon. On the grid, draw a shape that has this area. Choose from: triangle, rectangle, parallelogram (that is not a rectangle), trapezoid (that is not a parallelogram), and composite shape. Write the area (the number of square units) inside the shape.

- Players take turns. No one can repeat a shape until all shapes have been used once. If a player cannot make a shape with the given area, the player must pass.

- When two players in a row pass, the game is over. The player who has covered the most area wins.

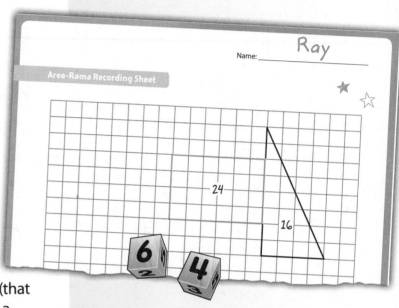

> As the grid gets filled up, I will have to draw shapes with smaller areas! I use mental math and area formulas to think about what numbers to make with the digits on the number cubes.

Name: _____

Geometry

In this unit you learned to:	Lesson
find the area of triangles, quadrilaterals, and other polygons.	22
solve problems with polygons in the coordinate plane.	23
use nets to find the surface area of three-dimensional figures.	24
find the volume of a rectangular prism with fractional edge lengths, for example: the volume of a cube with edges $\frac{1}{2}$ inch is $\frac{1}{8}$ cubic inch.	25

Use these skills to solve problems 1–6.

1 There are 25 desks in a classroom. Each desktop is the same as the one shown below.

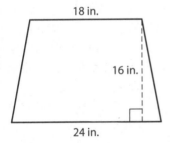

18 in.

16 in.

24 in.

What is the total area of all of the desktops?

Show your work.

Solution: _____

_____

2 A fish tank has the shape of a rectangular prism with dimensions as shown. The tank is open at the top.

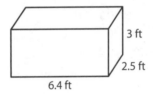

3 ft

2.5 ft

6.4 ft

How much glass was used to make the tank?

Show your work.

Solution: _____

_____

Solve.

3 What three-dimensional figure does the net represent?

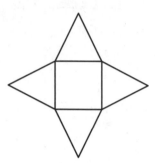

  A square pyramid

  B rectangular prism

  C triangular prism

  D cube

4 The area of the triangle is 24 square feet. What is the length of the base?

3 ft

  A 8 feet   **C** 21 feet

  B 16 feet   **D** 36 feet

5 Mildred has two cubes. The length of one side of the smaller cube is half the length of one side of the larger cube. How many of the smaller cubes would it take to fill the larger cube?

  A 2   **C** 8

  B 6   **D** 12

6 Henry drew a diagram of the front of his house on a coordinate plane.

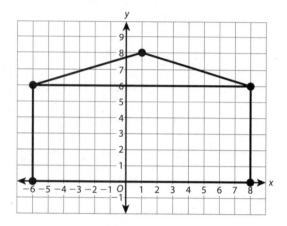

Part A: What is the area of the front of Henry's house on the diagram?

_____

Part B: There is a window with vertices at (−4, 2), (−4, 4), (−2, 2), and (−2, 4). There is a second window with vertices at (4, 1), (4, 5), (6, 1), and (6, 5). The front door has vertices at (−1, 0), (−1, 3), (1, 3), and (1, 0). Henry wants to paint the front of his house, but not the windows or the door. He drew the diagram so that 1 square unit = 9 square feet. What is the area that Henry wants to paint?

Show your work.

Solution: _____

_____

Name: _____

Answer the questions and show all your work on separate paper.

You are on the planning committee for the city road race. Your job is to plan a route for the race according to the rules below.

- The race has to be more than 3 miles but less than 5 miles in length.
- The race should start and stop at the same place.
- No part of the race can run through Central Avenue.

Here is a city map. Each city block (small square on the map) is 0.1 mile by 0.1 mile.

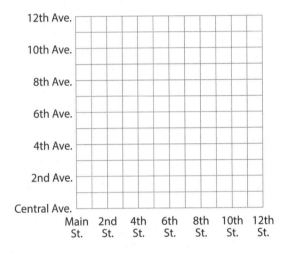

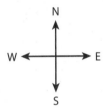

Use a coordinate grid to draw the race route. Label the vertices of the polygon that you draw with coordinate pairs. Show and explain why your route meets all of the rules. Then write a description of the route using directional words and street names.

Reflect on Mathematical Practices

After you complete the task, choose one of the following questions to answer.

1 **Use Structure** How did you use place value understanding to determine the length of the race route?

2 **Persevere** What was your plan for finding a possible race route?

Performance Task Tips

Word Bank Here are some words that you might use in your answer.

coordinate pair	polygon	north
x-axis	vertex	south
y-axis	perimeter	east
		west

Model Here is a model that you might use to find the solution.

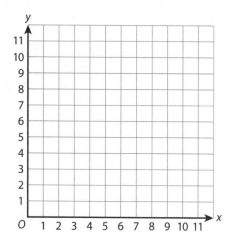

Sentence Starters Here are some sentence starters that might help you explain your work.

The race starts and ends _____

Start at _____, and travel _____

The perimeter of _____

Name: _____

My Examples

polygon

a closed plane figure whose sides are line segments that intersect only at their endpoints

base

the face of a geometric figure from which the height can be measured

net

a flat "unfolded" representation of a prism or pyramid

surface area

the sum of the areas of the faces of a figure

My Examples

triangular prism

a three-dimensional figure that has two parallel triangular faces that are the same size and shape

pyramid

a three-dimensiional figure whose base is a polygon and whose other faces are triangles

My Words

_____

_____

_____

_____

_____

_____

_____

Dear Family,

Your child is learning about statistical questions.

You are probably familiar with situations that involve statistics such as finance, sports, and weather.

A statistical question is a question that can be answered by collecting data. The answers to a statistical question will have some variety. Below are examples of statistical questions.

- What is your favorite TV show?

- How much time do you spend commuting to work each day?

A question that has a specific answer is not a statistical question. Below are examples of questions that are not statistical questions.

- When is the last day of school this year?

- How tall is the largest skyscraper in the U.S.?

Consider the following example:

Mr. Detrick wants to know how the people in his neighborhood use the park. He plans to ask some people in his neighborhood one statistical question. Which of these two questions should he ask?

- How many minutes per week do you spend at the park?

- On which street is the park?

The next page shows one way your child may determine whether a question is a statistical question or not.

NEXT

Mr. Detrick wants to know how the people in his neighborhood use the park. He plans to ask some people in his neighborhood one statistical question. Which of these two questions should he ask?

- How many minutes per week do you spend at the park?

- On which street is the park?

Decide whether each of the two questions is statistical or not.

Question	Does the question have a variety of answers?	Is the question statistical?
How many minutes per week do you spend at the park?	Yes	Yes
On which street is the park?	No	No

The first question is a statistical question. Mr. Detrick should ask it.

- The question will have a variety of answers.

- Mr. Detrick can use the data to find out how often people in his neighborhood use the park.

The second question is not a statistical question. Mr. Detrick should not ask it.

- The question only has one answer.

- Mr. Detrick cannot use the data to find out how people use the park.

Answer: Mr. Detrick should ask the question "How many minutes per week do you spend at the park?" because it is a statistical question that has a variety of answers. He can use the data to find out how people use the park. Another statistical question he could ask is "What time of day would you be most likely to visit the park?"

Name: _____

Prerequisite: How can you use a line plot to interpret data?

Study the example problem showing how to make a line plot. Then solve problems 1–7.

Example

Anna planted radish seeds in her vegetable garden. At the end of two weeks, she measured the height of each radish plant to the nearest $\frac{1}{2}$ inch and recorded her data in a table. How can Anna show this data in a line plot?

Make an X to stand for each plant in the table. For example, the line plot below shows that two plants were $\frac{1}{2}$ inch tall.

Height (inches)	Number of Plants
$\frac{1}{2}$	2
$1\frac{1}{2}$	3
2	8
$2\frac{1}{2}$	7
$3\frac{1}{2}$	2

```
                    x
                    x   x
                    x   x
                    x   x
                    x   x
                x   x   x
        x       x   x   x       x
        x       x   x   x       x
   +----+---+---+---+---+---+---+----+
   0   1/2  1  1 1/2 2  2 1/2 3  3 1/2 4
```

Height of Radish Plants (inches)

---

1 How can you use the line plot to tell how many plants are 2 inches tall?

_____

_____

2 Consider how the data in the line plot is clustered. What does the line plot say about the plant heights?

_____

_____

_____

Vocabulary

line plot a graph that uses Xs above a number line, or part of a number line, to show data. Line plots are useful for showing how data are grouped.

Solve.

Use this situation and the line plot for problems 3–6.

Colton puts grapes in plastic bags to sell at the farmer's market. He weighs each bag and records the weights in a line plot.

3 What is the difference in weight between the heaviest bag and the lightest bag of grapes?

Show your work.

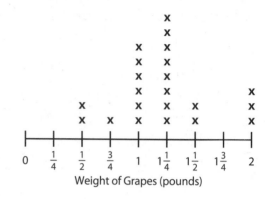

Weight of Grapes (pounds)

Solution: _____

4 How many bags of grapes weigh more than 1 pound and less than 2 pounds?

_____

5 Describe two different ways that a customer could buy $4\frac{1}{4}$ pounds of grapes.

_____

_____

6 Greg wants to buy two bags of grapes that have a total weight of $3\frac{3}{4}$ pounds. Is there a way that he can do this? Explain how you know.

_____

_____

_____

_____

7 Describe a different set of data that you could display on a line plot.

_____

_____

Name: _____

Identify Statistical and Non-statistical Questions

Study the example showing how to determine whether a question is statistical or not. Then solve problems 1–7.

Example

Abigail asked her classmates two questions. Are the questions statistical or not? Explain your answer.

What is your favorite after-school activity?

On what day does the computer club meet?

This is a statistical question because you can expect a variety of answers. You can use the answers to make a prediction about a larger group.

This is not a statistical question because no matter who you ask, the answer is always the same.

1 Explain how you can tell whether a question is statistical or non-statistical.

_____

_____

2 Maxwell asked 20 classmates these questions. Determine whether each question is statistical or non-statistical. Explain your answer.

a. How do you travel to school?

_____

_____

b. How many students in the class ride the bus to school?

_____

_____

c. What time do you get up on school mornings?

_____

_____

Vocabulary

statistical question a question that can have a variety of answers and can be used to make a prediction about a larger group.

Solve.

Use the following situation and table to solve problems 3–5.

Paulo asked 20 sixth graders a question and then displayed the results in this table.

Number of Pets	0	1	2	3	4	more than 4
Number of Students	2	8	5	2	1	2

3 What question could Paulo have asked?

_____

4 If Paulo asked 20 different sixth graders the same question, would he most likely get exactly the same results? Explain your thinking.

_____

_____

_____

5 Based on Paulo's results, what prediction could Paulo make about the sixth graders in his school?

_____

_____

6 Write a statistical question and a non-statistical question that you could ask your classmates about computer games.

statistical: _____

_____

non-statistical: _____

_____

7 Ariel wanted to ask her classmates a statistical question. She decided to ask them "How many books have you read this month?" Is Ariel's question statistical? Explain.

_____

_____

Name: _____

Reason and Write

Study the example. Underline two parts that you think make it a particularly good answer and a helpful example.

Example

Rebecca wants to collect statistical data about the amount of time that sixth graders in her school spend doing homework each school night.

What question could she ask? How many students might she ask? Describe the data she might collect, and draw a line plot to show an example of that data. Then explain how Rebecca can use this data to predict the results for all sixth graders in her school.

Show your work. Use a table or line plot, words, and numbers to explain your answer.

Possible answer is shown.

Rebecca could ask a group of 20 sixth graders a statistical question like: About how many hours do you spend doing homework each school night?

A line plot of data that she collects might look like this:

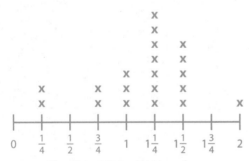

Time Spent Doing Homework on School Nights (hours)

Then she could see how the data clustered in the line plot and use that information to predict the number of hours that most sixth graders spend doing homework each school night. Based on this line plot, most sixth graders in my school spend $1\frac{1}{4}$ hours or $1\frac{1}{2}$ hours each school night doing homework.

Where does the example . . .
- answer all parts of the problem?
- use a table or line plot?
- use words?
- use numbers?
- explain how to use the data to make a prediction?

Solve the problem. Use what you learned from the model.

Dexter wants to collect statistical data about the weight of backpacks that sixth graders carry to school. Which is the better statistical question for Dexter to ask? Why?

- How much does your backpack weigh to the nearest half pound?

- Does your backpack weigh more than or less than 5 pounds?

How many students might he ask? Describe the data he might collect, and display the data in a table. Then explain how Dexter can use this data to predict the results for all sixth graders in his school.

Show your work. Use a table or line plot, words, and numbers to explain your answer.

Did you . . .

- answer all parts of the problem?

- use a table or line plot?

- use words?

- use numbers?

- explain how to use the data to make a prediction?

Dear Family,

> **Your child is learning about measures of center and variability.**

Measures of center are numbers that you can use to describe a set of data by its center, or middle. Some measures of center are:

- the *mean*, or average, of the data.

- the *median*, or middle number, of the data when it's organized from least to greatest.

- the *mode*, or most common value, of the data.

You can also describe the *variability* of a data set. Variability describes how the data varies or how spread out the data is.

- The *range* tells the span between the lowest and highest numbers in the data set.

- The *mean absolute deviation*, or *MAD*, tells the average distance of each number in the data from the mean.

Describing the way that a collection of statistical data varies can help you see a "big picture" of the data.

Consider the following example:

Ten families in a neighborhood donated money to a local community service club. A club member kept track of the amount of money each family gave and displayed the data in the line plot shown. Based on this data, what is the mean of the donation amounts?

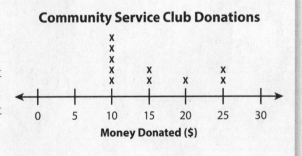

Community Service Club Donations

On the next page you will see two ways your child may find the mean, or average, of the community service club data.

Ten families in a neighborhood donated money to a local community service club. A club member kept track of the amount of money each family gave: $10, $10, $10, $10, $10, $15, $15, $20, $25, and $25. Based on this data, what is the mean of the donation amounts?

One way:
Apply the idea of fair sharing to find the mean.

Use the survey results to draw a graph that represents the amount of money that each of the 10 families donated. Think of each family as a letter.

```
                                   $   $
                               $   $   $
                       $   $   $   $   $
$   $   $   $   $   $   $   $   $   $
$   $   $   $   $   $   $   $   $   $
A   B   C   D   E   F   G   H   I   J
        $ = 5 dollars donated
```

Then, to show the mean, move the symbols on the graph so that each family donated an equal amount.

```
$   $   $   $   $   $   $   $   $   $
$   $   $   $   $   $   $   $   $   $
$   $   $   $   $   $   $   $   $   $
A   B   C   D   E   F   G   H   I   J
        $ = 5 dollars donated
```

The graph shows that the mean is 15.

Another way:
Add the data values.

$$10 + 10 + 10 + 10 + 10 + 15 + 15 + 20 + 25 + 25 = 150$$

Divide the sum by the number of data values.

$$\frac{150}{10} = 15$$

The mean is 15.

Answer: Both methods show that the mean, or average, of the community service club data is 15, which means that the average amount donated by a family to the community service club is $15.

Measures of Center and Variability

Name: _____

Prerequisite: Distribution of Data

Study the example showing how to interpret the distribution of data in a line plot. Then solve problems 1–8.

Example

There are several rare insects on display at the insect exhibit at a science museum. The line plot shows the lengths of the insects to the nearest $\frac{1}{8}$ inch. What is the distribution of the lengths of the insects?

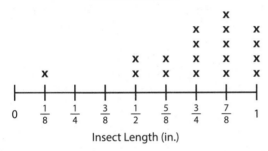

Insect Exhibit

Insect Length (in.)

Most of the data points are between $\frac{3}{4}$ and 1, so the insect lengths are clustered between $\frac{3}{4}$ and 1 inch.

---

1 The longest insect is how many times as long as the shortest insect? Write an equation to show your solution.

_____

2 Do any insects have a length that is very different from the rest of the insects? If so, what is the length?

_____

3 How would the line plot change if the insect lengths were clustered between $\frac{1}{8}$ and $\frac{1}{4}$ inch?

_____

_____

Vocabulary

distribution shows how spread out or how clustered data values are.

Solve.

Use the line plot for problems 4–8.

The line plot shows the amount of time it took some runners to finish a charity race to the nearest $\frac{1}{8}$ hour.

Fund-Raiser Run

```
                                      x
                                      x    x    x
                                 x    x    x    x
                            x    x    x    x    x
  x                    x    x    x    x    x    x
  +----+----+----+----+----+----+----+----+----+
  2   2⅛  2¼  2⅜  2½  2⅝  2¾  2⅞   3
```

Time (hours)

4 Tell whether each statement about the data in the line plot is *True* or *False*.

   a. None of the runners finished in exactly $2\frac{1}{2}$ hours. ☐ True ☐ False

   b. A time of 2 hours is uncommon. ☐ True ☐ False

   c. The most common time is $2\frac{3}{4}$ hours. ☐ True ☐ False

   d. Most runners finished in around $2\frac{7}{8}$ hours. ☐ True ☐ False

5 By how much do the times vary? Explain.

_____

6 Between which two times did most of the runners finish?

_____

7 Are any of the times very different from most of the times? If so, which time?

_____

8 Suppose the times for 10 additional runners were recorded, including a new slowest time and a new fastest time. What would be a set of reasonable times based on the data in the line plot? Explain.

_____

_____

_____

_____

Name: _____

Mean

Study the example showing how to describe the center of a data set using mean. Then solve problems 1–8.

Example

Ten people were asked how much money they plan to donate to the new library fund. Their answers were $20, $20, $20, $40, $40, $40, $40, $40, $40, and $100. What is the mean, or average, donation?

You can draw a graph that represents how much each person plans to donate. Then, to find the mean, move the symbols to show what each person would donate if all of them donated the same amount.

$ = 20 dollars donated

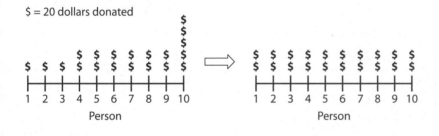

1. What is the mean donation? Explain how the graph on the right shows the mean.

   _____

   _____

2. Complete the equations to show another way to find the mean.

   ____ + ____ + ____ + ____ + ____ + ____ + ____ + ____ + ____ + ____ = ____

   _____ ÷ 10 = _____

3. Are there any outliers in the data? If so, calculate the mean without the outliers and explain how the mean is affected.

   _____

   _____

Solve.

Use the following situation to solve problems 4–6.

The numbers of hours that 12 students say they typically spend on homework in a week are 0, 2, 8, 8, 8, 8, 8, 8, 10, 10, 10, and 10.

4 What is the mean number of hours?

Show your work.

Solution: _____

5 What are the outliers in the data set? How do you know that they are outliers?

_____

_____

6 Explain how the outliers affect the mean. Then find the mean without the outliers to justify your answer.

_____

_____

_____

7 The mean of six values is 7. There is one outlier that pulls the mean higher than the center. What could the data set be? What is the mean without the outlier?

_____

8 Dee's scores for a computer game are 20, 18, 22, 12, 25, and 20. Li's scores are 21, 20, 20, 16, 21, and 16. Who has the higher mean score? By how much?

Show your work.

Solution: _____

Name: _____

Median and Mode

Study the example showing how to describe the center of a data set using median and mode. Then solve problems 1–8.

Example

A team's scores for ten basketball games are 46, 42, 43, 44, 42, 40, 42, 42, 44, and 43. Find the median and the mode of the basketball scores.

List the scores in order from least to greatest to find the median. The median is the middle number. When there are two middle numbers, the median is the mean, or average, of the two numbers.

40, 42, 42, 42, 42, 43, 43, 44, 44, 46

$42 + 43 = 85$ $85 \div 2 = 42.5$

The median score is 42.5.

The number that appears most often in a data set is the mode. The mode of this data set is 42.

1 Jason says that more than half of the values of any data set are above the median. Is he correct? Explain.

_____

_____

_____

2 What would the median score be if 40 were removed from the set of scores?

_____

3 The line plot shows the basketball scores from above. Explain how the line plot shows the mode.

_____

_____

Basketball Games

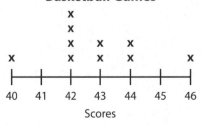

Scores

Solve.

Use the following situation to solve problems 4–6.

The heights, in inches, of some small trees for sale at a garden store are 62, 62, 59, 61, 59, 70, 59, and 62.

4 What is the median height?

Show your work.

Solution: _____

5 What is the mode? Explain.

_____

_____

6 What is the mean height? Explain why the mean height is different from the median.

_____

_____

7 Imena's math test scores are 83, 93, 78, 89, and 83. She has one more math test this semester. What score must she get on the test to have a median score of 85?

Show your work.

Solution: _____

8 Does the median of a data set have to be a value of the data set? Explain.

_____

_____

Name: _____

Variability

Study the example showing how to describe the spread of data sets. Then solve problems 1–10.

Example

Ten people donated the following amounts of money at a school fundraiser: $5, $30, $10, $10, $5, $5, $20, $30, $20, $15. What is the range of the data?

Range is the difference between the greatest and least values. Range gives you an idea of how spread out data values are. Here, the smallest donation is $5 and the largest donation is $30, so the range is $30 − $5 = $25.

1 MAD is another way to measure spread. It is the average distance each value is from the mean. The mean of the donation amounts in the table is 15.

a. Find the absolute value of each deviation. Write the answers in the table.

b. What is the MAD? Show how you found the MAD.

_____

_____

Donation	Deviation from Mean	Absolute Value of Deviation
5	−10	
5	−10	
5	−10	
10	−5	
10	−5	
15	0	
20	5	
20	5	
30	15	
30	15	

2 What does the MAD tell you about this data set?

_____

_____

3 Compare each deviation to the mean. When is the deviation positive? When is it negative? When is it zero?

_____

_____

_____

_____

Lesson 27 Measures of Center and Variability   **311**

Solve.

Use the table to solve problems 5–8.

The data values in the table represent the ages of children at a park.

Age (years)	Deviation from Mean	Absolute Value of Deviation
4	−4	4
6	−2	
6	−2	
8	0	
8	0	
8	0	
10	2	
10	2	
10	2	
10	2	

5 What is the range of the data values? Write an equation to show your solution.

_____

6 The mean of the data values is 8. Use the mean to complete the table.

7 What is the MAD?

Show your work.

Solution: _____

8 What does the MAD tell you about the data set?

_____

9 Could the MAD of a data set be a negative value? Explain.

_____

_____

10 The MAD of a set of six data values is 10. The mean is 20. What could the data values be? Show that the mean is 20 and the MAD is 10.

Show your work.

Solution: _____

Name: _____

Measures of Center and Variability

Solve the problems.

---

1 The lengths, in seconds, of eight commercials are 15, 15, 15, 15, 20, 20, 30, and 30. The mean of the times is 20 seconds. What is the mean absolute deviation (MAD)? What does the MAD tell you?

How do you find mean absolute deviation?

Show your work.

Solution: _____

_____

---

2 The line plot shows the number of books that each of 14 students checked out of the library.

Which statements are true? Select all that apply.

Library Books

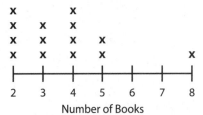

Number of Books

A The data points are clustered near 5.

B The range of the data is 6.

C The graph is skewed left.

D There are no outliers in the data set.

What does the distribution of the data in the line plot tell you?

---

3 A set of six data values have the same mean, median, and mode. The data values are not all the same. What could the data values and the mean, median, and mode be?

How can you find the median of a set of data with an even number of values?

_____

_____

Solve.

4 The line plot shows the ages of eight students on the track team.

Track Team

```
                    x
x           x   x
x           x   x           x
+---+---+---+---+---+---+---+
9   10  11  12  13  14  15
        Ages of Students
```

> What does each X in the line plot represent?

Tell whether each statement is *True* or *False*.

a. The modes are 9 and 12. ☐ True ☐ False

b. The median is 12.5. ☐ True ☐ False

c. The mean is 12. ☐ True ☐ False

d. The range is 13. ☐ True ☐ False

5 In a survey, 10 students and 10 teachers were asked how many hours of sleep they get at night. Here are the survey results:

Students: 6, 7, 8, 8, 9, 9, 10, 10, 10, 10

Teachers: 4, 5, 6, 6, 7, 7, 8, 8, 8, 8

What is the mean of each data set? What do the means tell you about each data set? Use the means to compare the data sets.

Show your work.

> Remember that the mean of a data set is the same as the average value.

Solution: _____

_____

Dear Family,

Your child is learning about displaying data using dot plots, histograms, and box plots.

The world today is full of data that is constantly being collected and distributed in various forms. Dot plots, histograms, and box plots are different ways of displaying data.

The dot plot at the right shows the number of songs downloaded in one month by a random sample of 15 teenagers. A dot plot shows all the data values in a data set.

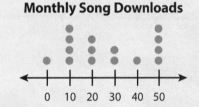

Monthly Song Downloads

The histogram at the right shows the same data as the dot plot above. The histogram shows the data grouped in intervals.

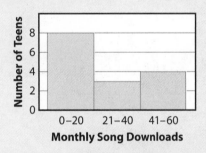

A box plot shows a 5-number summary of data. The box plot at the right is based on the same data as in the two displays above. The box plot describes the spread of data above and below the median, 20.

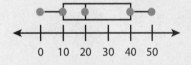

Consider the following example:

> Workers have the following commute times, in minutes:
>
> 15, 25, 25, 25, 30, 30, 30, 30, 30, 40, 40, 40, 45, 45, 45
>
> Construct a dot plot, histogram, and box plot to display and analyze the data.

The next page shows the three ways your child may display and analyze the data.

NEXT

Lesson 28 Display Data on Dot Plots, Histograms, and Box Plots **315**

Workers have the following commute times, in minutes:

15, 25, 25, 25, 30, 30, 30, 30, 30, 40, 40, 40, 45, 45, 45

Construct a dot plot, histogram, and box plot to display and analyze the data.

Dot plot: Display the data in a dot plot. The dot plot is best for finding out the most common commute time. The most common commute time is 30 minutes.

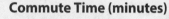

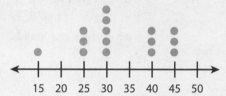

Commute Time (minutes)

Histogram: Display the data in a histogram. Choose intervals and organize the data.

Commute Time (minutes)	Number of Workers
0–14	0
15–29	4
30–44	8
45–59	3

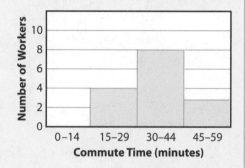

The histogram shows that 8 workers have a commute time between 30 and 44 minutes.

Box plot: Display the data in a box plot.

15, 25, 25, **25**, 30, 30, 30, **30**, 30, 40, 40, **40**, 45, 45, **45**

The *lower quartile* is the middle number between the minimum and the median. The *upper quartile* is the middle number between the median and the maximum.

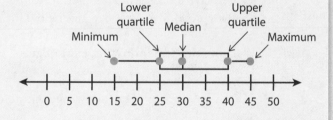

Answer: All three ways display the data about the workers' commuting times. They all give you at least an idea of what the shortest and longest commutes are, and that a commute of 30 minutes is typical.

Display Data on Dot Plots, Histograms, and Box Plots

Name: _____

Prerequisite: Mean, Median, and Mode

Study the example showing how to find the mean, median, and mode of a data set. Then solve problems 1–6.

Example

The weights, in pounds, of nine small dogs at a dog park are 26, 28, 20, 20, 22, 30, 28, 14, and 28. Find the mean, median, and mode of the weights.

To find the mean, add the values and divide by the number of values.

$26 + 28 + 20 + 20 + 22 + 30 + 28 + 14 + 28 = 216$

$216 \div 9 = \mathbf{24}$

To find the median, list the data points in order. The number in the middle is the median.

14, 20, 20, 22, **26**, 28, 28, 28, 30

To find the mode, look for the most common number.

14, 20, 20, 22, 26, **28** , **28** , **28** , 30

1 Why is the mean less than the median?

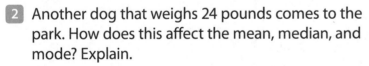

_____

_____

2 Another dog that weighs 24 pounds comes to the park. How does this affect the mean, median, and mode? Explain.

_____

_____

_____

_____

Vocabulary

mean is the average of the values in a data set.

median is the middle number in a data set.

mode is the number that appears most often in a data set.

7, 9, 10, 13, 15, 15, 15

The mean is 12.

The median is 13.

The mode is 15.

Solve.

Use the following situation to solve problems 3–5.

A group of sixth-grade students did sit-ups for
one minute. The number of sit-ups that each student
did is shown below.

62, 60, 56, 52, 63, 55, 58

3 Does the data set have a mode? Explain.

_____

4 What is the mean of the data set? What does it tell you
about the situation?

_____

_____

5 A group of seventh-grade students also did sit-ups for
one minute. They did the same mean number of sit-ups
in one minute as the sixth graders did, but they did a
total of 522 sit-ups. How is this possible? Explain.

_____

_____

_____

6 Claire and Gina kept track of the number of hours that
they practiced each week for an ice skating competition.
On average, who practiced more?

Claire: 12, 8, 10, 7, 8, 5, 8, 10, 12, 8

Gina: 10, 6, 12, 6, 10, 6, 10, 12, 6, 10

Show your work.

Solution: _____

Name: _____

Histograms

Study the example showing how to display data in a histogram. Then solve problems 1–9.

Example

Fifteen students were asked how much money they spent, to the nearest whole dollar, in the school cafeteria one week. Their responses are shown below. Display the data in a histogram.

2, 3, 5, 6, 9, 11, 11, 12, 12, 12, 14, 15, 15, 17, 19

First, choose the intervals you want to use and then make a table of the data using your intervals. Then use the table to make a histogram.

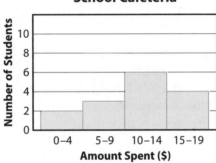

School Cafeteria

Amount Spent ($)	Number of Students
0–4	2
5–9	3
10–14	6
15–19	4

1 Do the table or the histogram show any individual data values? Explain.

No b/c it is in a range.

2 What does the height of a bar in a histogram represent?

# of students

3 The histogram at the right shows the data from above organized into larger intervals. What advantage might there be to using smaller rather than larger intervals in a histogram?

_____

_____

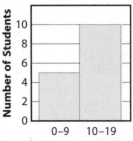

Solve.

Use the situation below to solve problems 4–8.

The times, rounded to the nearest whole minute, that thirteen students waited in line to buy a ticket to a new movie are shown below.

5, 5, 6, 6, 6, 9, 9, 9, 12, 14, 31, 34, 38

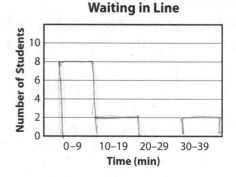

Waiting in Line

4 Complete the histogram to represent the data.

5 Describe how you drew the histogram in problem 4.

   I based it off how many numbers are in the interval

6 Is there a bar above every interval? Explain why or why not.

   NO, b/c there is not always a number

7 Can you use the histogram to tell how many students waited in line for less than 15 minutes? Explain.

8 Look at the data set at the top of the page again. If the histogram had twice as many intervals, what would it show about the spread of the data that is not shown in the histogram that you made?

9 The ages of nineteen people in a walkathon are shown below. Make a histogram of the ages. Choose intervals for the *x*-axis and a scale for the *y*-axis and label both axes.

   8, 8, 9, 9, 10, 10, 10, 11, 11, 12,
   14, 15, 16, 20, 20, 25, 25, 25, 28

Name: _____

Box Plots

Study the example showing how to display data in a box plot. Then solve problems 1–8.

Example

Fifteen students were asked how many hours they spent one week riding their bikes. Here are their responses, in order from least to greatest. Display the data in a box plot.

2, 3, 3, 3, 4, 5, 6, 8, 8, 9, 9, 10, 11, 12, 14

To display the data in a box plot, you need to find five values: the minimum, the maximum, the median, the lower quartile, and the upper quartile.

The minimum is the least value, 2. The maximum is the greatest value, 14. The median, 8, is the middle number. The lower quartile, 3, is the middle number between the minimum and the median. The upper quartile, 10, is the middle number between the median and the maximum.

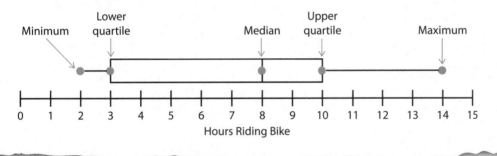

1 What do the lines that extend from the ends of the rectangular box represent?

_____

_____

_____

2 The interquartile range (IQR) is the difference between the upper and lower quartiles. What is the IQR for the data? What does it represent?

_____

_____

Solve.

Use this situation for problems 3–8.

A meteorologist reported the number of inches of snow that fell in each of nine weeks.

2, 3, 3, 4, 5, 6, 6, 6, 9

3 What are the minimum and maximum values in the data set?

_____

4 What is the median? _____

5 What are the lower quartile and the upper quartile? Explain how to find both values.

_____

_____

_____

6 Use your answers to problems 3–5 to draw a box plot using the given number line.

Snowfall (inches)

7 Omar says that the length of the rectangular box in the box plot represents the IQR. Is Omar's statement correct? Explain. What is the IQR?

_____

_____

_____

8 Would you use the range or the IQR to describe the spread of this data? Explain.

_____

_____

Name: _____

Display and Analyze Data

Study the example showing how to display and analyze data in a dot plot, histogram, and box plot. Then solve problems 1–6.

Example

The amounts of money that 13 students paid for used DVDs are shown below, in dollars. The price of each DVD is $5.

25, 15, 5, 20, 10, 25, 10, 15, 20, 20, 10, 20, 5

You can display the data in a dot plot, histogram, and box plot.

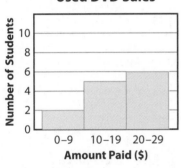

1 Which graph is easiest to use to find the median amount that students paid? Explain.

_____

_____

2 Which graph would you use if you wanted to know how many students spent less than $10? Explain.

_____

_____

3 Which graph shows the amount of money that the most number of students spent? Explain.

_____

_____

Solve.

The situation below and the three graphs at the right are from the example problem on the previous page. Use them to solve problems 4–5.

Used DVD Sales

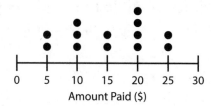

The amounts of money, in dollars, that 13 students paid for used DVDs are listed below and represented in the graphs. The price of each DVD is $5.

25, 15, 5, 20, 10, 25, 10, 15, 20, 20, 10, 20, 5

4 Every student who purchased 3 or more DVDs gets a free poster. How many students get free posters? Which graph can you use to solve the problem? Explain.

Used DVD Sales

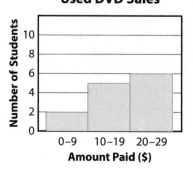

_____

_____

_____

_____

5 Layla says that she can use the histogram and the box plot to find the least and greatest amounts that students spent on DVDs. Is she correct? Explain.

Used DVD Sales

_____

_____

_____

_____

6 Students were asked how many movies they saw last year. Their responses are shown below.

20, 6, 12, 24, 12, 6, 12, 16, 8, 10, 18, 20, 22, 4, 22, 24

Display the data in a dot plot, histogram, or box plot. Write a question that can be easily answered using the graph you chose.

_____

_____

Name: _____

Display Data on Dot Plots, Histograms, and Box Plots

Solve the problems.

1 The following data represents the number of people who live in each of nine houses on a certain street: 8, 3, 3, 10, 5, 8, 6, 8, and 2. Use the partial number line to make a box plot of the data.

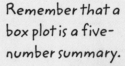

Remember that a box plot is a five-number summary.

```
 ├──┼──┼──┼──┼──┼──┼──┼──┼──┼──┤
 0  1  2  3  4  5  6  7  8  9  10
         Number of People
```

2 Students recorded how many hours of volunteer work they did one month. The dot plot shows the data.

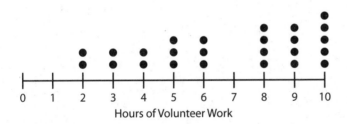

What does each dot represent?

```
 ├──┼──┼──┼──┼──┼──┼──┼──┼──┼──┤
 0  1  2  3  4  5  6  7  8  9  10
       Hours of Volunteer Work
```

Which of the following statements about the dot plot is true? Select all that apply.

A   There is a cluster of data points around 8, 9, and 10.

B   The mode of the data set is 8.

C   The total number of students is 25.

D   The range of the dot plot is 10.

Richard chose **D** as a correct answer. How did he get that answer?

_____

_____

Solve.

3 The box plot represents the number of inches of rainfall in one city during each of the last 12 months.

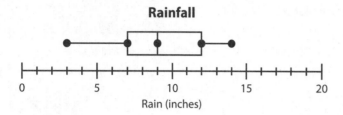

Rainfall

Rain (inches)

What information does a box plot show?

Can the box plot be used to answer the question? Choose *Yes* or *No*.

a. What is the median rainfall? ☐ Yes ☐ No

b. In how many months was the rainfall 6 inches or more? ☐ Yes ☐ No

c. What is the greatest amount of rainfall in the data set? ☐ Yes ☐ No

d. What is the IQR? ☐ Yes ☐ No

4 Students were asked how much money, to the nearest whole dollar, they spent on entertainment in one month. A total of 28 students responded. Nineteen students spent $20 or more. Twenty-five students spent $10 or more. Nine students spent between $30 and $39. No one spent more than $39. Draw a histogram that represents the data.

Make a list of the intervals and the number in each interval first.

©Curriculum Associates, LLC   Copying is not permitted.

Dear Family,

Your child is learning about analyzing numerical data.

Your child has already learned:

- that a data set can be described by measures of center, such as *mean, median,* and *mode.*

- that a data set can also be described by measures of variability, such as *range* and *mean absolute deviation.*

- how to display data in dot plots, histograms, and box plots.

Now your child is learning how to analyze a collection of data in order to make meaningful observations about the data.

Analyzing data is an important skill in today's world. Many jobs involve understanding and interpreting data, from analyzing customer service records to planning efficient railway or air transportation routes. Even routine tasks such as deciding which products to purchase or which healthcare plan to choose involve analyzing data.

Consider the following example:

A minor league baseball team conducted a survey of a random sample of spectators at one game. The table shows the ages of 15 spectators. What does the median tell you about the data? What does the interquartile range tell you about the variability in the ages of the spectators?

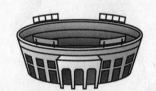

22	10	10	31	36	31	8	23
31	16	48	23	21	30	42	

On the next page you will see two ways your child may analyze this data using median and interquartile range.

A minor league baseball team collected data about the ages of spectators in a random sample of 15 spectators at one game:

22, 10, 10, 31, 36, 31, 8, 23, 31, 16, 48, 23, 21, 30, 42

What does the median tell the team about the data? What does the interquartile range tell about the variability in the ages?

One way: Find the median. Then find the quartile values to understand the interquartile range.

Make an ordered list of the data.   8, 10, 10, 16, 21, 22, 30, 23, 23, 31, 31, 31, 36, 42, 48

Identify the minimum, the lower quartile, the median, the upper quartile, and the maximum.

Minimum   Q1   Median   Q3   Maximum

⑧ 10 10 ⑯ 21 22 23 ㉓ 23 31 31 ㉛ 36 42 ㊽

Calculate the range between the upper quartile and the lower quartile to find the interquartile range (IQR): $31 - 16 = 15$.

The median age is 23. The interquartile range (IQR), 15, tells that the middle 50% of the ages are within a range of 15 years.

Another way: Draw a box plot to understand the interquartile range.

The median age is 23.

The box shows the interquartile range. It shows that half of the ages are between 16 and 31.

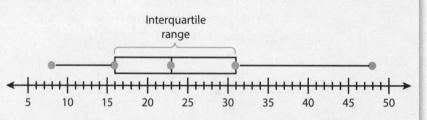

Interquartile range

5   10   15   20   25   30   35   40   45   50

Answer: Both methods show that the median age is 23 and the interquartile range is 15 years. The median age is 23 years old, so about 50% of the spectators are older than 23 and about 50% are younger. The interquartile range, 15, means about 50% of the spectators have ages between 16 and 31, about 25% are younger than 16, and about 25% are older than 31.

Analyze Numerical Data

Name: _____

Study the example showing how to display data in a box plot. Then solve problems 1–7.

Example

Fishermen recorded the lengths, in inches, of fifteen fish that they caught on a fishing trip: 22, 14, 15, 3, 9, 20, 20, 11, 9, 10, 18, 19, 10, 12, 15. Make a box plot of the data.

First, order the lengths from shortest to longest.

3, 9, 9, 10, 10, 11, 12, 14, 15, 15, 18, 19, 20, 20, 22

The minimum is the least value, 3. The maximum is the greatest value, 22. The median, 14, is the middle number. The lower quartile, 10, is the middle number between the minimum and the median. The upper quartile, 19, is the middle number between the median and the maximum.

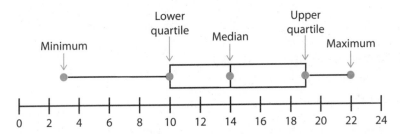

Vocabulary

box plot a five-number summary that includes the minimum, the lower quartile, the median, the upper quartile, and the maximum.

lower quartile the middle number between the minimum and the median in an ordered set of numbers.

upper quartile the middle number between the median and the maximum in an ordered set of numbers.

1 What is the interquartile range (IQR) of the data? Does the IQR include outliers? What does the IQR tell you about the fish lengths?

_____

_____

2 What is the range of the data? Does the range include outliers? What does the range tell you about the fish lengths?

_____

_____

Solve.

3 The number of pounds that each kitten or cat at an animal rescue center weighs is listed below. Display the data in a box plot.

1, 1, 2, 3, 3, 3, 3, 4, 4, 4, 4, 5, 5, 5, 5, 6, 8, 8, 10, 12

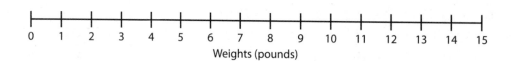

Weights (pounds)

4 What are the lower quartile, the upper quartile, and the IQR for the data in problem 3?

_____

5 Explain what the box that you drew in the box plot in problem 3 represents in terms of the weights.

_____

_____

6 Tomas listed the amounts that he deposited in his savings account each week for 15 weeks. Write the correct amount in each box below the box plot.

$25, $32, $32, $35, $35, $35, $35, $38, $40, $40, $43, $43, $44, $45, $55

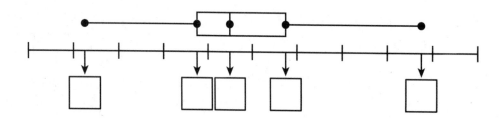

7 In problem 6, what do the lines to the right and to the left of the rectangular box in the box plot represent?

_____

_____

_____

Name: _____

Use Interquartile Range to Describe Data

Study the example showing how the IQR measures variability. Then solve problems 1–7.

Example

The heights of trees, in feet, in a city park are listed below.

3, 13, 16, 18, 19, 21, 21, 23, 25, 25, 27, 27, 31, 33, 43

What does the IQR tell you about the variability of the heights?

Draw a box plot to help you visualize the quartile values.

Height of Trees (ft)

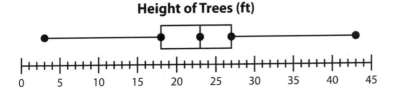

The IQR is $27 - 18 = 9$. It tells me that the middle 50% of the heights of the trees are in the 9-foot range between 18 feet and 27 feet.

---

1 What is the median of this data? What does the median tell you about the heights of the trees?

_____

_____

2 Are there any outliers in this data set? If so, what are they? Explain.

_____

_____

3 Explain why the median and IQR are not affected by outliers.

_____

_____

_____

Solve.

Use the following situation and box plot to solve problems 4–7.

The speeds of cars, in miles per hour, along a neighborhood street were recorded and are shown in the box plot.

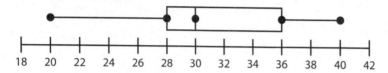

4   Can you tell from the box plot whether any one of the cars was traveling at a speed of 34 miles per hour?

_____

_____

_____

5   Does the box plot show the number of car speeds that were recorded? Explain.

_____

_____

_____

6   What is the range of data shown in the box plot? What is the IQR? Explain why it might be more helpful to use the IQR rather than the range to describe this data set.

_____

_____

_____

7   Write a question about the distribution of car speeds that you can answer by looking at the box plot. Answer your question.

_____

_____

_____

Name: _____

Use Mean Absolute Deviation

Study the example showing how to analyze data using the mean absolute deviation. Then solve problems 1–8.

Example

The table shows the number of points scored by a basketball team during the first 10 games of the season.

66	53	48	68	71
42	56	55	49	58

The mean of this data set is 56.6. Make a table to help you find the mean absolute deviation (MAD) of the data.

The mean absolute deviation (MAD) of a data set can help you understand the variability of the data in the set. To help you find the MAD, make a table that shows the data values in the set, their deviations from the mean, and the absolute values of those deviations.

Data Value	66	53	48	68	71	42	56	55	49	58
Deviation from Mean	9.4	−3.6	−8.6	11.4	14.4	−14.6	−0.6	−1.6	−7.6	1.4
Absolute Deviation	9.4	3.6	8.6	11.4	14.4	14.6	0.6	1.6	7.6	1.4

1 Look at the table. Explain how the deviation from the mean was calculated for the data values 66 and 53. Why is one deviation positive and the other negative?

_____

_____

2 What is the MAD of the data values in the example? Explain how you found the MAD.

_____

_____

3 What does the MAD tell you about the number of points scored?

_____

_____

Vocabulary

mean absolute deviation (MAD) average distance between each data value and the mean. It describes how spread out the data is.

Solve.

Use the data in the table to solve problems 4–8.

Price of Laptop Computers ($)				
390	230	290	350	270
340	320	890	220	400

4 What is the mean of this data?

Show your work.

Solution: _____

5 What does the mean tell you about the prices of the computers?

_____

6 What is the MAD of this data?

Show your work.

Solution: _____

7 What does the MAD tell you about the prices of the computers? Does the MAD tell you that there is a lot of variability in the prices or not?

_____

_____

_____

8 Which data value from the table would you delete to make the greatest change possible to the MAD? Explain.

_____

_____

Name: _____

Analyze Numerical Data

Solve the problems.

1 The dot plot shows the number of books that some sixth graders read last month. Find the mean and the median.

What does each dot on the plot represent?

Number of Books Read

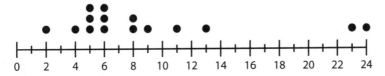

```
0   2   4   6   8  10  12  14  16  18  20  22  24
```

Show your work.

Solution: _____

2 In problem 1, is the mean or the median a better measure of center? Explain.

_____

_____

How do outliers affect the measures of center?

3 The histogram shows the time, to the nearest whole minute, that some students spend each week doing chores. How many students spend more than $\frac{1}{2}$ hour doing chores?

A 4 **C** 12

B 5 **D** 20

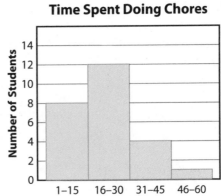

Time Spent Doing Chores

How many values are in each interval?

Solve.

4 The box plot shows the amount of money raised by some students for a school fund-raiser. Tell whether each statement is *True* or *False*.

> What are the five numbers represented in a box plot?

25 30 35 40 45 50 55 60 65 70 75 80 85
Money ($)

a. The variability of the middle 50% of the money raised is less than the variability of the lower 25%. ☐ True ☐ False

b. The box plot shows that 80 students raised money. ☐ True ☐ False

c. If the $30 value is replaced by a $50 value, the IQR will be the same. ☐ True ☐ False

5 What is the IQR in problem 4? What does it tell you about the data values in the box plot?

> In the box plot, what does the rectangular box represent?

_____

_____

_____

6 Josh recorded the amount of time, in minutes, that he exercised during the first 10 days of the month.

30, 45, 25, 25, 35, 5, 40, 35, 30, 20

The mean of the data is 29. Find the MAD of the data. What does the MAD tell you?

> What does mean absolute deviation measure?

Show your work.

Solution: _____

_____

Name: _____

Data Remix

What you need: Recording Sheet, Data Cards

Directions

- Your goal is to collect a set of data that best fits the Data Summary for each round on your Recording Sheet. Your cards are your data set.

- To start a round, shuffle and deal 7 cards to each player. Place the rest in a stack and turn one card faceup to start a discard pile.

- On your turn, you may draw 1 card from the stack, take the top card from the discard pile, or pass. If you take a card, you must discard one so that you end with 7 cards.

- In a round, each player gets to pick from the stack or discard pile 3 times. The resulting 7 cards make up the data set.

- To complete a round, write your data set on your Recording Sheet. Calculate and record the values listed in the Data Summary. The player whose data best matches the Data Summary gets 1 point.

- Play 5 rounds. The player with the most points wins.

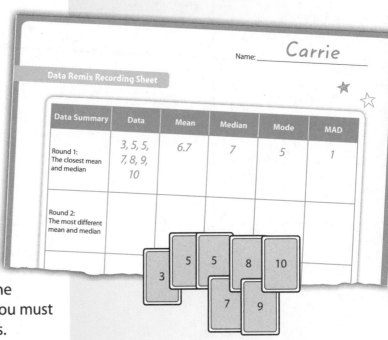

Name: **Carrie**

Data Remix Recording Sheet ★ ☆

Data Summary	Data	Mean	Median	Mode	MAD
Round 1: The closest mean and median	3, 5, 5, 7, 8, 9, 10	6.7	7	5	1
Round 2: The most different mean and median					

> I have to think about what numbers will help me meet the goal for each round. Sometimes I want numbers that are close together. At other times I need numbers that are more spread out.

Data Remix Recording Sheet

Data Summary	Data	Mean	Median	Mode	MAD
Round 1: The closest mean and median					
Round 2: The most different mean and median					
Round 3: The least MAD value					
Round 4: The greatest MAD value					
Round 5: No mode					

Points: _____ + _____ + _____ + _____ + _____ = _____

       Round 1   **Round 2**   **Round 3**   **Round 4**   **Round 5**   **Total**

1-10 Number Cards

1	2	3	4
5	6	7	8
9	10	1	2
3	4	5	6
7	8	9	10

1–10 Number Cards

1	2	3	4
5	6	7	8
9	10	1	2
3	4	5	6
7	8	9	10

Statistics and Probability

In this unit you learned to:	Lesson
recognize what makes a question a statistical question.	26
calculate measures of center such as mean and median.	27
calculate measures of spread such as range and mean absolute deviation.	27
display data accurately with a dot plot, histogram, or box plot.	28
describe data using measures of center and measures of spread.	29

Use these skills to solve problems 1–6.

1 You ask 20 students from the same class one of the survey questions below. Which question is a statistical question? Select all that apply.

A What was the highest score on the last math test?

B How long did you spend studying for the test?

C How many problems were on the last math test?

D What is your favorite subject?

2 Which of these can be determined from a box plot? Select all that apply.

A mean

B median

C mode

D range

E interquartile range

F mean absolute deviation

3 Create a set of six data values such that the mode is 6, the median is 6.5, and the mean is 7.

_____

4 For which data set is the median a better measure of center than the mean?

A 13, 14, 16, 16, 17, 18, 20

B 4, 12, 15, 16, 17, 19, 21

C 11, 13, 14, 15, 18, 19, 20

D 8, 10, 12, 14, 16, 18, 20

Solve.

5 Answer the questions about a histogram. Select *Yes* or *No*.

a. Is a histogram more useful than a dot plot to show data with a very large range? ☐ Yes ☐ No

b. Should each interval included in the histogram be the same size? ☐ Yes ☐ No

c. Is it always possible to find the mean using a histogram? ☐ Yes ☐ No

d. Is it always possible to find the median using a histogram? ☐ Yes ☐ No

e. Is it always possible to find the mode using a histogram? ☐ Yes ☐ No

f. Is it always possible to find the maximum and minimum values using a histogram? ☐ Yes ☐ No

6 The dot plot shows the number of students in different classrooms in East School.

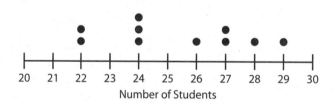

Number of Students

Select whether each statement is *True* or *False*.

a. There are 9 data values in the set. ☐ True ☐ False

b. The median is 25. ☐ True ☐ False

c. The mode is 24. ☐ True ☐ False

d. The mean is 25.3. ☐ True ☐ False

e. The mean absolute deviation is 2.24. ☐ True ☐ False

f. The interquartile range is 3. ☐ True ☐ False

Name: _____

Answer the questions and show all your work on separate paper.

Mr. Vila puts students in groups to time them in the 100-meter dash. He writes the times, in seconds, in the tables below.

Group A

14	16	17	15
13	13	16	14
17	16	20	18

Group B

15	13	19	17
14	14	16	14
18	15	18	16

Group C

13	19	16	14
16	19	15	18
16	15	16	18

Group D

13	17	16	15
14	13	15	14
17	14	17	15

Mr. Vila wants you to analyze the data he collected.
- Pick two groups of students.
- Organize the data in a display that will help you easily find the mean and median times for each group. Show how to find the mean and median for each data set.
- Calculate the mean absolute deviation for each group.
- Use the results to compare the running times of the two groups. Tell which group has the faster average time and which group has greater variability in times.

Reflect on Mathematical Practices

After you complete the task, choose one of the following questions to answer.

1 **Tools** What tools did you use to organize the data before completing your calculations? Why did you use these tools?

2 **Use Models** What data displays did you use to show the data? How did they help you find a solution?

Word Bank Here are some words that you might use in your answer.

mean	average	dot plot
median	mean absolute deviation	variability

Models Here are some models that you might use to find the solution.

Time							
Number of Students							

Sentence Starters Here are some sentence starters that might help you explain your work.

To find the median, _____

There is greater variability _____

By comparing the mean of each group, _____

My Examples

line plot

a graph that uses Xs above a number line to show data; line plots are useful for showing how data is grouped

statistical question

a question that can have a variety of answers and can be used to make a prediction about a larger group

distribution

shows how spread out or how clustered data values are

mean

the average of the values in a data set; the sum of all the values divided by the number of values.

7, 9, 10, 13, 15, 15, 15

The mean is 12.

My Examples

median

the middle number in a data set when all the values are listed from least to greatest

7, 9, 10, 13, 15, 15, 15

The median is 13.

mode

the number that appears most often in a data set

7, 9, 10, 13, 15, 15, 15

The mode is 15.

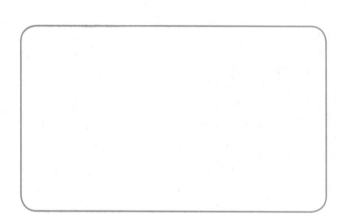

box plot

a five-number summary that includes the minimum, the lower quartile, the median, the upper quartile, and the maximum; shown graphically next to a number line

lower quartile

the middle number between the minimum and the median in an ordered set of numbers

upper quartile

the middle number between the median and the maximum in an ordered set of numbers

mean absolute deviation (MAD)

average distance between each data value and the mean; it is a way to tell how spread-out the data are.

My Words

_____

_____

_____

_____

_____

_____

_____

My Words

My Examples

Fluency Table of Contents

Compute with Percents—Skills Practice

Name: _____

Find the percent.

1 30% of 250 = _____

2 90% of 130 = _____

3 15% of 80 = _____

4 10% of 70 = _____

5 110% of 630 = _____

6 125% of 84 = _____

7 20% of 75 = _____

8 15% of 40 = _____

9 25% of 60 = _____

10 70% of 120 = _____

11 80% of 80 = _____

12 50% of 82 = _____

13 29% of 300 = _____

14 11% of 100 = _____

15 75% of 32 = _____

16 50% of 196 = _____

17 100% of 90 = _____

18 10% of 720 = _____

19 80% of 25 = _____

20 60% of 70 = _____

21 8% of 200 = _____

22 150% of 80 = _____

23 35% of 40 = _____

24 40% of 120 = _____

Compute with Percents—Skills Practice

Name: _____

Find the percent. Form B

1. 20% of 15 = _____

2. 140% of 55 = _____

3. 60% of 105 = _____

4. 90% of 170 = _____

5. 50% of 96 = _____

6. 25% of 116 = _____

7. 75% of 24 = _____

8. 100% of 80 = _____

9. 10% of 390 = _____

10. 25% of 480 = _____

11. 19% of 400 = _____

12. 40% of 35 = _____

13. 30% of 520 = _____

14. 70% of 40 = _____

15. 80% of 140 = _____

16. 50% of 122 = _____

17. 11% of 600 = _____

18. 90% of 260 = _____

19. 48% of 200 = _____

20. 75% of 148 = _____

21. 60% of 5 = _____

22. 110% of 80 = _____

23. 40% of 120 = _____

24. 25% of 40 = _____

Name: _____

Use the part and the percent to find the whole.

Form A

1 6 = 10% of _____

2 62 = 50% of _____

3 15 = 25% of _____

4 12 = 48% of _____

5 3 = 30% of _____

6 8 = 40% of _____

7 49 = 70% of _____

8 52 = 26% of _____

9 50 = 20% of _____

10 9 = 75% of _____

11 32 = 80% of _____

12 11 = 100% of _____

13 150 = 50% of _____

14 81 = 90% of _____

15 186 = 62% of _____

16 12 = 20% of _____

17 24 = 75% of _____

18 40 = 40% of _____

19 35 = 70% of _____

20 27 = 10% of _____

21 98 = 49% of _____

22 80 = 40% of _____

23 15 = 15% of _____

24 30 = 75% of _____

Compute with Percents—Skills Practice

Name: _____

Use the part and the percent to find the whole.   Form B

1 18 = 90% of _____   **2** 70 = 70% of _____   **3** 54 = 50% of _____

4 14 = 20% of _____   **5** 66 = 11% of _____   **6** 64 = 80% of _____

7 16 = 25% of _____   **8** 16 = 10% of _____   **9** 49 = 100% of _____

10 10 = 40% of _____   **11** 60 = 75% of _____   **12** 198 = 99% of _____

13 70 = 70% of _____   **14** 15 = 60% of _____   **15** 2 = 20% of _____

16 38 = 19% of _____   **17** 11 = 25% of _____   **18** 8 = 50% of _____

19 6 = 30% of _____   **20** 60 = 15% of _____   **21** 24 = 10% of _____

22 40 = 25% of _____   **23** 30 = 10% of _____   **24** 15 = 20% of _____

Compute with Percents—
Repeated Reasoning

Name: _____

Find patterns in percents.

Set A

1 60% of 20 = _____

2 60% of 30 = _____

3 60% of 40 = _____

4 50% of 20 = _____

5 50% of 30 = _____

6 50% of 40 = _____

7 40% of 20 = _____

8 40% of 30 = _____

9 40% of 40 = _____

10 30% of 20 = _____

11 30% of 30 = _____

12 30% of 40 = _____

Set B

1 8% of 25 = _____

2 16% of 25 = _____

3 24% of 25 = _____

4 8% of 50 = _____

5 16% of 50 = _____

6 24% of 50 = _____

7 8% of 75 = _____

8 16% of 75 = _____

9 24% of 75 = _____

Describe a pattern you see in one of the sets of problems above.

_____

_____

_____

Compute with Percents— Repeated Reasoning

Name: _____

Find place value patterns.

Set A

1 25% of 4 = _____   **2** 25% of 40 = _____   **3** 25% of 400 = _____

4 50% of 4 = _____   **5** 50% of 40 = _____   **6** 50% of 400 = _____

7 75% of 4 = _____   **8** 75% of 40 = _____   **9** 75% of 400 = _____

Set B

1 100% of 300 = _____   **2** 10% of 300 = _____   **3** 1% of 300 = _____

4 200% of 300 = _____   **5** 20% of 300 = _____   **6** 2% of 300 = _____

7 400% of 300 = _____   **8** 40% of 300 = _____   **9** 4% of 300 = _____

Describe a pattern you see in one of the sets of problems above.

_____

_____

_____

Compute with Percents— Repeated Reasoning

Name: _____

Find patterns using the distributive property.

Set A

1 30% of 10 = _____

2 20% of 10 = _____

3 50% of 10 = _____

4 30% of 20 = _____

5 20% of 20 = _____

6 50% of 20 = _____

7 30% of 30 = _____

8 20% of 30 = _____

9 50% of 30 = _____

Set B

1 2% of 50 = _____

2 4% of 50 = _____

3 6% of 50 = _____

4 20% of 50 = _____

5 40% of 50 = _____

6 60% of 50 = _____

7 200% of 50 = _____

8 400% of 50 = _____

9 600% of 50 = _____

10 220% of 50 = _____

11 440% of 50 = _____

12 660% of 50 = _____

13 222% of 50 = _____

14 444% of 50 = _____

15 666% of 50 = _____

Describe a pattern you see in one of the sets of problems above.

_____

_____

_____

Divide Fractions—Skills Practice

Find the quotient.

Form A

1 $\dfrac{2}{3} \div \dfrac{3}{6} =$ _____

2 $\dfrac{1}{2} \div \dfrac{1}{6} =$ _____

3 $\dfrac{2}{2} \div \dfrac{5}{6} =$ _____

4 $\dfrac{1}{4} \div \dfrac{1}{6} =$ _____

5 $\dfrac{2}{4} \div \dfrac{3}{6} =$ _____

6 $\dfrac{7}{4} \div \dfrac{3}{2} =$ _____

7 $\dfrac{8}{5} \div \dfrac{4}{10} =$ _____

8 $\dfrac{2}{3} \div \dfrac{5}{6} =$ _____

9 $\dfrac{5}{8} \div \dfrac{3}{4} =$ _____

10 $\dfrac{5}{4} \div \dfrac{10}{12} =$ _____

11 $\dfrac{4}{6} \div \dfrac{3}{6} =$ _____

12 $\dfrac{5}{4} \div \dfrac{1}{8} =$ _____

13 $\dfrac{1}{8} \div \dfrac{5}{4} =$ _____

14 $\dfrac{3}{2} \div \dfrac{6}{5} =$ _____

15 $\dfrac{9}{4} \div \dfrac{3}{2} =$ _____

16 $\dfrac{3}{10} \div \dfrac{6}{5} =$ _____

17 $\dfrac{6}{4} \div \dfrac{2}{8} =$ _____

18 $\dfrac{4}{8} \div \dfrac{5}{5} =$ _____

Divide Fractions—Skills Practice

Name: _____

Find the quotient.

Form B

1 $\dfrac{7}{4} \div \dfrac{1}{2} =$ _____

2 $\dfrac{2}{3} \div \dfrac{2}{3} =$ _____

3 $\dfrac{5}{6} \div \dfrac{4}{12} =$ _____

4 $\dfrac{8}{10} \div \dfrac{2}{5} =$ _____

5 $\dfrac{7}{8} \div \dfrac{6}{8} =$ _____

6 $\dfrac{5}{6} \div \dfrac{2}{3} =$ _____

7 $\dfrac{1}{10} \div \dfrac{1}{5} =$ _____

8 $\dfrac{3}{5} \div \dfrac{2}{3} =$ _____

9 $\dfrac{5}{3} \div \dfrac{4}{4} =$ _____

10 $\dfrac{4}{3} \div \dfrac{8}{6} =$ _____

11 $\dfrac{6}{12} \div \dfrac{1}{3} =$ _____

12 $\dfrac{3}{8} \div \dfrac{9}{4} =$ _____

13 $\dfrac{3}{10} \div \dfrac{2}{5} =$ _____

14 $\dfrac{6}{6} \div \dfrac{4}{3} =$ _____

15 $\dfrac{10}{4} \div \dfrac{5}{6} =$ _____

16 $\dfrac{2}{6} \div \dfrac{2}{5} =$ _____

17 $\dfrac{6}{5} \div \dfrac{3}{10} =$ _____

18 $\dfrac{1}{5} \div \dfrac{1}{3} =$ _____

Divide Fractions—Repeated Reasoning

Name: _____

Find patterns in fraction division.

Set A

1 $\frac{1}{2} \div \frac{1}{2} =$ _____

2 $\frac{3}{2} \div \frac{1}{2} =$ _____

3 $\frac{1}{2} \div \frac{1}{4} =$ _____

4 $\frac{3}{2} \div \frac{1}{4} =$ _____

5 $\frac{1}{2} \div \frac{1}{8} =$ _____

6 $\frac{3}{2} \div \frac{1}{8} =$ _____

7 $\frac{1}{2} \div \frac{1}{16} =$ _____

8 $\frac{3}{2} \div \frac{1}{16} =$ _____

Set B

1 $\frac{1}{2} \div \frac{1}{4} =$ _____

2 $\frac{3}{2} \div \frac{1}{4} =$ _____

3 $\frac{1}{2} \div \frac{2}{4} =$ _____

4 $\frac{3}{2} \div \frac{2}{4} =$ _____

5 $\frac{1}{2} \div \frac{3}{4} =$ _____

6 $\frac{3}{2} \div \frac{3}{4} =$ _____

7 $\frac{1}{2} \div \frac{4}{4} =$ _____

8 $\frac{3}{2} \div \frac{4}{4} =$ _____

Describe a pattern you see in one of the sets of problems above.

_____

_____

_____

Divide Whole Numbers—Skills Practice

Name: _____

Find the quotient.

Form A

1 $61\overline{)793}$

2 $25\overline{)675}$

3 $46\overline{)506}$

4 $30\overline{)510}$

5 $41\overline{)328}$

6 $80\overline{)5,680}$

7 $35\overline{)2,170}$

8 $22\overline{)7,040}$

9 $72\overline{)7,488}$

10 $63\overline{)53,865}$

11 $75\overline{)72,525}$

12 $40\overline{)9,240}$

13 $44\overline{)54,164}$

14 $15\overline{)15,810}$

15 $12\overline{)17,472}$

Divide Whole Numbers—Skills Practice

Name: _____

Find the quotient.

Form B

1 45)$\overline{4,410}$

2 25)$\overline{475}$

3 21)$\overline{189}$

4 81)$\overline{972}$

5 20)$\overline{960}$

6 54)$\overline{702}$

7 60)$\overline{8,520}$

8 33)$\overline{8,580}$

9 70)$\overline{3,570}$

10 64)$\overline{47,616}$

11 14)$\overline{14,168}$

12 15)$\overline{18,945}$

13 66)$\overline{89,958}$

14 75)$\overline{62,025}$

15 76)$\overline{8,208}$

Divide Whole Numbers—Repeated Reasoning

Name: _____

Find place value patterns.

Set A

1 $10\overline{)16,000}$

2 $100\overline{)16,000}$

3 $1,000\overline{)16,000}$

4 $5\overline{)16,000}$

5 $50\overline{)16,000}$

6 $500\overline{)16,000}$

Set B

1 $120 \div 10 =$ _____

2 $1,200 \div 10 =$ _____

3 $12,000 \div 10 =$ _____

4 $120 \div 20 =$ _____

5 $1,200 \div 20 =$ _____

6 $12,000 \div 20 =$ _____

7 $120 \div 30 =$ _____

8 $1,200 \div 30 =$ _____

9 $12,000 \div 30 =$ _____

10 $120 \div 40 =$ _____

11 $1,200 \div 40 =$ _____

12 $12,000 \div 40 =$ _____

Describe a pattern you see in one of the sets of problems above.

_____

_____

_____

Add Decimals—Skills Practice

Name: _____

Add.

Form A

1 22.098 + 14.103 = _____

2 6.07 + 12.149 = _____

3 3.1 + 4.904 = _____

4 8.062 + 7.189 = _____

5 11.802 + 32.4 = _____

6 13.765 + 6.23 = _____

7 76.147 + 5.07 = _____

8 63.98 + 0.031 = _____

9 0.093 + 0.02 = _____

10 5.2 + 0.871 = _____

11 41.82 + 7.593 = _____

12 2.76 + 27.959 = _____

13 8.91 + 0.092 = _____

14 33.99 + 24.002 = _____

15 1.099 + 0.038 = _____

16 2.08 + 0.671 = _____

17 9.7 + 0.345 = _____

18 1.999 + 52.651 = _____

19 17.76 + 8 + 45.309 = _____

20 68.821 + 15.34 + 1.009 = _____

©Curriculum Associates, LLC   Copying is permitted for classroom use.

Fluency Practice **365**

Add Decimals—Skills Practice

Name: _____

Add.

Form B

1. 23.189 + 15.014 = _____

2. 7.08 + 11.238 = _____

3. 2.7 + 3.603 = _____

4. 9.073 + 4.479 = _____

5. 13.732 + 36.5 = _____

6. 12.803 + 5.18 = _____

7. 67.258 + 9.05 = _____

8. 54.87 + 0.082 = _____

9. 0.058 + 0.08 = _____

10. 4.4 + 0.936 = _____

11. 52.64 + 4.865 = _____

12. 3.58 + 28.846 = _____

13. 7.92 + 0.084 = _____

14. 44.88 + 35.113 = _____

15. 1.077 + 0.034 = _____

16. 3.06 + 0.863 = _____

17. 9.4 + 0.762 = _____

18. 3.998 + 65.462 = _____

19. 14.45 + 7 + 48.602 = _____

20. 67.462 + 16.82 + 2.008 = _____

Add Decimals—Repeated Reasoning

Name: _____

Use patterns and mental math to add.

Set A

1 1.999 + 0.001 = _____   **2** 1.999 + 0.002 = _____   **3** 1.999 + 0.003 = _____

4 1.998 + 0.002 = _____   **5** 1.998 + 0.003 = _____   **6** 1.998 + 0.004 = _____

7 1.997 + 0.003 = _____   **8** 1.997 + 0.004 = _____   **9** 1.997 + 0.005 = _____

Set B

1 2.007 + 0.003 = _____   **2** 2.008 + 0.003 = _____   **3** 2.009 + 0.003 = _____

4 2.008 + 0.002 = _____   **5** 2.009 + 0.002 = _____   **6** 2.010 + 0.002 = _____

7 2.009 + 0.001 = _____   **8** 2.010 + 0.001 = _____   **9** 2.011 + 0.001 = _____

Describe a pattern you see in one of the sets of problems above.

_____

_____

_____

Subtract Decimals—Skills Practice

Name: _____

Subtract.

Form A

1 $0.09 - 0.072 =$ _____

2 $82.456 - 50.03 =$ _____

3 $53.5 - 0.094 =$ _____

4 $12.091 - 0.132 =$ _____

5 $0.8 - 0.341 =$ _____

6 $54.784 - 23.8 =$ _____

7 $25.76 - 4.213 =$ _____

8 $27.261 - 18 =$ _____

9 $10.002 - 0.004 =$ _____

10 $6.365 - 0.245 =$ _____

11 $4.598 - 2.46 =$ _____

12 $36.7 - 0.062 =$ _____

13 $68 - 6.218 =$ _____

14 $18.25 - 6.342 =$ _____

15 $1.087 - 0.3 =$ _____

16 $0.076 - 0.02 =$ _____

17 $48.1 - 9.354 =$ _____

18 $56.285 - 7.293 =$ _____

19 $2.89 - 0.089 =$ _____

20 $82.138 - 6.4 =$ _____

21 $21.98 - 13.761 =$ _____

Subtract Decimals—Skills Practice

Name: _____

Subtract.

Form B

1 $0.08 - 0.067 =$ _____

2 $94.281 - 40.05 =$ _____

3 $42.5 - 0.083 =$ _____

4 $14.082 - 0.243 =$ _____

5 $0.9 - 0.426 =$ _____

6 $76.892 - 34.9 =$ _____

7 $35.87 - 3.435 =$ _____

8 $28.831 - 19 =$ _____

9 $10.006 - 0.009 =$ _____

10 $8.496 - 0.356 =$ _____

11 $7.792 - 3.66 =$ _____

12 $32.8 - 0.074 =$ _____

13 $63 - 2.453 =$ _____

14 $14.36 - 2.538 =$ _____

15 $1.092 - 0.4 =$ _____

16 $0.084 - 0.06 =$ _____

17 $52.1 - 4.463 =$ _____

18 $52.156 - 5.163 =$ _____

19 $3.78 - 0.078 =$ _____

20 $96.286 - 7.8 =$ _____

21 $23.94 - 15.358 =$ _____

Use patterns and mental math to subtract.

Set A

1 $8 - 0.1 =$ _____

2 $8 - 0.2 =$ _____

3 $8 - 0.3 =$ _____

4 $18 - 0.1 =$ _____

5 $18 - 0.2 =$ _____

6 $18 - 0.3 =$ _____

7 $108 - 0.1 =$ _____

8 $108 - 0.2 =$ _____

9 $108 - 0.3 =$ _____

Set B

1 $20 - 0.01 =$ _____

2 $20 - 0.02 =$ _____

3 $20 - 0.03 =$ _____

4 $20 - 1.01 =$ _____

5 $20 - 1.02 =$ _____

6 $20 - 1.03 =$ _____

7 $20 - 2.01 =$ _____

8 $20 - 2.02 =$ _____

9 $20 - 2.03 =$ _____

Describe a pattern you see in one of the sets of problems above.

_____

_____

_____

Multiply Decimals—Skills Practice

Name: _____

Multiply.

1   2.1
  × 0.76

2   52.4
  × 4.5

3   4.52
  × 8.9

4   5.8
  × 7.4

5   0.97
  × 0.23

6   63.52
  × 4.7

7   2.7
  × 0.25

8   8.35
  × 0.46

9   0.813
  × 4.6

10   0.83
  × 5.8

11   12.3
  × 6.5

12   0.78
  × 42.5

13   912.5
  × 0.85

14   3.6
  × 8.14

15   0.64
  × 31.8

16   5.6
  × 21.42

Name: _____

Multiply.

1. 4.1
    × 0.87

2. 65.5
    × 3.2

3. 0.65
    × 3.9

4. 0.924
    × 6.2

5. 34.78
    × 0.12

6. 7.65
    × 0.28

7. 0.69
    × 0.34

8. 36.25
    × 7.3

9. 0.65
    × 24.6

10. 73.8
    × 42.9

11. 21.4
    × 5.6

12. 6.28
    × 3.65

13. 2.5
    × 7.39

14. 691.5
    × 0.75

15. 0.43
    × 61.5

16. 7.8
    × 34.16

Multiply Decimals—Repeated Reasoning

Name: _____

Find patterns in multiplying decimals.

Set A

1 $0.1 \times 0.3 =$ _____

2 $0.1 \times 0.6 =$ _____

3 $0.2 \times 0.3 =$ _____

4 $0.2 \times 0.6 =$ _____

5 $0.4 \times 0.3 =$ _____

6 $0.4 \times 0.6 =$ _____

7 $0.8 \times 0.3 =$ _____

8 $0.8 \times 0.6 =$ _____

9 $1.6 \times 0.3 =$ _____

10 $1.6 \times 0.6 =$ _____

11 $3.2 \times 0.3 =$ _____

12 $3.2 \times 0.6 =$ _____

Set B

1
$$\begin{array}{r} 34.5 \\ \times\ \ \ \ 5 \\ \hline \end{array}$$

2
$$\begin{array}{r} 34.5 \\ \times\ \ 0.5 \\ \hline \end{array}$$

3
$$\begin{array}{r} 34.5 \\ \times\ 0.05 \\ \hline \end{array}$$

4
$$\begin{array}{r} 34.5 \\ \times\ 0.005 \\ \hline \end{array}$$

5
$$\begin{array}{r} 3.45 \\ \times\ \ \ \ 5 \\ \hline \end{array}$$

6
$$\begin{array}{r} 3.45 \\ \times\ \ 0.5 \\ \hline \end{array}$$

7
$$\begin{array}{r} 3.45 \\ \times\ 0.05 \\ \hline \end{array}$$

8
$$\begin{array}{r} 3.45 \\ \times\ 0.005 \\ \hline \end{array}$$

9
$$\begin{array}{r} 0.345 \\ \times\ \ \ \ 5 \\ \hline \end{array}$$

10
$$\begin{array}{r} 0.345 \\ \times\ \ 0.5 \\ \hline \end{array}$$

11
$$\begin{array}{r} 0.345 \\ \times\ 0.05 \\ \hline \end{array}$$

12
$$\begin{array}{r} 0.345 \\ \times\ 0.005 \\ \hline \end{array}$$

Describe a pattern you see in one of the sets of problems above.

_____

_____

_____

Name: _____

Divide.

1 $0.08\overline{)3.84}$

2 $0.16\overline{)6.08}$

3 $5.9\overline{)2.183}$

4 $112.5\overline{)7.2}$

5 $614.5\overline{)3.687}$

6 $2.68\overline{)9.648}$

7 $5.9\overline{)10.62}$

8 $2.6\overline{)137.8}$

9 $1.486\overline{)66.87}$

10 $2.357\overline{)68.353}$

11 $2.85\overline{)267.9}$

12 $0.368\overline{)33.856}$

13 $1.125\overline{)240.3}$

14 $0.3\overline{)8.37}$

15 $0.008\overline{)2.3}$

16 $0.36\overline{)0.621}$

Divide Decimals—Skills Practice

Name: _____

Divide.

Form B

1 $0.04\overline{)2.24}$

2 $0.18\overline{)7.56}$

3 $0.9\overline{)3.69}$

4 $5.6\overline{)5.152}$

5 $114.5\overline{)3.206}$

6 $2.8\overline{)16.52}$

7 $2.56\overline{)8.192}$

8 $217.5\overline{)18.27}$

9 $812.5\overline{)6.5}$

10 $1.276\overline{)82.94}$

11 $6.95\overline{)375.3}$

12 $3.689\overline{)99.603}$

13 $3.225\overline{)566.31}$

14 $56.25\overline{)7.2}$

15 $0.734\overline{)60.922}$

16 $0.8\overline{)0.856}$

Divide Decimals—Repeated Reasoning

Name: _____

Compare dividends and quotients to find patterns.

Set A

1 $0.5\overline{)2}$

2 $0.5\overline{)4}$

3 $0.5\overline{)8}$

4 $0.5\overline{)20}$

5 $0.5\overline{)40}$

6 $0.5\overline{)80}$

7 $0.5\overline{)200}$

8 $0.5\overline{)400}$

9 $0.5\overline{)800}$

Set B

1 $1 \div 0.2 =$ _____

2 $2 \div 0.2 =$ _____

3 $3 \div 0.2 =$ _____

4 $10 \div 0.2 =$ _____

5 $20 \div 0.2 =$ _____

6 $30 \div 0.2 =$ _____

7 $100 \div 0.2 =$ _____

8 $200 \div 0.2 =$ _____

9 $300 \div 0.2 =$ _____

Describe a pattern you see in one of the sets of problems above.

_____

_____

_____

Find the greatest common factor.   Form A

1 24 and 20: _____   **2** 36 and 42: _____   **3** 16 and 32: _____

4 12 and 8: _____   **5** 80 and 70: _____   **6** 50 and 14: _____

7 100 and 75: _____   **8** 15 and 18: _____   **9** 14 and 21: _____

10 40 and 60: _____   **11** 25 and 45: _____   **12** 33 and 77: _____

13 36 and 81: _____   **14** 64 and 40: _____   **15** 35 and 28: _____

16 17 and 34: _____   **17** 15 and 28: _____   **18** 3 and 69: _____

19 18 and 28: _____   **20** 27 and 63: _____   **21** 20 and 45: _____

22 54 and 24: _____   **23** 18 and 45: _____   **24** 72 and 64: _____

Greatest Common Factors—Skills Practice

Name: _____

Find the greatest common factor.

1 21 and 28: _____

2 50 and 75: _____

3 15 and 30: _____

4 6 and 9: _____

5 60 and 80: _____

6 16 and 40: _____

7 30 and 48: _____

8 12 and 18: _____

9 16 and 24: _____

10 40 and 90: _____

11 44 and 24: _____

12 26 and 16: _____

13 12 and 25: _____

14 7 and 42: _____

15 35 and 55: _____

16 44 and 99: _____

17 27 and 72: _____

18 13 and 39: _____

19 45 and 81: _____

20 40 and 25: _____

21 20 and 42: _____

22 120 and 70: _____

23 22 and 77: _____

24 72 and 63: _____

Name: _____

Find the least common multiple.   Form A

1 4 and 7: _____   **2** 5 and 6: _____   **3** 3 and 8: _____

4 4 and 6: _____   **5** 6 and 9: _____   **6** 10 and 6: _____

7 2 and 8: _____   **8** 3 and 4: _____   **9** 5 and 7: _____

10 8 and 9: _____   **11** 12 and 8: _____   **12** 8 and 10: _____

13 9 and 7: _____   **14** 2 and 11: _____   **15** 6 and 12: _____

16 11 and 9: _____   **17** 9 and 4: _____   **18** 3 and 6: _____

19 5 and 9: _____   **20** 11 and 8: _____   **21** 10 and 5: _____

22 13 and 39: _____   **23** 4 and 16: _____   **24** 7 and 6: _____

Least Common Multiples—Skills Practice

Name: _____

Find the least common multiple.   **Form B**

1 4 and 5: _____

2 2 and 6: _____

3 3 and 11: _____

4 7 and 6: _____

5 12 and 9: _____

6 10 and 12: _____

7 8 and 12: _____

8 5 and 8: _____

9 3 and 5: _____

10 4 and 9: _____

11 10 and 3: _____

12 6 and 4: _____

13 7 and 8: _____

14 2 and 9: _____

15 4 and 11: _____

16 8 and 4: _____

17 3 and 7: _____

18 9 and 3: _____

19 4 and 10: _____

20 5 and 11: _____

21 12 and 2: _____

22 7 and 28: _____

23 8 and 6: _____

24 21 and 3: _____

Exponents—Skills Practice

Evaluate the expression.

Form A

1 $5^2 =$ _____

2 $3^2 + 7^2 =$ _____

3 $4^2 \times 3^3 =$ _____

4 $2^3(4^3 + 6^2) =$ _____

5 $7^3 =$ _____

6 $4^4(1^8 + 2^2) =$ _____

7 $4^3 + 5^4 =$ _____

8 $\dfrac{9^2 - 7^2}{2^4} =$ _____

9 $8^3 =$ _____

10 $3^5 + 2^7 =$ _____

11 $9^2 =$ _____

12 $2^6 - 3^3 =$ _____

13 $\dfrac{10^2 + 3^2}{1^{13}} =$ _____

14 $3^4 =$ _____

15 $\dfrac{6^2 - 2^5}{2^2} =$ _____

16 $5^3 - 2^3 =$ _____

17 $8^2 \times 6^2 =$ _____

18 $\dfrac{3^3 + 6^2}{3^2} =$ _____

19 $2^5 =$ _____

20 $\dfrac{10^3}{2^2 + 6^2} =$ _____

21 $6^3 =$ _____

Name: _____

Evaluate the expression.   **Form B**

1 $6^2 =$ _____

2 $4^2 + 8^2 =$ _____

3 $5^2 \times 3^3 =$ _____

4 $3^2(9^2 + 2^4) =$ _____

5 $9^3 =$ _____

6 $2^3(7^3 + 1^9) =$ _____

7 $5^3 + 3^5 =$ _____

8 $\dfrac{6^2 - 3^2}{3^3} =$ _____

9 $4^3 =$ _____

10 $2^5 + 7^3 =$ _____

11 $8^2 =$ _____

12 $3^4 - 2^4 =$ _____

13 $\dfrac{9^2 + 10^3}{1^{12}} =$ _____

14 $7^4 =$ _____

15 $\dfrac{10^2 - 8^2}{3^2} =$ _____

16 $4^4 - 5^2 =$ _____

17 $7^2 \times 9^2 =$ _____

18 $\dfrac{6^2 + 8^2}{5^2} =$ _____

19 $2^6 =$ _____

20 $\dfrac{10^4}{8^2 + 4^2} =$ _____

21 $4^5 =$ _____

Exponents—Repeated Reasoning

Name: _____

Look for patterns in expressions with exponents.

Set A

1 $10^2 \times 10^1 =$ _____

2 $10^2 \times 10^2 =$ _____

3 $10^2 \times 10^3 =$ _____

4 $10^3 \times 10^1 =$ _____

5 $10^3 \times 10^2 =$ _____

6 $10^3 \times 10^3 =$ _____

7 $10^4 \times 10^1 =$ _____

8 $10^4 \times 10^2 =$ _____

9 $10^4 \times 10^3 =$ _____

Set B

1 $\dfrac{10^7}{10} =$ _____

2 $\dfrac{10^7}{10^2} =$ _____

3 $\dfrac{10^7}{10^3} =$ _____

4 $\dfrac{10^8}{10} =$ _____

5 $\dfrac{10^8}{10^2} =$ _____

6 $\dfrac{10^8}{10^3} =$ _____

7 $\dfrac{10^9}{10} =$ _____

8 $\dfrac{10^9}{10^2} =$ _____

9 $\dfrac{10^9}{10^3} =$ _____

Describe a pattern you see in one of the sets of problems above.

_____

_____

_____

Order of Operations—Skills Practice

Name: _____

Evaluate the expression.

Form A

1 $7 + 6 \times 2 =$ _____

2 $0.25 \times 16 + 4 =$ _____

3 $26 - 3 \times 4 =$ _____

4 $18 + 14 \times 0.5 =$ _____

5 $18 \div 2 + 7 =$ _____

6 $8 + 6 \times 3^2 =$ _____

7 $18 - 8^2 \div 4 =$ _____

8 $12 - 8 \times 0.25 =$ _____

9 $9 + 25 \div 5^2 =$ _____

10 $6^2 \div 9 + 3 =$ _____

11 $48 \div 0.5 + 2 =$ _____

12 $42 + 0.2 \times 30 =$ _____

13 $36 \div 3 \times 4 =$ _____

14 $131 - 4 \times 2^3 =$ _____

15 $56 - 0.3 \times 40 =$ _____

16 $32 - 8 + 11 =$ _____

17 $96 \div 2^4 + 32 =$ _____

18 $35 - 0.5 \times 56 =$ _____

19 $10^2 \div 5 \times 4 =$ _____

20 $3^3 + 18 \div 3 =$ _____

Order of Operations—Skills Practice

Name: _____

Evaluate the expression.

1 $8 + 7 \times 2 =$ _____

2 $0.4 \times 20 + 5 =$ _____

3 $34 - 4 \times 8 =$ _____

4 $26 + 12 \times 0.5 =$ _____

5 $24 \div 2 + 6 =$ _____

6 $6 + 5 \times 4^2 =$ _____

7 $18 - 6^2 \div 3 =$ _____

8 $16 - 12 \times 0.25 =$ _____

9 $4 + 9 \div 3^2 =$ _____

10 $8^2 \div 2 + 6 =$ _____

11 $26 \div 0.5 + 6 =$ _____

12 $54 + 0.2 \times 60 =$ _____

13 $54 \div 6 \times 3 =$ _____

14 $191 - 2 \times 3^4 =$ _____

15 $48 - 0.3 \times 30 =$ _____

16 $46 - 7 + 14 =$ _____

17 $72 \div 2^3 + 1 =$ _____

18 $41 - 0.5 \times 46 =$ _____

19 $6^2 \div 9 \times 2 =$ _____

20 $4^3 + 32 \div 8 =$ _____

Evaluate the expression.

1 $s = 7; 6s^2 =$ _____

2 $x = 3; 4x^3 + 2 =$ _____

3 $n = \frac{1}{8}; \frac{2}{n} =$ _____

4 $x = \frac{1}{6}; 18x + 4 =$ _____

5 $x = 7; \frac{4x + 8}{2} =$ _____

6 $p = 0.5; 42 - 42p =$ _____

7 $x = 0.25; 48x - 3 =$ _____

8 $a = 3; a^3 =$ _____

9 $y = 84; \frac{y}{4} - 15 =$ _____

10 $c = 35; \frac{9c}{5} + 32 =$ _____

11 $n = 0.5; \frac{8}{n} + 8 =$ _____

12 $x = 3; 169 - 2x^4 =$ _____

13 $a = 3; 12a^2 =$ _____

14 $w = \frac{1}{5}; 38 - 15w =$ _____

15 $x = 9; 8x + 3 =$ _____

16 $m = 2; \frac{16}{2m} =$ _____

17 $x = 7; x^2 - 5^2 =$ _____

18 $p = 25; \frac{p}{100}(120) =$ _____

Evaluate Expressions with Variables—
Skills Practice

Name: _____

Evaluate the expression.

Form B

1 $s = 8$; $6s^2 =$ _____

2 $x = 2$; $7x^3 + 4 =$ _____

3 $n = \frac{1}{6}$; $\frac{4}{n} =$ _____

4 $x = \frac{1}{3}$; $12x + 7 =$ _____

5 $x = 8$; $\frac{6x + 9}{3} =$ _____

6 $p = 0.2$; $20 - 20p =$ _____

7 $x = 2$; $78 - 4x^3 =$ _____

8 $a = 2$; $a^3 =$ _____

9 $y = 96$; $\frac{y}{6} - 12 =$ _____

10 $c = 45$; $\frac{9c}{5} + 32 =$ _____

11 $n = 0.5$; $\frac{12}{n} + 15 =$ _____

12 $x = 2$; $24x \div 6 =$ _____

13 $a = 6$; $5a^2 =$ _____

14 $w = \frac{1}{2}$; $46 - 4w =$ _____

15 $x = 7$; $9x + 4 =$ _____

16 $m = 3$; $\frac{30}{5m} =$ _____

17 $x = 9$; $x^2 - 7^2 =$ _____

18 $p = 50$; $\frac{p}{100}(460) =$ _____

Name: _____

Use the distributive property to write an equivalent expression.   **Form A**

1 $5x + 20 =$ _____

2 $3(x + 6) =$ _____

3 $8(4n + 3) =$ _____

4 $7x - 35 =$ _____

5 $12x - 6 =$ _____

6 $20p + 16 =$ _____

7 $9(2x + 9) =$ _____

8 $5(6 + 13a) =$ _____

9 $36 + 9y =$ _____

10 $6(c + 8) =$ _____

11 $7(n - 3) =$ _____

12 $2(12 + 10x) =$ _____

13 $21 + 15a =$ _____

14 $4(5 - 4w) =$ _____

15 $32 - 12x =$ _____

16 $10(2m - 7) =$ _____

17 $8 + 36x =$ _____

18 $11(6 + 4p) =$ _____

19 $25(4n + 8) =$ _____

20 $20w + 30 =$ _____

Equivalent Expressions—Skills Practice

Name: _____

Use the distributive property to write an equivalent expression.   **Form B**

1 $6x + 18 = $ _____

2 $4(x + 7) = $ _____

3 $9(3n + 5) = $ _____

4 $4x - 32 = $ _____

5 $15x - 5 = $ _____

6 $30p + 18 = $ _____

7 $8(3x + 7) = $ _____

8 $7(9 + 12a) = $ _____

9 $42 + 6y = $ _____

10 $3(c + 4) = $ _____

11 $5(n - 8) = $ _____

12 $6(5 + 9x) = $ _____

13 $24 + 18a = $ _____

14 $11(8 - 6w) = $ _____

15 $42 - 36x = $ _____

16 $25(10m + 3) = $ _____

17 $6 + 14x = $ _____

18 $10(3p - 4) = $ _____

19 $2(7n + 6) = $ _____

20 $40w + 70 = $ _____

Solving Equations—Skills Practice

Name: _____

Solve the equation.

1 $x + 24 = 36$; $x =$ _____

2 $5 = 6y$; $y =$ _____

3 $\frac{5}{3} + x = 2$; $x =$ _____

4 $7w = 28$; $w =$ _____

5 $\frac{9}{5} = 1 + m$; $m =$ _____

6 $0.5x = 14$; $x =$ _____

7 $\frac{7}{2} = 4x$; $x =$ _____

8 $215 + p = 230$; $p =$ _____

9 $\frac{5}{6}x = 20$; $x =$ _____

10 $x + 32 = 45$; $x =$ _____

11 $c + \frac{2}{5} = 2$; $c =$ _____

12 $0.2 + x = 3$; $x =$ _____

13 $9 = 4y$; $y =$ _____

14 $x + 0.8 = 4.3$; $x =$ _____

15 $56 + n = 97$; $n =$ _____

16 $39 = 17 + x$; $x =$ _____

17 $0.6 + w = 4$; $w =$ _____

18 $9y = 189$; $y =$ _____

Solving Equations—Skills Practice

Name: _____

Solve the equation.

Form B

1 $x + 26 = 39$; $x =$ _____

2 $4 = 5y$; $y =$ _____

3 $\frac{7}{3} + x = 3$; $x =$ _____

4 $8w = 48$; $w =$ _____

5 $\frac{7}{4} = 1 + m$; $m =$ _____

6 $0.5x = 18$; $x =$ _____

7 $\frac{5}{2} = 3x$; $x =$ _____

8 $225 + p = 260$; $p =$ _____

9 $\frac{3}{4}x = 24$; $x =$ _____

10 $x + 41 = 63$; $x =$ _____

11 $c + \frac{2}{3} = 4$; $c =$ _____

12 $0.4 + x = 4$; $x =$ _____

13 $7 = 6y$; $y =$ _____

14 $x + 0.5 = 3.7$; $x =$ _____

15 $48 + n = 79$; $n =$ _____

16 $43 = 11 + x$; $x =$ _____

17 $0.8 + w = 5$; $w =$ _____

18 $4y = 248$; $y =$ _____